W9-AFX-417

"Cheryl Coon's book is a smorgasbord of information for the literate parent. I have seen nothing like it in my years as a psychologist for children. I find it fascinating because it provides a 'natural' approach to understanding the myriad situations that a parent and child will, hopefully, face together. Nothing seems to bond a child and parents so much as reading a favorite book together again and again."

—**Michael J Fulop**, Psy.D., Clinical Psychologist, Portland, OR

"*Books to Grow With* will be an invaluable tool for every parent, teacher and librarian who believes that sharing the right books with children can help them find relief from the sometimes frightening and always challenging adventure of growing up. I will place a copy in both the parent and professional collections in my school library and share it with colleagues, teachers, parents, guidance counselors, friends—everyone who loves books and cares for the well-being of children."

—**Diane Oesau**, Library Media specialist
Horace Mann Elementary School, Cherry Hill, N.J.

"An excellent tool. Parents, librarians, and teachers will be delighted."

—**GraceAnne A. DeCandido**, lecturer in Children's literature
Rutgers School of Information, Communication and Library Sciences

"A wonderful resource for parents with children who are facing difficult situations from bedwetting to new babysitters, from being the biggest child in a group to building new friendships when best friends move away. It is also a good tool for librarians who are faced with perplexed parents and teachers. The list of titles—and the inclusion of how to access the books—are great helps for the librarian."

—**Karen Topham**, Professor
Bankier Library, Brookdale Community College, Lincroft, N.J.

"A massive amount of research that many parents will benefit from. Books to Grow With should be endorsed by PTA groups, Parent's Magazine, Gerber's, the Head Start program, to name only a few..."

—**Dr. Al Siebert**, *The Survivor Personality* (Perigee Books, 1996)

"A well-researched and parent-friendly guide to picture books and fiction that can facilitate conversations in families about ordinary, everyday issues. The books indexed here present starters for grand and meaningful conversations. Parents who not only bring home the books, but also delight in the reading will discover much wisdom about the tough challenges of parenthood as well."

—**Sarah Borders**, Licensed Professional Counselor, Specialist in
Bibliotherapy, Faculty, Appalachian State University
Boone N.C., author of *Children Talking About Books*, Oryx Press 1993

"A clear and easy way to find books that deal with all types of situations I encounter. It's so nice to find a reference book that has multiple ways to find the right book for the right issue. This book is one you will want to keep close by."

—**Rochella Farnand**, Third Grade Teacher
Chapman Elementary School, Portland, OR

"A valuable tool for parents, educators and others. This resource will help children and their parents come to terms with the many and varied challenges facing children today."

—**Brynna Hurwitz**, Executive Director of the Children's Diabetes
Seminars and Support Network, Adjunct Faculty in Education
Lewis and Clark College, Portland, OR

"*Books To Grow With* takes a complex topic and organizes it very effectively into short, concise reviews with just the right amount of explanation about the story and the book format. I really appreciate the information and reasoning behind the selections. I plan to share it with teachers and parents who come to me with questions about these issues."

—**Barb Swanson Sanders**, Children's Literature Consultant, Portland, OR

"*Books to Grow With* is a wonderful, time-saving resource for busy parents who want to help their children learn and grow with literature. Coon includes only quality fiction books that have literary interest to engage a child's thinking. Themes both ordinary and sensitive can be gently introduced to children through stories, creating an opening for further discussion and exploration between parent and child. Coon has done her homework so parents don't have to—book listings are helpfully summarized and include key information to help find a suitable resource for a particular child. She offers practical tips for using literature to help children and includes indexes to help you find resources quickly. Homeschooling parents may find this book particularly useful."

—**Ann Lahrson-Fisher**, Author *Fundamentals of Homeschooling: Notes
on Successful Family Living* and columnist, *Home Education Magazine*

"A valuable tool for parents, counselors, librarians, and teachers."

—**Marvin Diamond**, Librarian, Congregation Beth Israel, Portland, OR

"What a great resource this book will be for parents, counselors, therapists, librarians—anyone who lives or works with children—to be able to find quickly several books they can read with their children to help them through life's challenges."

—**Sue Moshofsky**, PTA President, Chapman Elementary School, Portland, OR

BOOKS TO
GROW WITH

BOOKS TO GROW WITH

A Guide to Using
the Best Children's Fiction
for Everyday Issues
and Tough Challenges

by Cheryl F. Coon

lutra
PRESS

Lutra Press
Portland, OR

BOOKS TO GROW WITH:
A GUIDE TO USING THE BEST CHILDREN'S FICTION
FOR EVERYDAY ISSUES AND TOUGH CHALLENGES

Copyright © 2004 by Lutra Press

Publisher's Cataloging-in-Publication Data

Coon, Cheryl F.
    Books to grow with: a guide to using the best
children's fiction for everyday issues and tough
challenges / by Cheryl F. Coon.—1st ed.

    p.cm.
    ISBN: 0-9748025-7-3

    Includes bibliographical references and index.

    1. Children's Literature—Bibliography. 2. Social
problems in literature—Bibliography. 3. Children—Life
skills guides—Bibliography. 4. Childen—Books and
reading—United States. 5. Children's literature—
Stories, plots, etc.   I. Title.

Z1037.C66 2004   011.62
                           QB133-2008

Inquiries should be addressed to

Lutra Press
2939 NW 53rd Drive
Suite 400
Portland, Oregon 97210-1067

http://www.lutrapress.com

Cover design by Robert Aulicino, Cover art by Julia Noonan

Manufactured in the United States of America

First Edition: July 2004

ACKNOWLEDGMENTS

The idea of comforting and enriching ourselves through great books is an ancient one. In the last century, many experts in teaching, counseling, and parenting children have advocated the use of books to help children. I am indebted for their vision, scholarship, and persistence.

Many people encouraged me as I researched and wrote this book and I am grateful for their support and assistance. The Washington County Library system, particularly the Cedar Mill Library branch staff, and the Multnomah County Library system generously and uncomplainingly located and held for me more than 3,000 books during the course of my research.

To Jenny Martin, Librarian at Chapman Elementary School, who first believed in the value of this book; Sue Moshofsky who read drafts and encouraged me; Janet Zarem, whose wise counsel and generous advice aided me; Claire Austin, who offers support to children through Imaginative Resources for Children; Dr. Meg Eastman, Dr. Mike Fulop and Barb Swanson, who kindly offered to read drafts; Amy Johnson of Lift Communications; and to my dear friend Patti Aronsson who unfailingly encouraged me, my thanks.

To my grandparents and my dad, whose memory sustains me and to my mother, who shares with me her passion for books, my love and gratitude.

Above all, to my wonderful husband Jim, to my daughter Nora, who inspired and urged me to return to writing, and to my son Eli, who gave generously of his abilities with computers and making me laugh, my heartfelt love and thanks.

TABLE OF CONTENTS

INDEXES

FOREWORD

❦

*A book is a garden, an orchard, a storehouse, a
party, a company by the way, a counselor, a
multitude of counselors.*
—Henry Ward Beecher

The right fiction book can help children overcome their fears and anxieties, handle their anger, and learn the tools of problem-solving. It also can reassure them that they aren't alone in the experiences they're having. However, finding the right book can be frustrating. At your local library you may find lists of books or page through reference books. But you really won't know if a particular book is a good choice unless you read it yourself. That's time-consuming and limits the number of books you can consider.

When I began to write *Books to Grow With*, I had several goals. The most important was to make it easier for all of us to find the very best children's fiction on the many issues children encounter while growing up.

Deciding what topics to include was the easiest part. I began with the issues that most children face. Then, I decided to include more difficult and unusual issues, ones that perhaps fewer children were coping with personally but which some children will deal with in their lives. Later, when one of my children developed a chronic illness, I became aware of the paucity of fiction book choices featuring characters living with disabilities and chronic illness and included books on these topics as well.

As it turned out, not all of the topics I originally intended to include made it to the final version of *Books to Grow With*. The reason was simple. For some topics there weren't any books I could recommend, such as a number of books featuring characters with illnesses and disabilities. Often these books are overwhelmingly preachy and didactic.

To make *Books to Grow With* easy to use, I wanted the topics to be specifically defined. When I look for books dealing with "anger," I don't want to have to sort through books that feature many other emotions; I'm just looking for a book for a child who is angry. When I want to help a child who is having trouble with sharing, I don't want to have to look through all the sources of emotional challenges in a catchall category marked "Stress." *Books to Grow With* has very specific topic headings. If a book about teasing is also about siblings, it is listed in both sections so there's no chance of missing it.

Finally, I wanted to make it easy for an adult to find books on particular topics of interest. I include indices designed to make it easy to find the desired topic, a favorite author or illustrator, multicultural books, and books available in Spanish.

Although both teenagers and younger children can be helped through fiction, it is easier to find appropriate books that address the problems of elementary school children. Older children may benefit from some of the books I list, but as I limited the books reviewed to those with fewer than 100 pages, most of the books, with a few exceptions, will be too young for adolescents and teenagers. There definitely are exceptions, so don't hesitate to consider them for an older child for whom the book may be useful.

In addition to limiting recommended books to those under 100 pages, I also chose not to review nonfiction. Providing nonfiction to a child to help him can be a valid approach but I am not enthusiastic about it as a general rule. The critical element in children's fiction is a child's ability to identify with a fictional protagonist. This is what subtly reassures him that he is not alone and presents constructive options in a way less likely to encounter his resistance to direct, didactic instruction. Nonfiction can rarely do this.

I also chose to consider only children's fiction books that are widely available. By that I mean books available in new or used bookstores, in public libraries, or through online booksellers. Many books that are "out of print" can be easily located through one of these sources.

It's not easy to pick great books. We all know what leaves us cold and what makes us catch our breath with wonder, but in between there are lots and lots of books. There are explicit problem-solving books that are too direct for most children to swallow. There are books that are earnestly well-intended but will not captivate an audience of children. These books could not be recommended.

While no one can put together a wonderful book simply from a list of ingredients, it is possible to think about the elements that, taken together, may make a book both enjoyable and enlightening. Some of the qualities that make a fiction book especially useful for helping a child include:

- *Characters we care about and believe in.*
- *Characters with believable emotions and reactions.*
- *Humor, surprise, or suspense.*
- *Creative problem-solving.*
- *Engaging, eye-catching illustrations.*

It's been lots of fun reading all of these wonderful children's books. I hope that you will find, as I have, a world of good friends and counselors among these books, who are here to help your child on her journey through growing up.

Cheryl Coon

INTRODUCTION

We read to know we are not alone.
—C.S. Lewis

"Oh Mom, don't tell me you're going to give me a bunch of books to read about lying," my son Eli moaned as I came home one day with a stack of books. I had caught him in a lie and I responded by bringing home fiction about other children who had told lies.

On this particular occasion, my nine-year-old son had discovered the powerful allure of lying. Eli noticed that when he told the truth, particularly when it involved something he wanted to do or possess, the results did not seem to be rewarding. Often, he did not obtain the toy he wanted and, if he had broken a family rule, there was a consequence. So why not lie about it? Why not say that he had taken his vitamin even though he hadn't? Why not report that he had brushed his teeth when all he had done was rinse his mouth with water?

He needed to understand that there are consequences to lying, consequences more serious than the loss of television or parental approval. So off I went, hoping to find books with characters who also had succumbed to the temptation to lie. Perhaps, if I were lucky, I would find a book about a nine-year-old boy who had lied to his mom. I had discovered that reading about fictional characters and how they handle a problem offered my children a roadmap, not only to solutions to that particular problem but also to the very tools of problem-solving.

If you can find a book dealing with a fictional situation similar to your child's issue, you can accomplish two important things. First, you can offer your child the reassurance that he isn't alone, that other children have faced the same problem and found ways to deal with it. Second, with books, you can reach your child without preaching or lecturing. Is there a parent who hasn't experienced the glazed-eyes syndrome the moment she opens her mouth to deliver well-meant words of wisdom? When you provide the right book to your child, to be read-aloud together or read on his own, the glazed-eyes syndrome surrenders to engagement in the story.

What I knew from past experience was that even if my son recognized that I had deliberately given him a book to make a point, it still would help him. That was the case whether I read the book aloud to him or he read it to himself. We would talk, perhaps not about his own lies, but about the character and what the character did. We might talk about the long-term consequences and what they meant for that character. Or we might focus on how the character felt. Somehow the story would work its magic. It would reassure him that other children had tried lying and that giving in to the temptation to lie, while wrong, was not unusual or different. It might not change everything but it would start him thinking.

Years earlier, his sister Nora, when transitioning from diapers to the toilet, had been afraid to go to the bathroom alone at night. I was in despair about how to persuade her to give up her 3 a.m. escort. Although we lit the hallway with nightlights and offered her talismans to carry to the bathroom, Nora was reluctant to walk through the house alone at night.

Then I stumbled on Anna Grossnickle Hines's *All by Myself*, a story about a little girl who was afraid to go to the bathroom at night. After a few readings, Nora seemed empowered to conquer her fear. Was it the realization that another little girl had faced the same problem?

Was it that she could identify with the character and see that someone else could solve the problem, hence she could too?

When you think about it, seeking fictional characters with whom we can identify is something adults instinctively do for ourselves. Anyone who has had a friend with cancer will find Elizabeth Berg's *Talk Before Sleep* a compelling and powerful story. Similarly, other books have explored the territory of marital relationships, mothers and daughters, and extended families. When we experience impending motherhood or the empty-nest syndrome, we are naturally drawn to stories with characters facing the same issues.

When your child is adjusting to preschool, having trouble sharing with other children, or dealing with a bully, you want to help. But simply offering advice may not work. Perhaps your child is too young to understand explicit advice. Perhaps he's at that stage when your advice is the last thing he thinks he needs. You want to help your child solve the immediate problem and learn how to approach other problems that lie ahead. You want to reach your child and open the opportunity to discuss the issue. The right fiction can help.

An approach known as bibliotherapy uses books, both fiction and nonfiction, to help people. Some experts view traditional bibliotherapy as the exclusive province of trained librarians, psychologists and psychiatrists. Others distinguish between developmental bibliotherapy (for normal life stages or transitions) and clinical bibliotherapy (for especially difficult emotional issues).

Although traditional bibliotherapy may be carried out by a therapist, using fiction to help children isn't limited to that setting. It's simple common sense. As children read fiction and observe the behavior of the characters, they learn how to solve problems or at least that problems can be solved. A parent, a teacher, a librarian or a counselor who knows a particular child need not shy away from finding an appropriate fiction book for that child. Reserving bibliotherapy to specialists means foregoing a valuable tool to help kids with resources available to all of us.

The critical element is always the choice of book. The entire process depends on choosing a book whose characters a child truly can relate to and identify with, a book that assures a child he is not alone and offers him the opportunity to consider and discuss different strategies for handling a problem. Only then can the book work its magic.

How to Use Fiction to Help Children

Books are the quietest and most constant of friends:
they are the most accessible and wisest of counselors,
and the most patient of teachers.
—Charles W. Eliot

Whether you are a parent, teacher, school librarian, or school counselor, the first step is to find the right book for a particular child and the issue he is facing. *Books to Grow With* includes a variety of organizational tools to help you. Your first stop should be the Table of Contents, to look for the topic that interests you. From there, you'll want to read the reviews of the recommended books to find the ones that you think will interest your child.

Perhaps you are looking for books with multicultural characters or which are available in Spanish. If so, you can check the Index that specifically lists those books. If your child is especially fond of *Berenstain Bear* books, you may want to use the Titles Index. Or maybe you'd like to look for a favorite author or illustrator, in which case the appropriate index will assist you.

Once you have selected the book, you'll want to read it, together or separately. You may read the book with just one child or with a group of children. Not every child will be enthusiastic about reading a book you've selected. A child may not show interest in the book and there's no point in insisting. I always found it remarkably effective simply to leave the book on the kitchen table. Sooner or later, I would see my child pick it up and become engrossed.

After you both have read the book you will naturally be ready to talk about it. But not every child will want to talk. Discussion is not critical to success with fiction. As any teacher knows, there are approaches other than talking for following up on reading. Some of the options both for individual children and for groups include drawing, story telling, acting the story out, creating a diary for a character in the story, writing a letter from one character to another, composing an alternate ending, or producing a puppet show from the story.

If you do have a conversation about the book, be open to the possibility that it may go in many directions, depending on the child's maturity, interest, and personality. Children enjoy giving their opinions on books and often will respond to your question about a particular element of the plot or perhaps an especially funny part of the story.

Ask your child what she liked or disliked about the story. Give her a chance to talk about the main character and the problem he is facing. Ask your child what he thinks the character is feeling and what he might do to solve the problem. Sometimes it's engaging to consider other ways the book might have ended or other approaches a character might have tried.

There are a few pitfalls to avoid. Most of them call for simple common sense and kindness. No child wants to face scrutiny as the designated representative of a particular issue:

> *"So, Tommy, is that how it feels to you?"*
> *"So, Mary, now do you see ways to stop bullying?"*

It is neither fair nor effective to embarrass a child and force him to discuss a problem. You may be surprised at how well you can communicate when the focus isn't on your own child's behavior but on a fictional character.

Listen to what your child tells you. It may offer you valuable hints on how to help him progress with his issue. Remember, it's not so much the solution that the fictional character discovers as it is that your child is learning that the problem can be addressed. By the way, these conversations often work best in the car or at bedtime.

What You Will Find in the Book Reviews

Your time is valuable. You want to spend it helping your child, not searching for books. The goal of *Books to Grow With* is to help you find books quickly. Every review begins with the same factual information in the same format: title, author, illustrator, publisher, publishing date, number of pages, and a brief description of the illustrations.

Every book review contains a plot summary that indicates whether the main character is a girl or a boy, the main character's approximate age, and the theme of the story. The reviews also indicate whether a book features multicultural characters and whether a Spanish language translation is available. For any book that has received recognition from one of the many organizations that annually recognize excellence in text, illustration, or both, you will find in the listing what awards the book has received.

Every book is suitable for reading aloud. Children enjoy being read to long after they are capable of reading on their own. Sometimes, in fact, a good way to entice a child to try a book is to begin as a read-aloud and then let a child continue it on his own.

Books to Grow With is organized by issue rather than by age group. Many children's books designate a reading level based on age or grade. But it's important to remember that older children may enjoy a picture book and younger children may enjoy listening to a chapter book. Some picture books may be suitable only for advanced readers due to different fonts, use of cartoon bubbles and other factors. Similarly, some transitional chapter books feature limited, simple text and may be suitable for courageous beginning readers. Each review will provide you with the information you need to determine how best to share the book.

Because the recommended books may be read together or separately, you will find *ratings based on the skill of the reader*.

The designations are: beginning readers (very limited vocabulary and text), intermediate readers (still limited vocabulary but significantly more text), and advanced readers (challenging vocabulary).

The recommended books include toddler books (sometimes in a board book format), picture books (generally fewer than 32 pages in length with color illustrations on every page or every other page), transitional chapter books (short chapters) and chapter books up to 100 pages.

You will also find *ratings based on age*, in parentheses at the end of each review. These designations should used only as a guideline. Do consider a book designated for a different age group if it otherwise sounds interesting for your child.

Recommended Books

---

*It was books that taught me that the things that
tormented me most were the very things that
connected me with all the people who were alive,
or who had ever been alive.*
—James Baldwin

The Early Childhood Transitions

Moving From a Crib to a Big Bed

The change from a crib to a "big kid bed" is
momentous for many children. It is a big change and perhaps the first recognition that a child is growing up. For
many children, it is both exciting and scary to leave the
cozy safety of a crib. Children wonder "will I fall out?" and
"am I ready for this?"

Billy's Big-Boy Bed
by Phyllis Limbacher Tildes.
Whispering Coyote Press, 2002. 32 pages.
Cheerful watercolors.
Read-aloud or intermediate readers.

Billy, a toddler, is outgrowing his clothes, his shoes,
and his crib. His parents suggest a new bed and they buy
one despite Billy's ambivalence. But they wisely do not
insist that he make the move. Instead, his new bed is
installed in his room and his mother puts a cozy quilt on
top. But Billy continues to sleep in his crib. By the third
night, Billy has moved all his stuffed animals except one

1

into the new bed and, in the morning, his parents come in to find that Billy and his last stuffed animal slept in the new bed. Billy is proud of himself, as are his parents. A warm, reassuring look at the transition to a big-boy bed. (Ages 2-4)

My New Bed
by Stan and Jan Berenstain.
Random House, 1999. 14 pages.
Familiar Berenstain bear cartoon figures.
Board book format.
Read-aloud or intermediate readers.

In a simple, first person narrative, a little bear (gender unspecified) talks about how his crib suited him when he was little, helped him learn to stand, and kept him safe. But as he recognizes, he is bigger now and has more stuff so his crib doesn't suit him anymore. He shows enthusiasm and excitement about moving to his "grand new, brand-new" bed. While the book doesn't express any hesitation or concern by the little bear, it does give him the chance to matter-of-factly explain why a crib no longer works for him. (Ages 2-4)

My Own Big Bed
by Anna Grossnickle Hines.
Illustrated by Mary Watson.
Greenwillow Books, 1998. 22 pages.
Soft but realistic oil paints.
Read-aloud or intermediate readers.
Parent's Choice Award winner.

A little girl is proud that she is about to sleep in her own big bed, but she also thinks about her fears (falling out, getting lonely, getting lost, getting scared). For each fear, she devises a simple solution and expresses confidence in her ability to solve the problem. An outstanding choice for a child transitioning from crib to bed. (Ages 2-5)

POTTY TRAINING

Few transitions are more difficult for both parent and child than potty training. For a parent, it is the hope that an unpleasant chore is over. For a child, it is the beginning of true independence and control over himself, a self that he increasingly recognizes to be separate from his parent.

Everyone Poops
by Taro Gomi.
Translated by Amanda Mayer Stinchecum.
Kane/Miller 1993. 26 pages.
Vivid, distinctive illustrations.
Read-aloud or intermediate readers.
Multicultural. Available in Spanish.
This book tells a simple story, that every living creature poops. Its references to potty training are indirect. After observing the ways and places animals poop, the book shows grown-ups and children pooping in "special places" and notes that while some children poop on the potty, "others poop in their diapers." The rest of the pictures with humans show them pooping in the toilet. The message, while not the lead theme of the book, is that pooping in the toilet is our special way of doing it. (Ages 2-4)

I Have to Go
by Anna Ross.
Illustrated by Norman Gorbaty.
Random House, 1990. 24 pages.
Brightly-colored Sesame Street characters.
Read-aloud or intermediate readers.
Little Grover hurries past all of his friends, who invite him to stop and play. To each invitation he responds, "No, thank you. I have to go," leading them to wonder where he is headed. Finally he reaches his mother, who

helps him unfasten his straps. He then uses the potty all by himself, and his mother shares his pride. Suitable for the youngest of children, especially Sesame Street fans, this book conveys the pleasure Little Grover and his mother feel at his growing independence. (Ages 2-4)

Koko Bear's New Potty
by Vicki Lansky.
Illustrated by Jane Prince.
Book Peddlers, 1997. 32 pages.
Pen and ink drawings.
Read-aloud only, due to advice for adults.

Koko Bear decides to try the potty because he enjoys the way a dry diaper feels. But when he tries to use the potty, nothing happens. His mother reassures him and the next time he tries he succeeds. His rewards are his own happiness, brand new "Big-bear" pants, and his mother's pride in him. Though he later has an accident, his mother again reassures him that this is okay. The story line is thin but it covers many of the classic concerns and motivations about using a potty. The approach of the Koko Bear series is to present a "read-together book" with a story, as well as practical tips for parents on each page. (Ages 2-4)

Max's Potty
by Harriet Ziefert.
Illustrated by Emily Bolam.
DK Publications, 1999. 18 pages.
Bright primary colors.
Read-aloud; Lift-the-flaps format.
Out of print but available in libraries and used bookstores.

Max, a toddler, wears a diaper and finds many funny uses for the potty. But eventually Max figures out what to do with a potty, remembers to wash his hands, and wears "big boy underwear." Humorous questions and illustrations in bold primary colors invite the reader to consider whether various animals use a potty and then whether Max does. Very simple, suitable for the youngest of children. (Ages 2-4)

On Your Potty
by Virgina Miller.
Candlewick Press, 2000. 22 pages.
Dreamy watercolors. Board book format.
Read-aloud or beginning readers.

A large bear named George tries to enlist the cooperation of Bartholomew, a baby bear, to get ready in the morning by pooping on his own, but Bartholomew resists. When George insists that Bartholomew sit on his potty, nothing happens. But after Bartholomew goes outside to play, he suddenly has the urge to go and remembers his potty. He reaches his potty just in time and gets a big hug from George. Simple story line emphasizes both the young bear's stubborn determination to do what he wants and the pride he feels when he is able to use a potty successfully. (Ages 2-4)

Sam's Potty
by Barbro Lindgren.
Illustrated by Eva Eriksson.
William Morrow & Company, 1986. 32 pages.
Simple but humorous drawings.
Read-aloud or beginning readers.

Sam tries to entice his dog onto the potty but soon he sees that it just isn't right for Doggie. He solves the problem by sitting on the potty (and using it) while holding Doggie on his lap! A delightful story for the youngest readers about a little boy who doesn't seem to want to sit on his potty. (Ages 2-4)

The Princess and the Potty
by Wendy Cheyette Lewison.
Illustrated by Rick Brown.
Aladdin Library, 1998. 40 pages.
Humorous evocative watercolors.
Read-aloud or intermediate readers.

Once upon a time, a princess refused to use her potty despite entreaties from her royal parents. The King and Queen commissioned unique potties (polka dot, musical, glow-in-the-dark) but the princess refused to use any of them. A wise man counseled patience and advised that the princess would use the potty when it pleased her to do so. Finally, the princess decided to use the potty because it enabled her to wear new "pantalettes" and that mattered more than resisting her parents. A good book for young girls because it has an amusing story and eye-catching illustrations. (Ages 2-4)

GIVING UP COMFORT OBJECTS

A familiar thumb, a pacifier, a fuzzy blanket—these are the things that so many young children find reassuring. But there comes a time when a child gives up these comforts, either because they get in the way of more active pursuits or perhaps because a parent urges a child to do so. Even the most mature child may find it hard to give up sucking a thumb or pacifier, or carrying a blanket, and may need some loving assistance.

THUMB-SUCKING

Danny and his Thumb
by Kathryn F. Ernst.
Illustrated by Tomie de Paola.
Prentice-Hall, 1973. 32 pages.
Simple, charming illustrations.

Read-aloud or intermediate readers.
Out of print but available in libraries and used
bookstores.

Danny has sucked his thumb since he was a baby. There are various places where Danny enjoys sucking his thumb. Now that school has started, Danny doesn't like doing it as much. Noticing other children don't do it any-more, he decides that he doesn't have the time for it either because of his many activities. The simple story does not offer any practical advice. Instead, it focuses on the more grown-up and interesting things Danny now has in his life. A nice reminder that giving up thumb-sucking may simply happen in its own good time. (Ages 4-8)

Donald Says Thumbs Down
by Nancy Evans Cooney.
Illustrated by Maxie Chambliss.
Putnam Publishing Group, 1987. 32 pages.
Bright, colored illustrations.
Read-aloud or intermediate readers.
Out of print but available in libraries and used book-
stores.

Donald experiences the frustration and embarrass-ment of wanting to quit sucking his thumb and being unable to do so. He devises his own strategies: wearing mittens, putting a bad taste on his thumb, sitting on his hands. When his ideas fail, his mother comforts him. They decide to play a game, "Donald Says," in which Donald directs their activities. Eventually Donald applies the game to his thumb-sucking and tells himself, "Thumbs down." Using this approach, Donald succeeds. It's helpful for children to see that it isn't always easy to give up thumb-sucking. Sometimes you have to try lots of strate-gies before you find the approach that works for you. (Ages 4-8)

Harold's Hideaway Thumb
by Harriet Sonnenschein.
Illustrated by Jurg Obrist.
Aladdin Library, 1993. 32 pages.
Colorful, active illustrations.
Read-aloud or intermediate readers.

Harold, the little bunny, is growing up. But he just can't seem to give up sucking his thumb. He tries to hide his thumb but that doesn't work. Then he tries wearing a balloon or a bell to remind himself, as well as posting pictures of himself sucking his thumb in every room in the house. One day he overhears his parents talking about how he has forgotten thumb sucking and he proudly answers that he remembers but he is a big bunny now. Simple story emphasizes Harold's own desire to move on and his ingenious attempts at a solution. (Ages 4-8)

The Quitting Deal
by Tobi Tobias.
Illustrated by Trina Schart Hyman.
Viking Press, 1975. 27 pages.
Simple line drawings.
Read-aloud or intermediate readers.

The story contrasts an older child's thumb sucking with her mother's smoking addiction. They decide to quit together and, in a series of vignettes, they try a variety of approaches including holding hands, substituting candy, paying a fine, and so on. Despite their efforts, both cheat at times. Finally they decide that neither of them can quit altogether, but each will try to do it less often. Useful for older children but somewhat pessimistic in its message. (Ages 5-9)

PACIFICERS

The Last Noo-Noo
by Jill Murphy.
Candlewick Press, 1995. 32 pages.
Humorous illustrations.
Read-aloud or intermediate readers.
1995 Nestle Smarties Award winner.

Marlon, a charming green monster, loves his pacifier, which he calls a "noo-noo." But his grandmother warns his mother of dire consequences unless he stops using it. His mother hides all the noo-noos but Marlon also hides noo-noos throughout the house: under the armchair, in the back of the breadbox, in the toe of his boot, and so on. Mom and Granny warn him that the other monsters will tease him but even teasing doesn't discourage him. As his supply dwindles, Marlon plants one of his last ones in the garden, hoping it will grow others. When the other little monsters snatch his last noo-noo, it's okay with Marlon. He has a secret, his noo-noo tree! A delightful lighthearted look at pacifiers and control struggles. (Ages 4-8)

Little Bunny's Pacifier Plan
by Maribeth Boelts.
Illustrated by Kathy Parkinson.
Albert Whitman & Company, 2001. 32 pages.
Bright, busy watercolors and ink.
Read-aloud or intermediate readers.

Little Bunny loves his pacifier. In fact, he has learned to do just about everything with his pacifier in his mouth. But his dentist suggests that it's time to put it away and he has some suggestions about how to succeed. Little Bunny follows the dentist's suggestions. He tries keeping the pacifier in his room and then progresses to keeping it on a chair. His struggles are shown, as well as the loving support of his parents. Eventually Little Bunny stops wanting the pacifier and, when his cousin is born, he wraps it up and gives it to her as a present. A practical solution that may interest your child. (Ages 4-8)

STUFFED ANIMALS

Dogger
by Shirley Hughes.
HarperCollins Juvenile Books, 1993. 32 pages.
Gentle, sepia-toned illustrations.
Read-aloud or intermediate readers.
1977 Kate Greenaway Award winner.

Dave's most cherished possession is his soft old stuffed animal, Dogger. Dave takes Dogger with him everywhere, pulling him on a leash, carrying him, and giving him rides in a wagon. Unlike his sister and brother who enjoy lots of toys, Dave loves only Dogger. Then one day Dave loses Dogger. He is heartbroken until he spies Dogger on a toy stand at the school summer fair. While he races to find his parents, another child buys Dogger. But Dave's sister saves the day, giving up the prize she has won to buy Dogger back for her brother. The classic about a lost stuffed animal, the story is all the more touching for its lack of preachy tone and for the genuine kindness it portrays between siblings. (Ages 3-8)

I Lost My Bear
by Jules Feiffer.
HarperTrophy, 2000. 40 pages.
Bright, aggressive ink and watercolors.
Read-aloud or advanced readers.
1998 New York Times Best Illustrated Children's Books of the Year winner.

A little girl loses her stuffed bear and seeks help from her family to find it. Her mother suggests that she "think like a detective." Her father suggests that she figure it out for herself and her sister suggests that she try throwing another stuffed animal, hoping it will land in the same place. While none of these approaches is successful, she does find many other lost items. The little girl is sad and feels a little guilty when she realizes that the search itself has distracted her from remembering her lost bear. When she goes to bed, she cries about how no one in her family would help her. Then she finds her bear waiting in her bed. No strategies here, but reassurance that sometimes lost things turn up even when you've given up looking for them. (Ages 4-8)

BLANKETS

D. W.'s Lost Blankie
by Marc Tolon Brown.
Little, Brown and Company, 2000. 24 pages.
Familiar illustrations from the television series.
Read-aloud or intermediate readers.

In this story focusing on D.W., Arthur's little sister, a beloved blanket is misplaced. Everyone helps D. W. search for it but when it isn't found D. W. faces a night without blankie. However, Mother comes to the rescue with the blanket, freshly laundered, and D.W. is able to fall asleep. No message about giving up a blanket, but a nice recognition of the importance of comfort objects and the fact that they have to be cleaned sometimes! (Ages 2-4)

Geraldine's Blanket
by Holly Keller.
William Morrow & Company, 1988. 32 pages.
Simple, humorous drawings.
Read-aloud or beginning to intermediate readers.
Available in Spanish.

Geraldine's pink blanket goes everywhere with her and she literally loves it to pieces! Despite her parents' disapproval, Geraldine refuses to give her blanket up. No matter what strategies they try, including giving her a new doll, Geraldine stubbornly remains attached to her blanket. When her parents insist that she give it up, Geraldine neatly solves the problem by making it into a dress for the new doll! A story children will love because, in the end, Geraldine keeps her blanket in her own determined way. (Ages 2-4)

Owen
by Kevin Henkes.
Greenwillow Books, 1993. 32 pages.
Gentle, reassuring watercolors.
Read-aloud or intermediate readers.
Available in Spanish.
1994 Caldecott Award winner; 1994 Boston Globe-Horn Honor Award winner.

Owen loves his fuzzy blanket. He takes it everywhere. But his mother thinks he's too old for it and tries different strategies to persuade him to give it up. Owen refuses to give it up and insists on taking it to school. Then Mom comes up with a winning idea. She cuts the blanket into handkerchiefs. Now Owen can take it everywhere again. A kind and loving recognition that even when a child seems too old for a comfort object, he may need a way to keep it with him. (Ages 3-8)

NEW EXPERIENCES

LOOSE TEETH

"I lost my tooth!" is the triumphant and universal cry as a child turns an important corner in his development. Early grade school years are punctuated by lost teeth as children lose twenty teeth during their grade school years. It is a happy time but it can be stressful too.

If everyone else in your class has lost a tooth and you still have a full smile of baby teeth, life is worrisome. This is one of those times parents can anticipate a child's concerns and provide him with good books that address this event as well as celebrate a memorable occasion.

Arthur's Tooth
by Marc Brown.
Joy Street Books, 1985. 32 pages.
Familiar illustrations from the series.
Read-aloud or intermediate readers.

Arthur has a problem. Everybody in his class has lost a baby tooth except him. Now that he is seven years old he expects to lose a tooth too. His friends are happy to help. The Brain invents a Tooth Remover and Binky offers to sock it out. Arthur waits and waits to lose his first tooth. Funny but realistic, this story would work well for Arthur fans. It also reassures that teeth will fall out when they're ready and not before. (Ages 4-8)

Little Rabbit's Loose Tooth
by Lucy Bate.
Illustrated by Diane de Groat.
Crown Publications, 1988. 28 pages.
Homey, detailed illustrations.
Read-aloud or intermediate readers.

When Little Rabbit has her first loose tooth she thinks she cannot eat her carrots and beans for dinner. "You can chew on your other teeth," says her father. When her tooth comes out in a bowl of chocolate ice cream, she considers what she might do with it, such as making it into a necklace, drawing stars around it and hanging it on her wall, or trying to buy some candy with it. Ultimately she decides to put her tooth under her pillow for the Tooth Fairy. This book celebrates the fun of losing a tooth in a gentle and sweet way. (Ages 4-8)

Madlenka
by Peter Sis.
Frances Foster Books, 2000. 48 pages.
Unusual, appealing illustrations.
Read-aloud or intermediate readers.
Multicultural.
2000 Parenting Best Books of the Year Award winner.

Madlenka walks, runs, struts, and rushes around her block in New York City to tell her multinational neighbors the wonderful news that her tooth is loose! While this book does not deal with any concerns, it offers opportunities to emphasize the exciting side of losing a tooth. (Ages 4-8)

My Loose Tooth
by Stephen Krensky.
Illustrated by Hideko Takahashi.
Random House, 1999. 32 pages.
Bright, distinctive illustrations; rhyming verse.
Read-aloud or beginning readers.

A little boy discovers that his tooth is loose. He wonders how to make it come out and whether animals have the same problem. Finally he loses his tooth. He reassures himself at the end that a brand-new tooth will take the place of the one he has lost. A good story for generating discussion with a child experiencing his first loose tooth. (Ages 4-8)

My Tooth is Loose!
by Martin Silverman.
Illustrated by Amy Aitken.
Puffin Books, 1994. 32 pages.
Appealing drawings.
Read-aloud or intermediate readers.

Georgie's tooth is loose and he isn't sure what to do about it. His friends suggest ideas for getting his tooth to fall out but Georgie is afraid that it will hurt. Finally he goes to his mother, who reassures him that his tooth will fall out all by itself. A simple story that reassures. (Ages 4-8)

Teeth Week
by Nancy Alberts.
Little Apple, 1993. 76 pages.
Occasional black-and-white drawings.
Read-aloud or intermediate readers.
Out of print but available in libraries and
used bookstores.

Everyone in Liza's second grade classroom has lost at least one tooth except for Liza. When her teacher announces the beginning of Teeth Week, Liza is hopeful that perhaps a tooth will finally fall out. Various adventures ensue, including dealing with a teasing boy, finishing an art project for Teeth Week, dealing with substitute teachers, and finally, losing a tooth in a most unexpected way. Most of the books that deal with losing a tooth are written for very young children so it's helpful to find a book on the topic aimed at older children. (Ages 7-9)

BABYSITTERS

Early experiences with babysitters are difficult for many children. Perhaps this is the first time that parents have left a child in someone else's care. The babysitter may be a stranger unaccustomed to the usual comforting home routines. Children may be afraid of being alone with someone they don't know well who cannot meet their needs the way parents can. A little advance talking about babysitters can go a long way to allay these fears and pave the way for a successful experience. These stories, filled with all kinds of kids with all kinds of babysitters, offer opportunities to begin your discussions.

Bear and Mrs. Duck
by Elizabeth Winthrop.
Illustrated by Patience Brewster.
Holiday House, 1988. 32 pages.
Gentle, humorous watercolors.
Read-aloud or intermediate readers.
Out of print but available in libraries and
used bookstores.

Bear's best friend Nora has to go to the store. Bear isn't happy about being left with Mrs. Duck, a babysitter, so he plans to sit and wait for Nora's return. After Mrs. Duck succeeds in coaxing him into some fun, Bear realizes that even though he'd prefer to be with Nora, being with Mrs. Duck also is enjoyable. A nice message that it's okay to enjoy your babysitter even if you'd prefer that your family were at home. (Ages 3-8)

The Berenstain Bears and the Sitter
by Stan & Jan Berenstain.
Random House, 1981. 32 pages.
Familiar Berenstain cartoon illustrations.
Read-aloud or intermediate readers.
Available in Spanish.

When Mama and Papa Bear decide to attend an important neighborhood meeting and none of the usual family babysitters is available, Mama Bear calls Mrs. Grizzle. "I understand Mrs. Grizzle has raised seven cubs of her own," says Mama reassuringly, "and I'm pretty sure she's a perfectly good back scrubber, story reader, and tucker-inner." But the kids remember that Mrs. Grizzle looked grumpy when Sister's ball went into her garden. When Mrs. Grizzle arrives with a bag full of cards and games, the evening goes just fine. And she turns out to be a perfectly good back scrubber, story reader, and tucker-inner. This story reassures children that first impressions of a babysitter may turn out to be mis-impressions. (Ages 4-8)

Eleanor and the Babysitter
by Susan Hellard.
Joy Street Books, 1991. 32 pages.
Soft, expressive watercolors.
Read-aloud or intermediate readers.
Out of print but available in libraries and used bookstores.

Eleanor, a young aardvark, is dismayed to hear that she will be staying home with a babysitter and angrily points out that she is not a baby. She proceeds to reject every suggestion her babysitter makes. Finally, Eleanor shuts herself in a closet and becomes terrified by the shapes in the dark until the babysitter comes to her rescue. Eleanor has just begun to enjoy being with her babysitter when her parents come home. A good message that even older kids can have fun with a babysitter. (Ages 4-8)

An Evening at Alfie's
by Shirley Hughes.
Lothrop, Lee & Shepard, 1984. 32 pages.
Comfy, colorful drawings.
Read-aloud or intermediate readers.
Out of print but available in libraries and used bookstores.

Alfie and his baby sister Annie Rose have a great teenaged babysitter, Maureen, from down the street. After his parents leave Alfie snuggles up for a story with Maureen. Soon Alfie is ready to go to sleep but he hears a dripping sound. He and Maureen find a bucket to catch the drip. When that isn't enough Maureen calls her parents to help and her father shuts off the broken pipe. The positive message is that having a babysitter can be a comfortable and loving experience and if there's a problem, everyone will pitch in and take care of it until parents are home. (Ages 3-8)

The Good-Bye Book
by Judith Viorst.
Illustrated by Kay Chorao.
Aladdin Library, 1992. 32 pages.
Impressionistic, detailed watercolors.
Read-aloud or intermediate readers.

In a monologue by a little boy, we see his desire for his parents to stay home, his anger that they are leaving him home with a babysitter, his pleading and his bargaining. He even resorts to threats, including that he will never say goodbye. In the end, after they leave and his babysitter distracts him with a good book, we hear him say goodbye. This simple story may work both with the youngest of children as a way to spur discussion about the feeling of being left behind as well as with older children who may find the monologue interesting. (Ages 4-8)

Howard and the Sitter Surprise
by Priscilla Paton.
Illustrated by Paul Meisel.
Houghton Mifflin, 1996. 28 pages.
Cartoon pictures.
Read-aloud or intermediate readers.

Howard doesn't like babysitters and apparently they don't like him because they never return after the first experience. Finally, Howard's mom finds a special babysitter, Sarah. Sarah lives in the woods behind the family house and they call her with a whistle because she is a bear! Howard tries all his tricks, including climbing on top of the refrigerator and holding his breath when he wants something. But Sarah wins him over and she has an important message for Howard. It's not that parents don't love their kids when they leave them with a babysitter, it's that "big bears need to do big bear business and have big bear fun." An engaging story that conveys its message in a gentle way. (Ages 3-8)

Koko Bear's New Babysitter
by Vicki Lansky.
Illustrated by Jane Prince.
Bantam Doubleday Dell Books, 1987. 32 pages.
Read-aloud only due to advice for adults.
Out of print but available in libraries and used bookstores.

Although Koko is nervous about a new babysitter, his parents have left a surprise snack in the fridge and the babysitter brought a puppet to read a story. One in a series called Practical Parenting, this book offers a story as well as tips for parents. The book is engaging enough to be included in our recommendations although it is an explicitly problem- solving book. (Ages 3-7)

Shoes like Miss Alice's
by Angela Johnson.
Illustrated by Ken Page.
Orchard Books, 1995. 28 pages.
Lively, realistic paintings.
Read-aloud or intermediate readers.
Out of print but available in libraries and used bookstores.

Sara's new babysitter, Miss Alice, turns out to be lots of fun. Miss Alice has shoes for dancing, shoes for walking, and fuzzy slippers for naptime. Since she has no special shoes for drawing, she and Sara draw pictures of everything they did during the day in their bare feet. The story reassures a child that she can have a fun day with a new babysitter. (Ages 3-7)

Thomas's Sitter
by Jean Richardson.
Illustrated by Dawn Holmes.
Simon and Schuster, 1991. 32 pages.
Soft, dreamy watercolors.

Read-aloud or intermediate readers.
Out of print but available in libraries and used bookstores.

Thomas is unhappy that his mother is returning to work and that he will have to stay home with a sitter. Usually his behavior is enough to discourage sitters but this time the sitter turns out to be a young man, Dan. To Thomas' surprise and delight, Dan is happy to do all the outdoor play that Thomas loves. A good choice for a child with a babysitter who is just a little different from the usual. (Ages 4-8)

What Kind of Babysitter is This?
by Dolores Johnson.
Pearson Higher Education Publishing, 1991. 26 pages.
Realistic watercolor and colored pencil illustrations.
Read-aloud or intermediate readers.
Multicultural.

Kevin, an African-American boy, is angry with his mother for leaving him at home. He is certain that his new babysitter will ignore him as all his other babysitters have. When the babysitter begins watching television, his fear seems to be confirmed. But the television program turns out to be his favorite, a baseball game. What's more, she begins to read a baseball book softly as well. Intrigued, Kevin snuggles up to her and they end up enjoying themselves. An unusual story that features an older African-American child as the main character. (Ages 4-8)

HAIRCUTS

We all remember a haircut that didn't turn out the way we had hoped. For children, the visit to the barbershop, the beauty parlor or the hair cutter, carries some real uneasiness. What about those cold scissors so close to your head or that loud buzzer coasting down your neck? The smells, the itchy hairs that fall into your shirt, the admonition to "hold still" all add to the anxiety about the experience. Is being transformed, even superficially, a comfortable, even exciting experience or is it a little scary?

The Day of the Bad Haircut
by Eva Moore.
Illustrated by Meredith Johnson.
Cartwheel Books, 1997. 32 pages.
Colorful, evocative illustrations.
Read-aloud or intermediate readers.

Molly's mother insists that she have a haircut despite Molly's protests. Mom is enthusiastic about the results but Molly is horrified because now she looks like a boy. Molly forgets about her hair until a construction crew begins work next door and a construction worker asks Molly and her brother, "Do you boys live here?" Molly angrily points out that she is a girl with a bad haircut and the construction worker is sympathetic. Mom apologizes and Molly feels better knowing that the haircut really isn't that important. A good story for every girl who has ever been mistaken for a boy because of her short hair. (Ages 4-8)

Jeremy's First Haircut
by Linda Walvoord Girard.
Illustrated by Mary Jane Begin.
Albert Whitman & Company, 1986. 24 pages.
Impressionistic drawings.
Read-aloud or intermediate readers.

Dad thinks that Jeremy is ready for his first haircut but Mom postpones it, until she finally decides to cut it herself. When Jeremy looks at himself afterwards in a mirror, he is delighted to see that now he looks like a big boy. Jeremy feels good about his haircut and thinks that he won't ever worry about a haircut again because he knows now that it's fun. A gentle and reassuring exploration of a little boy's feelings about his first haircut and his parents' different attitudes as well. (Ages 4-8)

Katy's First Haircut
by Gibbs Davis.
Illustrated by Linda Shute.
Houghton Mifflin Company, 1985. 32 pages.
Colorful, expressive drawings.
Read-aloud or intermediate readers.

Katy loves her long hair but sometimes it can be a nuisance to comb out the tangles. Katy decides to have it cut. She enjoys the haircut until she sees that people mistake her for a boy. So she hides her hair under a hat when she goes to school. When the other kids ask her why she's wearing a hat, she remembers why she decided to cut her hair in the first place and her teacher congratulates her on making a big decision and going through with it. Later she has an opportunity to reassure another child who is about to get her hair cut. A good story for a child whose issue is the way she feels about a haircut afterwards. (Ages 4-8)

Mike's First Haircut
by Sharon Gordon.
Illustrated by Gioia Fiammenghi.
Troll Associates, 1989. 30 pages.
Humorous tri-color drawings.
Read-aloud or beginning readers.
Out of print but available in libraries and used bookstores.

Mike's hair keeps growing until it covers his eyes and ears. Mother tells him it's time for a haircut but Mike worries about how it will look. But when the barber is done Mike is delighted to see that his haircut looks just like him! Simple reassurance that you won't emerge from a haircut no longer looking like yourself. (Ages 4-8)

Will Gets a Haircut
by Olof and Lena Landstrom.
Translated by Elisabeth Dyssegaard.
R & S Books, 2000.
Unusual, expressive drawings.
Read-aloud or intermediate readers.

Will is headed for a haircut but he isn't sure how he feels about it. He finds a picture in a magazine and shows it to the barber. The barber combs and cuts and the haircut is just what Will wanted. Mama looks a bit aghast but Will is pleased. Later he is the center of attention among his friends. The last page shows the barber giving a similar cut to another customer. A nice story about how a haircut sometimes becomes your own chosen transformation, one that you can have control in shaping. (Ages 4-8)

AIRPLANE TRIP

Airplane trips can be a great adventure, but adventures also have the potential to cause anxiety for some children. The chaos of the airport, the sensation of takeoff and landing, the strange pressure in your ears, and the turbulence call for some preparation beforehand. Some children will take their first flight alone, which has its own challenges. These books address both the details of the flight and the experience of flying alone.

First Flight
by David McPhail.
Joy Street Books, 1987. 32 pages.
Ink and watercolors.
Read-aloud or intermediate readers.

A little boy is going to take his first airplane trip to visit his grandmother. He describes in careful detail all the steps of his trip including finding his seat, listening to the safety rules, and relaxing during takeoff. As he calmly experiences the trip, a large bear seated next to him finds the experience difficult, and the little boy's presence soothes him. Nice for a younger child, especially in its use of the large bear to express the child's fears and concerns. (Ages 4-8)

I Fly
by Anne Rockwell.
Illustrated by Annette Cable.
Crown Publishers, 1997. 30 pages.
Detailed, realistic pictures.
Read-aloud or intermediate readers.
Multicultural.

The narrator, a young boy, describes in detail the experience of flying in an airplane to visit his cousins. His descriptions of everything from the way the plane feels as it coasts for takeoff to the feeling of ears popping to the food that is served are comforting in their matter-of-fact tone. Although he never mentions any concerns or fears, the story covers many aspects of flying and offers opportunities for questions and discussion. (Ages 4-8)

SLEEPOVERS

Perhaps nothing so signifies independence as the willingness and ability to be comfortable at night away from home and parents. For some children the first sleepover may occur at a young age, perhaps at a relative's home. For others, it may not come until the later elementary school years. Even when a child is close friends with another, the thought of falling asleep without familiar comforts and away from home can raise anxieties.

Arthur's First Sleepover
by Marc Brown.
Little, Brown and Company, 1996. 32 pages.
Familiar illustrations from the series.
Read-aloud or intermediate readers.
Available in both board book and paper.
Available in Spanish.

Arthur is busy preparing for his friend Buster to sleep over even though the date is still days away. When the big night arrives, Arthur and Buster are scared by a news article about spaceships and aliens. That night they're certain that they hear a space alien until they realize it's just D.W., Arthur's little sister. They pay her back with a dose of her own medicine and enjoy the rest of their night. A gentle way to reassure that nighttime sounds may be nothing to worry about and that everyone has a few anxieties on their first sleepover. (Ages 4-8)

Best Friends Sleep Over
by Jacqueline Rogers.
Scholastic, 2000. 31 pages.
Detailed, realistic watercolors.
Read-aloud or intermediate readers.

Gilbert, an endearing little gorilla, is both excited and worried about his first sleepover. He wonders whether he will be able to find the bathroom in the dark or have trouble falling asleep without his goodnight song. His mother counsels him to bring along his toy clown. Gilbert has a great time enjoying pizza, games, and a pillow fight but at bedtime he misses his mom and realizes he forgot his toy clown. Nothing comforts him until his friends lend him their teddy bear. After that, he has no trouble falling asleep. A sweet reminder that your child won't be alone; he will have his good friend to keep him company in the dark. (Ages 4-8)

Franklin Has a Sleepover
by Paulette Bourgeois.
Illustrated by Brenda Clark.
Scholastic, 1996. 30 pages.
Vividly colored illustrations.
Read-aloud or intermediate readers.

Franklin feels ready for his friend Bear to sleep over. Franklin and Bear are excited although Bear's parents voice some concern about Bear's readiness. The friends have a wonderful evening but when it's time to go to sleep Bear feels homesick. Franklin suggests they move to his room and gives Bear's bunny a goodnight hug just like Bear's mother always does. A warm story that shows children helping their friends through loving acceptance. (Ages 4-8)

Ira Sleeps Over
by Bernard Waber.
Houghton Mifflin, 1973. 48 pages.
Messy, childlike watercolors.
Read-aloud or intermediate readers.
Available in Spanish.

As Ira excitedly contemplates his sleepover at Reggie's house, his sister worries him by asking him how he will sleep without his teddy bear. Ira wonders what Reggie's reaction would be if Ira brought his bear. Once again Ira's sister causes him to doubt the wisdom of bringing his bear and he goes to the sleepover without it. After the boys scare themselves with ghost stories, Ira discovers that Reggie too has a teddy bear and he hurries home to get his own. A reminder that your child probably isn't alone in his feelings about his stuffed animal. (Ages 4-8)

Pajama Party
by Amy Hest.
Illustrated by Irene Trivas.
Beech Tree Books, 1994. 48 pages.
Soft watercolors.
Read-aloud or intermediate readers.

Three eight-year-old girls persuade their mothers to let them have a sleepover. Told in a first-person narrative by one of the girls, the story describes what happens when one of the girls is too homesick to spend the night. The other girls try to persuade her to stay but when she insists on leaving, they accept her need to go. She returns in the morning and is welcomed by the other girls. A story about being accepted by one's friends and about being ready to sleep away from home. (Ages 7-9)

Porcupine's Pajama Party
by Terry Webb Harshman.
Illustrated by Doug Cushman.
HarperTrophy, 1990. 64 pages.
Simple, limited illustrations.
Read-aloud or intermediate readers.

Porcupine invites both Owl and Otter to a sleepover. But both of them already have special plans (to watch a scary movie, to bake cookies) so Porcupine suggests they do all the activities together. The cookie dough gets eaten, the scary movie scares them, but the three friends help each other with their fears and have fun. Another story that accepts the feelings kids might have at a sleepover and offers the solace of good friends. (Ages 4-8)

Sarah's Sleepover
by Bobbie Rodriguez.
Illustrated by Mark Graham.
Viking Children's Books, 2000. 32 pages.
Soft, muted watercolors.

Read-aloud or intermediate readers.

    A sleepover story with a new twist—the hostess, Sarah, is blind. At first Sarah feels bad that she can't play certain games that require sight. But after her parents leave for a visit to nearby friends, the cousins enjoy a pillow fight until the lights unexpectedly go out. Then Sarah takes charge, reassuring the other girls about the dark and, in the process, feeling good about herself and her role in the group. A fine story for sleepovers and for children with disabilities. (Ages 4-8)

Somebody's New Pajamas
by Issac Jackson.
Illustrated by David Soman.
Dial Books for Young Readers, 1996. 30 pages.
Vivid watercolors.
Read-aloud or intermediate readers.
Multicultural.
Out of print but available in libraries and used bookstores.

    At his new friend's home for a sleepover, Jerome is embarrassed that he has no pajamas. He borrows his friend's pajamas and is impressed with the silk material as well as the affluence of his friend's house. When he returns home he is unhappy with the difference between his friend's wealthier home and his simple surroundings but sensitive handling by his parents helps Jerome to feel good about the way his family does things. This book is unusual: its sleepover story features boys and the socio-economic contrast between the two families, and its main characters are all African-American. (Ages 4-8)

The Tapping Tale
by Judy Giglio.
Illustrated by Joe Cepeda.
Green Light Readers, 2003. 16 pages.
Bright, bold illustrations.

Read-aloud or beginning readers.
Multicultural.

Two little girls have a sleepover but the guest hears a tapping noise and is afraid. Both girls investigate and discover that it's the pet dog under the bed, wagging his tail. A simple story in limited language that manages to convey all the main points about sleepovers. (Ages 4-8)

ILLNESS/A VISIT TO THE DOCTOR

Being sick transports all of us to a realm where we feel helpless. Most of the time, it just takes rest and time to get well, but sometimes a doctor's visit is necessary. Even as adults, many people feel anxiety about visiting the doctor. For little ones, the anxiety may begin with a story from an older sibling about shots or other unpleasant procedures. Or a child may visit a doctor when he is already sick and feeling out of sorts. These books present characters who face a trip to the doctor and discover that it's not as bad as they feared.

The Berenstain Bears Go to the Doctor
by Stan and Jan Berenstain.
Random House, 1981. 32 pages.
Familiar Berenstain Bear illustrations.
Read-aloud or intermediate readers.

The Berenstain bear cubs are headed for their annual exam and they aren't happy about it. Papa Bear assures them that it's nothing to worry about although he never goes because he's so healthy. He sneezes as they drive to the doctor's office, a hint that he soon may find out for himself what an exam is like. The cubs get full exams and then it's time for shots. Before the cubs can protest, the clever Dr. Grizzley calls in other cubs to watch "a brave little cub who's going to show you all how to take a shot." They are on their way out when Papa's sneezing catches the doctor's attention, and she insists on giving him medicine. A gentle poke at adults and their fears while reassuring kids. (Ages 4-8)

Big Bird Goes to the Doctor
by Tish Sommers.
Illustrated by Tom Cooke.
Western Publishing Company, 1986. 25 pages.
Familiar Sesame Street muppet illustrations.
Read-aloud or intermediate readers.
Out of print but available in libraries and used bookstores.

It's time for an annual checkup and Big Bird is worried that he will have to have a shot. Even though the doctor is interrupted frequently by other Sesame Street characters, the checkup goes well until it's time for Big Bird's shot. Big Bird attempts to avoid it but ultimately submits to the shot and later tells a friend that it hurt only briefly. For fans of the Sesame Street characters, Big Bird offers a familiar friend with whom they can identify. (Ages 4-8)

Corduroy Goes to the Doctor
by Don Freeman.
Illustrated by Lisa McCue.
Viking Press, 1987. 12 pages.
Cheerful reassuring illustrations.
Read-aloud in board book format.

Corduroy the Bear is a cuddly and expressive little guy. In this brief tale of his trip to the doctor, Corduroy enjoys the toys in the waiting room and most of the exam. When it's time for a shot Corduroy winces visibly but later he gets a balloon, a button, and praise for his bravery. For the youngest of children, a reassuring tale about what happens at the doctor. (Ages 2-4)

Hello Doctor
by David F. Marx.
Illustrated by Mark A. Hicks.
Children's Book Press, 2000. 24 pages.
Simple ink drawings; limited text.
Read-aloud or beginning readers.

A little boy at the doctor's office demonstrates all the things he can do, including saying "Ahhh," blowing out, bending over, and collecting a urine sample. But when it's time for a shot he voices his first uncertainty about whether he can "do this." He's worried that it will hurt. In the next drawing, the shot is over and he compliments himself on being brave. The story offers a good opportunity for very young children to talk about a doctor's visit. (Ages 4-8)

It's O.K.! Tom and Ally Visit the Doctor
by Beth Robbins.
Illustrated by Jon Stuart.
DK Publications, 2001. 32 pages.
Bright, cheerful illustrations.
Read-aloud or intermediate readers.
Out of print but available in libraries and used bookstores.

Tom and Ally, boy and girl kittens, worry about an upcoming visit to the doctor, especially after Ally unhelpfully explains to Tom what a shot is. Dad reassures them that if they think about something else, the shot will be over "in a flash" and he promises to have a bowl of fresh-picked strawberries waiting for them when they get home. In the cheery waiting room, other animals also are waiting to see the doctor, including a frog with a bucket stuck on his head and chicks with chicken pox. Tom and Ally enjoy playing with all the toys so much that they forget about the visit until it's their turn. The friendly elephant doctor lets them listen to each other's hearts with her stethoscope. Her instruments are realistically drawn, although the syringe is quite large.The shot is quickly over and the kittens happily return home only to find that their dad has injured himself. That gives them the chance to accompany him to the doctor and watch his reaction to the news that he needs a tetanus shot. Although the book risks preaching, the mostly realistic illustrations and humor make it a helpful addition. (Ages 4-8)

Pooh Gets a Checkup
by Kathleen W. Zoehfeld.
Illustrated by Robbin Cuddy.
Random House Disney, 2001. 24 pages.
The classic Pooh characters from the books and Disney films.
Read-aloud or intermediate readers.

Pooh is due for his "animal checkout" and he also feels "a bit rumbly" in his tummy. So it's time to go see Dr. Owl. But Pooh worries about getting a shot. During the examination Dr. Owl carefully explains each step in the process. When the time comes for Pooh's shot, Owl encourages him to bring in Piglet to hold his hand. Pooh bravely says later that it didn't hurt too much and to Pooh's delight, Dr. Owl prescribes a large pot of honey. The story offers familiar animal characters with whom children can identify in working through their fears. (Ages 4-8)

Robby Visits the Doctor
by Martine Davison.
Illustrated by Nancy Stephenson.
Random House, 1992. 30 pages.
Detailed ink and watercolors with close-ups of medical instruments.
Read-aloud or intermediate to advanced readers.
Multicultural.

Out of print but available in libraries and used bookstores.

Robby wakes up with a bad earache and feels anxious about visiting the doctor when he isn't feeling well. His parents try to reassure him but even in the waiting room he worries. Then he sees his friend and hears about shots, causing him to worry more. The nurse and doctor carefully explain each step of the examination and even let Robby examine them. He learns that all he has to do is take medicine and his ear will feel better. A calm and realistic look at how it feels to be sick and visit the doctor. (Ages 4-8)

When Vera Was Sick
by Vera Rosenberry.
Henry Holt and Company, 1998. 32 pages.
Unusual ink drawings.
Read-aloud or intermediate readers.

Vera has the measles so she moves into another room away from the rest of the family. She feels lonely and scared, but her family brings her a special pillow, ointment for her skin, and a book. Still, Vera wishes she could be part of the family's activities. As time drags by, her family sing to her, play with her, and do crafts with her. Finally, Vera is well again and she celebrates exuberantly. A fine tale that explores being sick and the pleasure of getting well. (Ages 4-8)

A VISIT TO THE DENTIST

Even as adults, many of us dread a visit to the dentist more than any other type of medical examination. What is there about "opening wide" that evokes such fear? Perhaps the mere sight of the tray of gleaming instruments or the dental chair is enough to scare anyone. Nowadays, many dentists emphasize gentle, painless care and perhaps the next generation will fear it less. In the meantime, here are some stories that talk about what to expect.

A Visit to the Dentist
by Eleanor Fremont.
Illustrated by Andy Mastrocinque.
Simon Spotlight, 2002. 24 pages.
Pastel illustrations based on the television series.
Read-aloud or intermediate readers.
Multicultural.

    Little Bill's tummy feels strange when he thinks about his upcoming visit to the dentist. But his friends April and Bobby remind him of the fun things, like the chair that moves up and down and the teeth cleaning machine. In the dentist's office, Little Bill is reassured by the hygienist when he worries about an X-ray, and he gets praise from the dentist for his good dental care. When Little Bill comes back to the waiting room he is able to reassure another child about what to expect. A nice addition because of its emphasis on children helping other children. (Ages 4-8)

Curious George Goes to the Dentist
by Margaret and H. A. Rey.
Adapted from the Curious George film series.
Houghton Mifflin, 1989.
Familiar illustrations of everyone's favorite mischievous monkey.
Read-aloud or intermediate to advanced readers.
Out of print but available in libraries and used bookstores.

    Every Curious George story has an adventure he experiences because of his endless curiosity. Here George is curious about the dentist's office. Not only will your child relate to George's curiosity about the levers and knobs on the dentist's chair, your child may also be intrigued, just as a little girl in the story is, by what George discovers. George finds the results humorous and so does the little girl, enough to help her get over her fear of the dentist. (Ages 4-8)

Just Going to the Dentist
by Mercer Mayer.
Golden Books Publishing Company, 2001. 24 pages.
Whimsical illustrations.
Read-aloud or intermediate readers.

Mayer's little monster (unspecified gender) has a mildly sarcastic and funny take on every new experience and the dentist's office is no exception. The hygienist shows off her teeth, the exam room looks like a spaceship, and there's even a sink in which to spit. Everything is going well until the dentist brings out a shot. But the little monster closes his eyes and counts to ten and the shot is done. After that, it's fun to not feel a thing. Great humor for the occasion. (Ages 4-8)

Milo's Toothache
by Ida Luttrell.
Illustrated by Enzo Giannini.
Puffin, 1997. 40 pages.
Soft, impressionistic watercolors.
Read-aloud or intermediate readers.

Milo, a young pig, realizes he has a toothache while he's playing with his friend, Dan. Although Milo initially isn't afraid of the dentist, Dan hints at horrors ahead. Dan insists on accompanying Milo to the appointment later that day and enlists their friend Amy to come as well. Amy enlists Pam, and when all the friends turn up at the appointment, Milo has nowhere to sit. When the friends overhear the dentist telling Milo to open wide, they become so agitated they end up getting injured. Now it's Milo's turn to accompany them to the doctor's office. A humorous take that gives children a chance to identify with fearless Milo as well as his fearful but loyal friends. (Ages 4-8)

Molly at the Dentist
by Angie Sage.
Peachtree Publishers, 2001. 12 pages.
Bright, playful illustrations
Read-aloud or intermediate readers in board book
format.

Molly, a young green monster, has two teeth and
now she must go to the dentist for a checkup. But she
balks at his request to open her mouth until he offers her
a look at her teeth with his tiny mirror. After that the visit
is a success and Dr. Brushwell even gives her a new toothbrush. A lift-the-flap format makes this book an active,
engaging winner for very young children. (Ages 2-5)

The Berenstain Bears Visit the Dentist
by Stan and Jan Berenstain.
Random House, 1981. 32 pages.
Familiar Berenstain Bear cartoon characters.
Read-aloud or intermediate readers.

Sister Bear has a loose tooth, which gives Brother an
excuse to tease her with the idea that Dr. Bearson, their dentist, will yank it out. By the time of the appointment with Dr.
Bearson, Sister's tooth still hasn't fallen out, so Sister decides
to watch Brother's examination, including a filling. Then Dr.
Bearson tells her it's her turn. Sister is dreading the "big
yankers" but instead Dr. Bearson gently extracts her tooth
with a bit of gauze. There's something about the bears and
their adventures that many children find very enjoyable,
although adults may tire of these books. (Ages 4-8)

A TRIP TO THE HOSPITAL

A visit to the doctor's office is an experience every
child will have but a stay in the hospital may be an experience none of your child's friends have had. Your child
may need a way to work through his fears and develop a
realistic picture of what it will be like. These books offer
familiar characters going to the hospital for the first time.

Betsy and the Doctor
by Gunilla Wolde.
Random House, 1992. 21 pages.
Ink and colored pencil drawings.
Read-aloud or intermediate readers.
Out of print but available in libraries and used bookstores.

Betsy falls from a tree and hits her head on a stone. She goes to the emergency room and there is so much to see she forgets to worry about the doctor. When the doctor arrives, he checks for broken bones, tells Betsy she will need stitches, and then explains she will need a shot first. Although the shot stings, Betsy realizes that even the stitches don't hurt because of the anesthesia. Later Betsy discovers that having stitches removed doesn't hurt either. A reassuring look at a visit to an emergency room and getting stitches. (Ages 4-8)

Franklin Goes to the Hospital
by Paulette Bourgeois.
Illustrated by Brenda Clark.
Scholastic, 2000. 32 pages.
Bright colors.
Read-aloud or intermediate readers.
Available in Spanish.

Franklin, a little boy turtle, is about to go to the hospital for the first time. He has a crack in his shell that requires an operation. Everyone compliments Franklin on his bravery but he confesses to his doctor how scared he feels. His doctor reassures him that fear has nothing to do with being brave and Franklin feels better. The operation goes smoothly and Franklin wakes up in his hospital room feeling better. The story offers an opportunity to talk about everything from the need for an empty stomach, to sitting in a wheelchair, to x-rays. A nicely detailed story for a child facing a trip to the hospital. (Ages 4-8)

Koko Bear's Big Earache
by Vicki Lansky.
Illustrated by Jane Prince.
Book Peddlers, 1990. 24 pages.
Simple, colored ink drawings.
Read-aloud or intermediate readers.

Koko, a bear of unspecified gender, wakes at night crying and finds it hard to hear during the day. Although the doctor gives Koko medicine, she also suggests ear tubes, carefully explaining that they are very tiny. The entire procedure in the hospital is done with great sensitivity to Koko's feelings. Although this book is unashamedly problem-solving, its story and thoughtful details make it a good book for starting a discussion with your child. Another entry in the Practical Parenting series, the story is accompanied by suggestions for parents. (Ages 3-8)

Miffy in the Hospital
by Dick Bruna.
Kodansha International, 1999.
Very simple line drawings.
Read-aloud or intermediate readers.

Miffy, a girl bunny, has a sore throat. At the doctor's office she learns that she will need to go to the hospital to have her tonsils removed. Miffy cries because she is scared to go to the hospital and stay there alone. But a kind nurse reassures her and the shot that she gives Miffy doesn't hurt much. Although having tonsils out and staying alone in the hospital may be an outdated practice, this book has a simple, gentle story line suitable for very young children facing this procedure. (Ages 3-8)

Paddington Bear Goes to the Hospital
by Michael Bond and Karen Jankel.
Illustrated by R.W. Alley.
HarperCollins Juvenile Books, 2001. 40 pages.

Detailed, colorful drawings.
Read-aloud or intermediate readers.

Paddington Bear has hurt his arm so the Brown Family takes him to the hospital. Paddington Bear experiences all that a hospital visit involves, from riding on a stretcher to x-rays to operations. Throughout his experience Paddington is curious and funny, which helps defuse anxiety about what is happening to him. Although Paddington's injury may not be universal, his reactions are, and that makes for a fun and reassuring story. (Ages 4-8)

New Skills

Learning to Swim

Learning to swim comes naturally for some children but for others it can be difficult to master. Beginners' swim classes, with fun names like Guppies and Tadpoles, are filled with chilly, goose-bump covered kids and many of them have reservations about jumping in. Many adults still remember the fear of putting our faces in the water. We also recall the thrill of opening our eyes under water for the first time. These stories talk about what to expect.

Edward in Deep Water
by Rosemary Wells.
Dial Books for Young Readers, 1995. 22 pages.
Bright illustrations.
Read-aloud or intermediate readers.
Available in Spanish.

Edward is on his way to Georgina's swim birthday party when his parents suggest that he leave his water wings at home. But Edward doesn't feel comfortable without them even after he hears Georgina and her friend whisper that water wings are for sissies. After he falls in the pool without his water wings on and is rescued by the alert lifeguard, he goes home, "just not ready for this kind of party." Edward's mom and dad are sensitive and know that "not everyone is ready for the same things at the same time." If your little swimmer is just not ready, this book can open discussion. (Ages 4-8)

Freddie Learns to Swim
by Nicola Smee.
Barron's Juveniles, 1999. 20 pages.
Pastels and watercolors.
Read-aloud or beginning readers.
Out of print but available in libraries and used bookstores.

Freddie wants to learn to swim like his goldfish so he goes with his mom to the learner's pool. Freddie is ready to learn but his teddy bear is fearful. His bear watches from the side of the pool as Freddie gets in and has trouble getting used to the water, coughing when water goes in his mouth. But Freddie keeps practicing and soon floats and paddles on his own. On the last page his bear is ready to give it a try. The story covers typical concerns and provides openings to discuss them with your worried young swimmer. (Ages 4-8)

Froggy Learns to Swim
by Jonathan London.
Illustrated by Frank Remkiewicz.
Puffin, 1997. 32 pages.
Bright cartoon illustrations.
Read-aloud or intermediate readers.

Although his mother says that he is a "natural born" swimmer, Froggy doesn't want to swim. When he finally gets in the water, his mother's patient encouragement, some silly songs, and lots of practice turn Froggy into a swimmer who can't be coaxed out of the water. An opportunity to talk about being patient with yourself as well as some ideas for making the learning process more fun. (Ages 4-8)

Last One In is a Rotten Egg
by Leonard Kessler.
HarperTrophy, 1999. 64 pages.
Color illustrations.
Read-aloud or intermediate readers.
Multicultural. Available in Spanish.

Freddy is always the last one in because he can't yet swim in the deep end. Tom, the lifeguard, teaches Freddie to swim the right way. Freddy soon is comfortable swimming anywhere in the pool. He is even able to face two bullies who teased him when he was not as good at swimming. A good depiction of possible problems that kids may find at a crowded public pool such as being pushed into the water, not being able to keep up with the deep water games of other kids, bullies, and fear of diving. (Ages 4-8)

Sidney Won't Swim
by Hilde Schuurmans.
Whispering Coyote Press, 2001. 24 pages.
Humorous watercolors.
Read-aloud or intermediate readers.
Parents' Choice Award winner.

Sidney, an endearing little dog, is going with his class to their first swim lesson and he is afraid. He tries various strategies to get out of swimming: he doesn't feel good until his mom offers to take him to the doctor; he "forgets" his swim bag, and he hides until his teacher gently insists that he come to the pool. The swimming instructor is sensitive and kind but some of Sidney's friends bring on a near disaster. Still, they are the ones who help him finally warm up to swimming. If your child doesn't want to learn to swim, if he thinks swimming is dumb or if he has secret fears and reservations, this is the story for him. (Ages 4-8)

Swim like a Fish
by Ellen Schecter.
Illustrated by John Emil Cymerman.
Gareth Stevens, 1998. 48 pages.
Bright colors.
Read-aloud or intermediate readers.

Annie and her mom go to the community pool. Annie is scared but her mom helps her float like a fish, paddle like a puppy, dive like dolphins, and sneak through the water like a shark. Now she can swim just like a big, brave, grown-up girl. Annie uses her imagination to help conquer her fears about the water. A good choice for offering concrete strategies to overcome fear. (Ages 4-8)

Swimming Lessons
by Betsy Jay.
Illustrated by Lori Osiecki.
Rising Moon, 1998. 32 pages.
Lively, original illustrations.
Read-aloud or intermediate readers.

Jane does not want to learn to swim and she comes up with many good reasons not to learn. But Mom buys her a new bathing suit and insists that Jane sit on the bleachers with the other novice swimmers. Jane's attitude changes when the neighbor boy, Jimmy, teases her that girls can't swim and that she is a chicken. Jane musters her courage to swim on behalf of girls everywhere and even gets back at Jimmy with a great joke. Lots of opportunities to talk about reasonable (and unreasonable fears) about learning to swim. (Ages 4-8)

Tuck in the Pool
by Martha Weston.
Houghton Mifflin, 2000. 28 pages.
Bright illustrations.
Read-aloud or intermediate readers.

Tuck's favorite part of swim lessons is "going home."

He has some very real fears about swim class: "They make you get your head wet so water gets in your ears and feels awful and water gets in your eyes, too." Tuck bravely enters the pool but he keeps his head out of the water and uses the kickboard with his chin held high. The teacher cannot convince him to put his face in the water. When his lucky spider toy falls into the pool, Tuck takes a deep breath and opens his eyes underwater to find it. A good opportunity to discuss fears about learning to swim, and how to overcome them. (Ages 4-8)

LEARNING TO RIDE A BICYCLE

What can compare with the thrill of riding a bike, especially a first bike? Yet this thrilling experience can be accompanied by many worries. The following books can help you discuss common fears and problems with your bicyclist, including the most common problem—making the transition from training wheels.

Hello, Two-Wheeler!
by Jane B. Mason.
Illustrated by Davie Monteith.
Grosset & Dunlap, 1995. 48 pages.
Humorous watercolors.
Read-aloud or intermediate readers.
A young boy loves to ride his bicycle with training wheels but now all of his friends are on two-wheelers. Every night he practices riding in the parking lot and every night he rides home with his training wheels still on. When his friends ask him to go biking, he always makes an excuse. Finally, he follows his friends to the pond on his bike and just before he gets there, he removes the training wheels. On the way home he discovers that he can ride a two-wheeler just like everyone else. The story is believable and provides opportunities for dialogue about giving up training wheels. (Ages 4-8)

Julian's Glorious Summer
by Ann Cameron.
Illustrated by Dora Leder.
Scott Foresman, 1999. 64 pages.
Black-and-white illustrations.
Read-aloud or advanced readers.
Multicultural.

Julian is a young African-American boy who is afraid to learn to ride a bicycle because of his fear of falling off and who occasionally tells lies. When his best friend Gloria not only learns to ride but also gets a new bike, the pressure is on. To avoid learning to ride, Julian tells Gloria that he's too busy to ride because he wants to make money that summer. Hearing that, his father puts him to work on a series of paid chores. Later, Julian confides his predicament to his understanding mother. His father surprises him with a reward for all his work--a brand new bike. Now Julian has to learn to ride and he admits the truth to Gloria. Once Julian tells Gloria the truth, he succeeds at riding his bike. A good way to talk about the fear of falling off a bike. (Ages 7-10)

Tom and Pippo and the Bicycle
by Helen Oxenbury.
Candlewick Press, 1997. 16 pages.
Soft watercolor and pencil drawings.
Read-aloud or intermediate readers.
Out of print but available in libraries and used bookstores.

Tom and his toy monkey Pippo enjoy riding his tricycle. However, when Tom goes over bumps, Pippo falls off the tricycle. An older friend, Stephanie rides by on a "big bike" and gives Pippo a ride. Tom observes that he needs a bike like that and that eventually he will get a big bike. The story reassures children that it's okay to be riding a small bike. At the same time, it offers gentle assurance that when the time comes, a child will make the transition. (Ages 3-7)

Two Wheels for Grover
by Dan Elliott.
Illustrated by Joe Mathieu.
Random House, 1984. 33 pages.
Familiar Sesame Street characters.
Read-aloud or beginning readers.
Out of print but available in libraries and used bookstores.

When Grover goes to visit his cousins, Rosie and Frank, they are excited about the prospect of riding bicycles together. They even have an old bike to loan to Grover. But Grover doesn't know how to ride a bike. Embarrassed to admit it, Grover comes up with a new excuse each day for why he can't ride. Finally he admits to Frank that he tried once to learn but he just couldn't. Frank is patient. He promises Grover that he will run along beside him and catch him if he falls. Frank also confides that he was seven before he learned to ride. With Frank's help and lots of practice, Grover finally is able to go on a great bicycling adventure. An encouraging story, particularly for kids who are discouraged about learning to ride a bike. (Ages 4-8)

SCHOOL-AGE KIDS

STARTING PRE-SCHOOL

In recent years, starting school often means pre-school or daycare rather than kindergarten. Either way, it's the first time a child has been away from home on a regular basis. There are lots of other kids to play with and to get along with. Often there is structured learning. Entering daycare and starting school are milestones for every child and every parent and, of course, it is a big change.

Bernard Goes to School
by Joan Elizabeth Goodman.
Illustrated by Dominic Catalano.
Boyd's Mill Press, 2001. 32 pages.
Charming, colorful illustrations.
Read-aloud or intermediate readers.

Bernard arrives for his first day of preschool already ready to go home! Bernard isn't interested in the toys, blocks, or paints but his family is intrigued and participates in some of the activities. Papa builds with blocks, Mama paints, and even Grandma participates in a tea party. Bernard is alone until his teacher entices him into feeding the fish and meeting a new friend. As Bernard becomes more comfortable, he announces to his family that it's time for them to leave. A nice twist on a child's ambivalence about preschool and his family's enthusiasm. (Ages 2-5)

Don't Go!
by Jane Breskin Zalben.
Clarion Books, 2001. 32 pages, including
advice to parents.
Detailed, colorful watercolors.
Read-aloud or intermediate readers.

Daniel, a young elephant, is off with his mother to his first day of preschool. Daniel is afraid to go into the classroom and he asks his mother not to leave. Even after they enter and the teacher welcomes Daniel, he still does not want his mom to go. Eventually he agrees and the teacher finds a welcoming place for Daniel on the story rug. Daniel makes new friends and, when his mother comes to pick him up, he presents her with a picture and two pumpkin cookies. A reassuring story about first days and feeling anxious about separation from mom. (Ages 2-5)

D. W.'s Guide to Preschool
by Marc Brown.
Little, Brown and Company, 2003. 32 pages.
Cheerful, familiar illustrations from the Arthur television and book series.
Read-aloud or intermediate to advanced readers.

D.W., Arthur's impudent little sister, is starting preschool and she narrates a cheery welcome to her school. Along the way she mentions some common concerns (saying goodbye to parents, bathroom breaks, sharing, eating unfamiliar foods, getting lost) and responds to those concerns in a reassuring way. For fans of Arthur and D.W. this is a good way to review and discuss concerns about starting school. (Ages 2-5)

Pete and Polo's Big School Adventure
by Adrian Reynolds.
Orchard Books, 2000. 32 pages.
Blurry watercolors.
Read-aloud or intermediate readers.

Pete is enthusiastic about his first day at school but his stuffed bear Polo isn't so sure. Pete encourages Polo to give it a try. Pete has fun and so does Polo. A nice approach that allows a child to identify with both characters' feelings. (Ages 2-5)

Will I Have a Friend?
by Miriam Cohen.
Illustrated by Lillian Hoban.
Aladdin Library, 1989. 26 pages.
Simple watercolors.
Read-aloud or intermediate readers.

As Jim goes to school on the first day, he worries aloud to his father whether he will have a friend at school. When he arrives, he feels uncomfortable. The boys are noisily playing and the girls are laughing. Everyone seems to have a friend already. Gradually he begins to play with the other children and they include him. By the end of the day, he has made several new friends. A gentle and reassuring story that conveys the idea that making friends is a process that takes time and patience. (Ages 2-5)

Will You Come Back for Me?
by Ann Tompert.
Illustrated by Robin Kramer.
Albert Whitman & Company, 1992. 26 pages.
Soft, gentle watercolors.
Read-aloud or intermediate readers.

Now that Suki is four years old, her parents decide that her mother will go back to work and Suki will go to daycare. Suki brings her stuffed animal, Lulu Bear, for a visit and sees all the children playing. But when her parents ask what she thinks, Suki is silent. The next morning, Suki tells her mother about a bad dream she had in which she took Lulu Bear to childcare and Lulu Bear was upset when it came time for Suki to leave. Suki's mother helps Suki express her fears, including whether her mother will come back for her. A thoughtful story for children afraid that they'll be forgotten. (Ages 2-5)

STARTING KINDERGARTEN

There is something very special about starting kindergarten even when a child has already been away from home. Many kindergartens are part of a larger elementary school. There is noise, confusion, and lots of big kids. It's the beginning of formal learning, a time when a child must meet external standards. Every child needs preparation for this big transition and there are many good books to help your child feel ready.

Annabelle Swift, Kindergartner
by Amy Schwartz.
Orchard Books, 1988. 28 pages.
Whimsical, humorous drawings.
Read-aloud or intermediate readers.

Annabelle's older sister Lucy has carefully prepared her for her first day of school. Unfortunately, much of Lucy's advice turns out to be wrong. But Lucy's training on math helps Annabelle earn the privilege of taking the milk money to the cafeteria. Charming and realistic sibling interactions add to this story of first day jitters. (Ages 5-7)

First Day, Hooray!
by Nancy Poydar.
Holiday House, 1999. 29 pages.
Detailed, full-page color illustrations.
Read-aloud or intermediate readers.

Ivy Green is ready to start school with new shoes and her own lunchbox. But Ivy begins to worry about all the "what ifs," including whether she will miss the bus and how she will find her classroom. The unusual twist in this story is that all over town everyone is getting ready, including the bus driver (who worries about all the stops she has to learn) and the teacher (who worries about getting everything ready in time). Each of them is shown getting ready for the first day, even having nightmares. A humorous reminder that everyone is a little scared the first day, not just kids. (Ages 5-7)

First Day Jitters
by Julie Danneberg.
Illustrated by Judy Love.
Charlesbridge Publishing, 2000. 28 pages.
Detailed, expressive drawings.
Read-aloud or intermediate readers.
Multicultural

Sarah Jane Hartwell worries whether she'll be liked, whether she will like school, and about everything that could go wrong. Her concerns are very familiar to any child starting school. By the end of the story, we sympathize thoroughly, and it's a delightful touch when we discover that Sarah Jane Hartwell is the new teacher, not a new student! A great way to remind your child that everyone has fears. (Ages 5-7)

Franklin Goes to School
by Paulette Bourgeois.
Scholastic, 1995. 29 pages.
Bright, cheerful illustrations.
Read-aloud or intermediate readers.
Available in Spanish.

Franklin, the little boy turtle, is going to school for the first time. Even though he knows how to count by twos and tie his shoes, he still is worried. On the bus he listens to his friends' worries. His teacher compliments his artistic skills and gets Franklin involved in lots of fun activities and it turns out to be a good day after all. A reassuring reminder that everyone has worries. (Ages 5-7)

I Am NOT Going to School Today!
by Robie H. Harris.
Illustrated by Jan Ormerod.
Margaret K. McElderry, 2003. 32 pages.
Bright color illustrations.
Read-aloud or intermediate readers.

A young boy carefully prepares for the first day of school but that night he has misgivings. In the morning, he tells his parents that he's not going because, on the first day, there are so many important things you don't know. His parents wisely do not argue. As they get ready and he continues to refuse to go, Mom comes up with the idea that he bring his stuffed animal Hank with him. At school, the little boy learns all of the things he had worried about not knowing. Now he announces to his parents that he will go to school the next day as long as Hank comes along too. A warm and realistic look at children's concerns. (Ages 5-7)

The Kissing Hand
by Audrey Penn.
Child Welfare League of America, 1993. 27 pages.
Gentle illustrations.
Read-aloud or intermediate readers.

This loving story depicts a little boy raccoon who doesn't want to go to school. He'd rather stay home with his mother, play with his friends and toys, and be in familiar surroundings. His mother counsels him that sometimes we all have to do things we don't want to do, even strange and new things, but eventually we find that we can enjoy them. Then she teaches him a secret way to carry her love with him always -- the kissing hand. Reassured by his mother's talisman, Chester finds the strength to try something new. A warm story that provides reassurance about new experiences. (Ages 5-7)

Look Out Kindergarten, Here I Come!
by Nancy Carlson.
Puffin, 2001. 32 pages.
Big, bright illustrations.
Read-aloud or intermediate readers.

Henry is so eager to leave for his first day of kindergarten that he almost forgets to wash his face, eat a good breakfast, or pack his school supplies. On the way to school, he questions his mother about school. When they arrive, Henry begins to worry that he might get lost. His mother reminds him that he already found his room and cubby during Roundup and that a teacher is there to help. But when he arrives at his classroom and sees all the new faces, he gets scared again. The sight of familiar toys, letters, and numbers reassures him and, after he finds someone to play with, he is enthusiastic again. A nice depiction of a child who is initially enthusiastic but begins to worry when confronted with a new place and new children. (Ages 5-7)

Lunch Bunnies
by Kathryn Lasky.
Illustrated by Marylin Hafner.
Little, Brown and Company, 1996. 29 pages.
Soft, whimsical drawings.
Read-aloud or intermediate readers.

Clyde's worries about his first day of school are focused on the lunchtime part of school. Will he be able to carry the tray? Will anyone sit with him? His older brother unhelpfully tells him scary stories about the cafeteria food and the lunch ladies. When lunchtime comes, it's not Clyde but another bunny that falls down, and Clyde comes to her assistance, making a new friend as well. A sweet story about a little-discussed feature of starting school. (Ages 5-7)

Off to School, Baby Duck!
by Amy Hest.
Illustrated by Jill Barton.
Candlewick Press, 1999. 24 pages.
Simple watercolors.
Read-aloud or intermediate readers.

It's the first day of school and Baby Duck has a jittery tummy. She worries about a mean teacher, not making friends, and being alone in a new place. But Grandpa understands and helps Baby Duck by reminding her of her many skills. Then Grandpa goes with Baby Duck to meet her new teacher. They reassure Baby Duck that lots of fun is in store for her at school. A sweet reminder of the special role that grandparents can play in allaying fears. (Ages 5-7)

Sumi's First Day of School Ever
by Soyung Pak.
Illustrated by Joung Un Kim.
Viking Children's Books, 2003. 32 pages.
Delicate watercolors.
Read-aloud or intermediate to advanced readers.
Multicultural.

Sumi arrives at school knowing two things her mother has taught her: what people will say when they are asking her name and how to respond. Despite the preparation, Sumi finds school to be a lonely, scary, and mean place for a child who is different. Then a kind teacher and the universal language of drawing in the dirt bring new friends and the hope that school won't be lonely after all. Gentle words and pictures acknowledge the difficulty of being new, especially when one is from a different culture, but reassure a child that it's still possible to fit in. (Ages 5-8)

Timothy Goes to School
by Rosemary Wells.
Viking Children's Books, 2000. 29 pages.
Soft watercolor and pastel illustrations.
Read-aloud or intermediate readers.

Timothy is going to school for the first time and he feels great about it. His teacher introduces him to Claude, who makes fun of what Timothy is wearing. The next day, Timothy wears different clothes and Claude teases him again. On the third day, they turn up in the same clothes but despite Timothy's hopes that Claude will get his come-uppance, Claude seems to have lots of friends. Things get better when Timothy makes a new friend. Deft handling of the problem of encountering children who aren't friendly. (Ages 5-7)

Tom Goes to Kindergarten
by Margaret Wild.
Illustrated by David Legge.
Albert Whitman & Company, 2000. 32 pages.
Vivid watercolors.
Read-aloud or intermediate readers.

    Tom, a cuddly panda, can't wait to go to kindergarten. His whole family accompanies him and when he suddenly panics, they decide to stay for the day. As it turns out, his father, mother, and sibling have so much fun that they want to return the next day. But now Tom is ready for independence. A humorous look at first fears and how much fun school can be. (Ages 5-7)

Vera's First Day of School
by Vera Rosenberry.
Henry Holt and Company, 1999. 29 pages.
Striking watercolors.
Read-aloud or intermediate readers.

    Vera can't wait for her first day of school. Because she has older sisters, she is familiar with the school. But when she arrives, the sight of so many older kids overwhelms her and she doesn't go inside. Then the bell rings and Vera realizes she is late. Horrified, she hurries home where she is able to go upstairs unnoticed by her mother. When her mother finds her, Vera's dress is a mess and her face is tearstained. This time Mother walks her to school and enters the building with her, helping with the transition. This story explores the perspective of the usually confident child who suddenly finds a new experience scary. (Ages 5-7)

Wemberly Worried
by Kevin Henkes.
Greenwillow Books, 2000. 32 pages.

Watercolors and black pen.
Read-aloud or intermediate readers.
Available in Spanish.
2000 NAPPA Award winner; 2000 Parenting Best
Books of the Year Award winner.

Wemberly, a little girl mouse, worries about everything. She worries all the time and everywhere she goes so it's no surprise that the very thought of school worries her. On the first day of school she meets a new friend, Jewel, with whom she shares a lot in common. By the end of the day Wemberly's worries aren't gone but she is worrying less. Wemberly is a child many parents and kids will recognize. It's helpful to have a funny, well-written book in which to explore the limits of worrying. (Ages 4-8)

LEARNING TO READ

Reading is the key for every child to a life of imagination and information. For some children reading comes easily but for others learning to read comes only after great difficulty. Here are some terrific reads about learning to read, especially for the child who is wondering when he will acquire the skill.

Arthur's Prize Reader
by Lillian Hoban.
HarperTrophy, 1984. 64 pages.
Cheerful, expressive drawings.
Read-aloud or intermediate to advanced readers.

Arthur, a young chimpanzee, has a younger sister who tells him she can read. Arthur tells her that if she can only read easy words, she can't really read. But as Arthur himself unwittingly proves later, his sister is the better reader! A satisfying read for every younger sibling who has tried to keep up with an older sibling's reading accomplishments. (Ages 4-8)

Arthur's Reading Race
by Marc Brown.
Random Library, 1996. 24 pages.
Familiar characters from the series.
Read-aloud or beginning to intermediate readers.
Garden State Children's Book Award winner.

Arthur is proud that he can read and offers to teach his sister D. W. how to read too. But to Arthur's surprise, D. W. turns down his offer, telling him that she already knows how. He challenges her to prove it, with a reward of an ice cream cone if she can read ten words. D. W. successfully reads ten words as they walk around town. Your child may be surprised to find how many words he too already knows how to read. (Ages 4-8)

Grover Learns to Read
by Dan Elliott.
Illustrated by Normand Chartier.
Children's Television Workshop, 1999. 29 pages.
Familiar Sesame Street characters.
Read-aloud or intermediate to advanced readers.

Grover loves having his mother read to him at bedtime. But when she casually comments that he soon will be reading books all by himself, Grover is alarmed. He decides to conceal his reading ability from his mother. But he longs to tell her and, finally, he's unable to resist. He also confesses his concern and that gives her an opportunity to reassure him that she will always read to him, but now he can sometimes read to her, too. A sound premise that may reassure your early reader that there's no downside to learning to read. (Ages 4-8)

Marvin One Too Many
by Katherine Paterson.
Illustrated by Jane Clark Brown.
HarperTrophy, 2003. 48 pages.
Soft watercolors.

Read-aloud or intermediate to advanced readers.
2001 Parenting Best Books of the Year Award winner.

Marvin is new to his school and to first grade. When his teacher greets him by saying, "One more? That is one too many," Marvin concludes that his teacher does not like him. Marvin also has concerns about reading. His teacher asks him to ask his parents to read with him every day but Marvin worries that they are too busy with their dairy farm. Marvin is teased and gets into trouble until he finally confesses his reading problem to his parents. His father reassures him that he too was the last one to read in his class and that he's sure Marvin will learn how. With parental help, Marvin soon learns to read. Simple yet realistic portrayal of how Marvin is teased and gets into trouble. (Ages 4-9)

Read Me a Story (Yoko & Friends)
by Rosemary Wells.
Illustrated by Jody Wheeler.
Hyperion Press, 2002. 31 pages.
Soft, appealing watercolors.
Read-aloud or intermediate to advanced readers.

Yoko, a little kitten, is afraid of losing her reading time with her mother if her mother finds out that Yoko has learned to read! So Yoko conceals her reading ability even from her teacher at school. Her secret is discovered when her school receives a response to a letter Yoko had written about a cereal offer for a secret decoder ring. Yoko finally confesses her secret to her mother and is reassured. A good choice for an early reader who worries that now he won't be read to. (Ages 4-8)

Today Was a Terrible Day
by Patricia Reilly Giff.
Illustrated by Susanna Natti.
Puffin, 1984. 26 pages.
Simple, expressive drawings.

Read-aloud or for intermediate reader.

Ronald Morgan has a terrible day at school. He is in second grade and is placed in a reading group for kids who haven't yet learned to read. When Ronald's teacher wonders aloud whether Ronald will be promoted to third grade because of his behavior, Ronald's classmate taunts him, saying, "Ronald Morgan may never get to third grade anyway. He still can't read." At the end of his terrible day his teacher gives him a note to take home and suggests, "Try to read it by yourself. If you can't, I'm sure your mother will help you." Ronald tries to read the note and when he succeeds, he realizes that he is learning to read. A good opportunity to talk about the obstacles facing new readers. (Ages 5-9)

When Will I Read?
by Miriam Cohen.
Illustrated by Lillian Hoban.
Bantam Doubleday Dell, 1996. 32 pages.
Cheerful illustrations.
Read-aloud or intermediate readers.
Multicultural.

Jim is eager to read but his teacher counsels patience, telling him that he will learn when he is ready. As the children go about their schoolwork and play, Jim wonders when he will ever start reading. When Jim notices that the sign on the hamsters' box is torn, he hurries to tell his teacher that because it is torn, the sign mistakenly reads, "Do let the hamsters out." His teacher makes a new sign and congratulates Jim that he is now reading on his own! Reassurance for a child who feels that reading skills are coming too slowly. (Ages 4-8)

READING PROBLEMS

Sometimes learning to read is very difficult for reasons that aren't immediately apparent. In those cases, dyslexia or other issues must be explored. Your child will need extra help understanding that he is not alone and that even these obstacles can be conquered, as the heroes and heroines of these books demonstrate.

The Flunking of Joshua T. Bates
by Susan Shere.
Random House, 1995. 96 pages.
Limited black-and-white illustrations.
Read-aloud or advanced readers.

Joshua Bates must repeat third grade because of his reading problems. He contends with bullies and teasing about being held back. Fortunately, his teacher is sensitive and helps him gain the admiration of his class by assigning him the task of helping other children in the class. The teacher also helps him with his problem with bullies. Realistic dialogue and a sense of Joshua's feelings and family interactions make this helpful for late readers. (Ages 7-11)

Kelly's Creek
by Doris Buchanan Smith.
Illustrated by Alan Tiegreen.
HarperCollins Children's Books, 1989. 71 pages.
Black-and-white illustrations.
Read-aloud or advanced readers.
Out of print but available in libraries and used bookstores.

Nine-year old Kelly has a learning disability. But his parents and teacher think that he isn't trying hard enough and he faces teasing as well. Kelly has a place where he excels and where he knows that he's smart, the Georgia tidal marsh where he and his older friend, Phillip, a biologist, study the tidal creatures. But his parents don't understand and they forbid him from going to the marsh or seeing Phillip. Ultimately Kelly's association with Phillip and the knowledge he has gained from the marsh win him the respect of his teacher and classmates. The ending is somewhat uneven but this is a great story for reminding kids that there are all kinds of ways to learn and be smart. (Ages 7-11)

Leo the Late Bloomer
by Robert Kraus.
Illustrated by Jose Aruego.
HarperCollins Children's Books, 1994. 32 pages.
Exuberant, full-page illustrations; limited text.
Read-aloud or beginning readers.
Available in Spanish.

      Leo is a sad little tiger because he can't read, write, draw, or talk. His father worries but his mother calmly reassures him that there's nothing wrong, it's just that Leo is a "late bloomer." His mother asks his father to be patient and his father tries not to worry. Still, Leo doesn't acquire these skills. But then "one day, in his own good time, Leo bloomed!" Leo's pride is evident and the message of being patient with oneself is skillfully conveyed. For a young child, this book may be just the right fit to understand why he will learn to read or write at his own pace. (Ages 5-9)

Thank you, Mr. Falker
by Patricia Polacco.
Philomel Books, 2001. 35 pages.
Beautiful paintings.
Read-aloud or intermediate readers.
Available in Spanish.
1998 Parenting Best Books Award winner; 2000
Alabama Emphasis on Reading Award winner;
2000 Rhode Island Children's Book Award winner;
2001 South Carolina Children's Book Award winner.

Trisha comes from a family of readers who value education. Trisha can't wait to go to school. She goes to kindergarten and loves it but she doesn't learn to read and the problem continues through first and second grade. Trisha becomes adept at fooling teachers and class-mates into thinking she can read. In third grade Trisha moves to California. A bully in her new class teases her about her inability to read. Her teacher, Mr. Falker, puts an end to the teasing and explains to Trisha that "you don't see letters or numbers the way other people do." He begins to work with her every day after school. "You're going to read, I promise you that," he tells her. After months of hard work, Trisha reads a paragraph and feels like Mr. Falker had "unlocked a door and pulled (her) into the light." An inspirational and reassuring story for children struggling with reading. (Ages 7-11)

STUTTERING

Many children stutter as they learn to talk. Stuttering is more likely to occur in children who are under stress, such as after starting day care, moving, or the birth of a sibling. Although parents worry about it, most children will out-grow stuttering. But a small group of children will deal with stuttering throughout their childhood and into their adult years. If your child is facing this issue or knows other children who stutter, these books will help spark discussion.

Mary Marony and the Snake, **Mary Marony Hides Out**, **Mary Marony**, **Mummy Girl**
by Suzy Kline.
Illustrated by Blanche Sims.
Putnam Publishing Group, various publication dates.
75-80 pages.
Limited but expressive black-and-white illustrations.
Read-aloud or intermediate readers.
All of the Mary Marony series books feature a hero-

ine who stutters, although the books listed above especially emphasize her stuttering. In *Mary Marony Hides
Out*, second-grader Mary hesitates to have dinner with her
favorite author because she is ashamed of her stuttering.
In *Mary Marony and the Snake*, Mary is terrified when
the teacher in her new school asks each child to stand up,
say his name, and tell one thing about himself. As Mary
fears, some of the children laugh at her stuttering. In *Mary
Marony, Mummy Girl*, Mary wants to prove to her classmate Marvin, who teases her about stuttering, that she can
create a great costume for Halloween. In all of these stories Mary is a realistic, spunky heroine who suffers with
her stuttering but manages to make friends and to make
progress in her speech. An inspiring yet fun read for kids
with the same problem. (Ages 9-12)

BOREDOM

Children may experience boredom at school but it
is just as likely that the familiar complaint, "Mom, there's
nothing to do. I'm bored!" will be heard at home. For all
the parents who endure that statement and think how
much they would enjoy being "bored," here are some good
books to help your child look at boredom in a new way,
discover new pursuits, or just escape boredom by reading
books about it.

Bored—Nothing to Do!
by Peter Spier.
Doubleday, 1987. 42 pages.
Detailed drawings; limited text.
Read-aloud or beginning to intermediate readers.
**Out of print but available in libraries and used
bookstores.**
In a charming tale, two bored brothers decide to
build an airplane. Their task requires lots of parts, which
they borrow from the baby carriage, the car, the clothes-

line, the television, and more. Their plane works and they have a great ride but their parents aren't pleased with their pilfering. So they are told to put everything back and, just as we saw them borrowing it all, we see the plane being dismantled and everything put away. Another testament to the things we can do when we're bored. (Ages 4-9)

In the Attic
by Hiawyn Oram.
Illustrated by Satoshi Kitamura.
Henry Holt and Company, 1988. 26 pages.
Distinctive, almost surreal images.
Read-aloud or intermediate readers.
Available in Spanish.

A young boy is bored as he sits on the floor surrounded by an impressive number of toys. He explains that he "had a million toys, but I was bored." From this intriguing beginning, the story takes us up into the attic to a wide range of fantastic places and creatures. As we learn in the end, it all happens in the boy's imagination--or does it? A good reminder that our toys can disappoint us but our imaginations always keep us entertained. (Ages 4-9)

Nothing to Do
by Russell Hoban.
Illustrated by Lillian Hoban.
HarperCollins Children's Books, 1964. 32 pages.
Simple pen and ink drawings.
Read-aloud or intermediate to advanced readers.
Out of print but available in libraries and used bookstores.

Walter Possum is bored. His father tries to give him ideas (play with toys, rake leaves) but Walter rejects all of them. The next day when Walter complains of boredom, his father gives him a "something-to-do" rock, telling him that whenever you have nothing to do, you rub the rock and it will give you something to do. Walter's first attempts don't work but his subsequent tries yield ideas until he accidentally loses the rock. Then Walter realizes that even without the rock he can think of things to do and he helps his sister find things to play as well. A nice idea for parents and children—that sometimes a magic talisman helps a child feel empowered to accomplish things on his own. (Ages 4-8)

On My Island

by Marie-Louise Gay.
Groundwood Books, 2001. 35 pages.
Unusual, quirky ink and watercolors.
Read-aloud or intermediate readers.

A boy lives alone on his island with animals for company. As he complains that nothing ever happens, all around him exciting things are occurring. Volcanoes erupt, elephants fly through the sky, sea serpents appear, and shark-riding cowboys cavort nearby. A delightful and humorous way to remind your child that boredom is a state of mind. (Ages 4-9)

Once Around the Block

by Kevin Henkes.
Illustrated by Victoria Chess.
William Morrow, 1987. 18 pages.
Gentle, expressive watercolors and ink.
Read-aloud or intermediate to advanced readers.
Out of print but available in libraries and used bookstores.

Annie is bored. Her best friend is away, her mother is busy with the baby, there's nothing on television, and her dog has fleas. So she sits on the porch waiting for her father to come home. Her mother suggests that to make the time go by, she take a little walk, "once around the block." Annie's walk leads to talking and spending enjoyable time with many friendly neighbors. Before she knows it, she's home and her father is waiting for her. Another gentle tribute to the notion that right within a child's own home or own neighborhood many ways exist to chase away boredom. (Ages 5-9)

There's Nothing to Do!
by James Stevenson.
William Morrow, 1986. 30 pages.
Cartoon drawings with bubble conversations.
Read-aloud or intermediate to advanced readers.
Out of print but available at libraries or used bookstores.

Mary Ann and Louie complain to Grandpa that they are bored. This reminds Grandpa of when he and his brother visited their grandfather and they were bored. Grandpa's reminiscences entertain his grandchildren and provide a terrific story. The message is that in the most seemingly boring setting, kids with imagination can find lots to do. (Ages 4-9)

Tidy Up, Trevor
by Rob Lewis.
Random House of Canada, 1998. 27 pages.
Bright, detailed illustrations.
Read-aloud or intermediate readers.

Trevor, a little boy turtle, is bored. He has done something fun on all the other days of the week but now it's Friday and he doesn't know what to do with himself. His family has suggestions for him but he remains bored and grumpy. Then Dad suggests a trip down the river and Trevor turns that down. Mom tells him that in that case, he must clean his closet! At first Trevor is furious but as he begins to clean, he finds lots of stuff he'd forgotten and has a wonderful time. Another good idea for combating boredom. (Ages 4-8)

Homework

Look here for books that sympathize with your child's lack of interest in doing his homework or his problems doing it in a timely way. Some books even offer your child suggestions as well as the reality that homework just has to be done.

Arthur in a Pickle
by Marc Brown.
Random House, 1999. 23 pages.
Familiar characters from the series.
Read-aloud or beginning readers.

When Arthur's teacher, Mr. Rathburn, asks what happened to his homework, Arthur tells a lie. Mr. Rathburn says, "You are in a pickle now," and tells him to see the principal in the morning. At home Arthur fidgets with his dinner and that night he has pickle nightmares. Finally he wakes up, goes to his desk, and does his late homework. When he sees the principal the next morning, he admits that he had not finished his homework but he now he has completed it. Many children will identify with Arthur's guilty feelings as well as his lies. (Ages 7-10)

The Berenstain Bears and the Homework Hassle
by Stan and Jan Berenstain.
Random House, 1997. 32 pages.
Familiar Berenstain Bear characters.
Read-aloud or intermediate readers.

Brother Bear is watching television, talking on the cell phone, and listening to his boom box with his school books open in front of him when his parents read a note from his teacher saying he is behind in his homework. When Brother Bear appeals to his grandparents for understanding, they remember that his dad had the same kind of problem with putting off homework. They assure him that

he will catch up just like his dad did. In fact, Papa Bear is behind right now too with his taxes. He and his son sit across from each other at a table and both try to get caught up. The story offers good advice: just do it.
(Ages 7-10)

Jingle Bells, Homework Smells
by Diane de Groat.
HarperTrophy, 2003. 28 pages.
Bright, realistic illustrations.
Read-aloud or intermediate readers.

Gilbert is excited about the winter holiday coming up so he delays doing his homework. Instead he bakes cookies and watches television. Then he goes skating with his friends who also plan to do their homework tomorrow. But when tomorrow comes, he and his dad go to pick out a Christmas tree, which then has to be decorated. Anyone who has put off doing something will sympathize with Gilbert on Monday morning when he realizes that he has forgotten to do his homework. A cautionary tale about the consequences of procrastination, delivered with humor.
(Ages 7-10)

PRESSURE

It's a common problem in our society, not enough time for all the things we have to or want to do. Sometimes children feel stressed by their parents' pressures. Sometimes children feel burdened by the things they have committed themselves to do. Either way, it's always a good idea to talk about the problem and search together for solutions.

The Berenstain Bears and Too Much Pressure
by Stan Berenstain and Jan Berenstain.
Random House, 1992. 32 pages.
Familiar Berenstain Bear characters.
Read-aloud or intermediate readers.

Brother and Sister Bear are busy with school and outside activities like ballet class, horseback riding, swimming, and computer club. While each activity is fun, keeping track of the schedule is difficult and Mama Bear is overwhelmed. The family has a meeting and agrees to no more than two after-school activities per week for each cub. The family discovers that by limiting activities they have more time to enjoy each other and their everyday lives. The Berenstain series may be utterly predictable and moralistic but kids love them. What more can you ask? (Ages 7-10)

Gifted Kids

Being different is never easy, even when the difference is that a child is especially gifted at math or writing. While some children revel in being special in this way, others are reluctant to be singled out from their classmates. Current educational approaches include separating children into special programs and this can create friction with other children. Sometimes the friction comes from within the family, where one child is identified as especially gifted and another child is not. The fiction books on this subject are limited but among them are several good ones that can help your child talk about this issue.

213 Valentines
by Barbara Cohen.
Illustrated by Wil Clay.
Henry Holt & Company, 1993. 55 pages.
Pen and ink drawings.
Read-aloud or intermediate to advanced readers.
Multicultural.

Wade, a young African-American boy, is selected for the Gifted and Talented program at another school. He's not enthusiastic about leaving his friends but his parents encourage him. At the new school he feels very alone, both because of his skin color and his intelligence. When his teacher announces a valentine exchange, Wade worries that no one will send him any. So he decides to make 213 valentines addressed to him from famous people. In the course of carrying out his plan he learns some things about true friends and loyalty. A nice story about the ambivalence your child may feel at being singled out for his intelligence. (Ages 8-11)

Alvin Webster's Surefire Plan for Success (and How it Failed)
by Sheila Greenwald.
Minstrel Books, 1989. 95 pages.
Occasional pen and ink drawings.
Read-aloud or intermediate to advanced readers.

Alvin is a fifth-grader in the gifted program at his school. His parents are expecting a new baby (which makes Alvin feel jealous and competitive) and his teacher has assigned him to help another student in math. Unfortunately, the student is Robertson Bone, "the dumbest of the dumb." But Alvin conceives a plan to win back his parents' attention. With many ups and downs, Alvin discovers that even gifted kids can learn something important. The story isn't really about being gifted as much as sibling rivalry but it offers an opportunity for discussion about the good and bad things about being gifted. (Ages 8-11)

Archibald Frisby
by Michael Chesworth.
Farrar, Straus and Giroux, 1996. 30 pages.
Delightful, scientifically-precise watercolors.
Read-aloud or intermediate readers.

Archibald Frisby thinks like a scientist, whether he is looking at his cat, taking apart appliances, or dissecting flowers. His mom worries that he doesn't know how to play so she sends him to camp and suggests that he forget about science and just have a good time. But old habits are hard to break and whether it's campfire or crafts,

Archibald can't help being himself. The great thing is that his scientific bent ends up making everything more interesting for the other kids. He even helps win the camper/staff ballgame by calculating the angle of maximum distance. A wonderful and encouraging story about being gifted and having confidence that you can be yourself and still make friends. (Ages 7-10)

I Hate Being Gifted
by Patricia Hermes.
G. P. Putnam's Sons, 1990. 122 pages.
No illustrations.
Read-aloud or advanced readers.
Out of print but available in libraries and used bookstores.

K.T., a sixth-grade girl, finds herself spending afternoons with all the "brainy kids" in a special program called LEAP for which she has qualified. But being smart isn't an honor among K.T.'s friends. In fact, most of the popular kids shun the "LEAP Creeps." K.T. wants her parents to let her drop the LEAP program, especially after her friends join a rival club that makes fun of LEAP kids. But when her parents agree to let K.T. drop the program, she has second thoughts. A realistic portrayal of the difficulties of bright adolescent girls. (Ages 10-13)

RELATIONSHIPS WITH OTHER CHILDREN

MAKING FRIENDS

Most children worry at one time or another about whether they will have friends in a new situation. Whether your child is adept in social interactions, a little shy, or even a little aggressive, he can always benefit from good books that explore how to make and keep friends.

First Friends
by Lenore Blegvad.
Illustrated by Erik Blegvad.
HarperCollins Children's Books, 2000. 24 pages.
Cheerful, old-fashioned illustrations.
Read-aloud or beginning readers.

Individual children are pictured, each with a toy. The simple text introduces the idea that all the children came here to school to play. Each child is pictured offering to share his toy. For the very youngest children, this book offers an opportunity to talk about how it will feel to share and how sharing can help make a new friend. (Ages 2-5)

The Other Emily
by Gibbs Davis.
Illustrated by Linda Shute.
Houghton Mifflin, 1990. 32 pages.
Simple illustrations.
Read-aloud or advanced readers.
Out of print but available in libraries and used bookstores.

Emily is looking forward to her first day of school and her parents have a present for her, a T-shirt that says "The One and Only Emily." It's appropriate, because Emily loves her name and never misses a chance to write it, carve it, draw it, or turn household objects into an E. But at school Emily discovers that there's another Emily in her class. She feels less special and not at all friendly toward the other Emily. Eventually she discovers the pleasure of sharing even her name with someone else and makes a new friend. A nice little book for every child who discovers to his surprise that there are others with his name. (Ages 4-8)

Who Will Be My Friends?
by Sydney Hoff.
HarperTrophy, 1985. 32 pages.
Cheerful, childlike sketches.
Read-aloud or beginning readers.

Freddy moves into a new house and is happy, but he wonders who will be his friends. He tries to play ball with a dog and then a cat but it's not what he'd hoped for. The policeman, mailman, and street cleaner tell him they will be his friends but they're too busy to play. Freddy finds some other boys at the playground but they ignore him. Undaunted, Freddy proceeds to play ball by himself until his skills and confidence gain the attention of the other boys and they invite him to join their play. This is a great opportunity to talk about how to make friends and to hear a child's ideas about what to expect in a new place. (Ages 4-8)

Other titles of interest, described elsewhere:
Will I Have a Friend?
Lunch Bunnies
Sumi's First Day of School Ever
Wemberly Worried
Timothy Goes to School
Yoko

BEST FRIENDS

Finding someone to be your best friend is a special experience, an experience that some children long for. For some children, once they have found a best friend, other friends feel unnecessary. But best friends change, move away, or even find other best friends. Learning to enjoy a best friend while remaining open to new friends is a skill and these good books have something to say about it.

Best Friends
by Miriam Cohen.
Illustrated by Lillian Hoban.
Aladdin Library, 1989. 27 pages.
Cheerful drawings.
Read-aloud or intermediate readers.

As school begins, Paul and Jim are best friends. But when two other children compete to be Jim's best friend, Paul fears that Jim doesn't like him anymore. Then a school crisis causes Paul and Jim to work together, and their friendship is reaffirmed. A lovely little story to reassure your child about the ebb and flow of friendships. (Ages 4-8)

Best Friends Think Alike
by Lynn Reiser.
Greenwillow Books, 1997. 28 pages.
Bold, colorful illustrations.
Read-aloud or intermediate readers.

Two young girls plan an afternoon in the park. They decide to play horse and rider but both of them want to be the horse. They are able to solve their problem when they decide that each can be both a horse and a rider. The premise of this entertaining story is that best friends don't always think alike and that's okay too. This book can be read aloud or, as the author suggests, read as a play with characters. A fun way to talk about the need for compromise with a good friend. (Ages 4-8)

George and Martha Round and Round
by James Marshall.
Houghton Mifflin, 1991. 48 pages.
Simple, happy illustrations.
Read-aloud or intermediate readers.

George and Martha are two hippo friends who have their ups and downs in the five vignettes included in this book. Although there is a hint of romance, friendship is the predominant theme, because these two large creatures have very sensitive feelings. They experience the problem of giving and receiving a gift that the recipient doesn't like and their feelings about practical jokes. They also learn how to respond tactfully to a friend's artistic endeavors. Through all their experiences, their friendship triumphs in the end. A good book for discussion about your child's best friend and how they support and respond to each other. (Ages 6-9)

The Hating Book
by Charlotte Zolotow.
Illustrated by Ben Shecter.
HarperTrophy. 1989. 32 pages.
Humorous drawings.
Read-aloud or beginning to intermediate readers.

The narrator, a little girl, begins her story by saying, "I hate hate hated my friend." Her friend is mean at school but the narrator is afraid to ask why. Her mother urges her to ask but she is afraid that her friend may respond with something cruel like, "You're ugly and dumb. Being with you was never fun." When the narrator finally gets the courage to ask, she discovers that it's all a misunderstanding. A nice reminder that sometimes, other kids' behavior has to do with their hurt feelings too. (Ages 6-9)

Hunter's Best Friend at School
by Laura Malone Elliott.
Illustrated by Lynn Munsinger.
HarperCollins Children's Books, 2002. 29 pages.
Humorous watercolors.
Read-aloud or advanced readers.

Hunter and Stripe are two young raccoons who are best friends. They like the same things and at school they do everything together. But when Stripe feels mischievous, Hunter has to decide whether to go along with him or be different. His dilemma is explored in a sensitive way in an entertaining story. It offers an opportunity for Hunter's mom to talk about whether being a best friend means always following along, a question you may want to broach with your child. (Ages 7-10)

Let's Be Enemies
by Janice May Udry.
Illustrated by Maurice Sendak.
HarperTrophy, 1988. 28 pages.
Delightful little illustrations; limited text.
Read-aloud or beginning to intermediate readers.

Two little boys, James and John, are best friends until one day John announces that James is his enemy because James is bossy and doesn't share. Right after his announcement, John can't resist suggesting that they roller-skate together and James happily agrees. A humorous way to talk to your young child about the ups and downs of friendship. (Ages 4-8)

Maude and Sally
by Nicki Weiss.
Viking Press, 1988. 27 pages.
Whimsical illustrations.
Read-aloud or advanced readers.
Out of print but available in libraries and used bookstores.

Maude and Sally feel as though they could be twins. There isn't room in their friendship for anyone else and that suits them just fine. But when Sally goes away to camp, Maude explores a new friendship with Emmylou. When Sally returns, Sally and Maude are still close but their friendship expands to include Emmylou. Whether your child's experience with a changing friendship is as easy as the experience of the girls in this story, it offers an opportunity to explore the issue of exclusivity and new friends versus old friends. (Ages 4-8)

My Best Friend
by Pat Hutchins.
Greenwillow Books, 1993. 26 pages.
Vibrant, full-size illustrations.
Read-aloud or intermediate readers.
Multicultural.

The narrator, a preschooler, shares the reasons he's glad that his friend is his best friend. In his eyes, she's fast and strong and brave. But when she becomes frightened at night by the darkness, he is the one who finds a solution. Now she's glad that he's her best friend. Sometimes friendship is just about kindness and in this loving book we're reminded of just that. (Ages 3-5)

Patrick and Ted
by Geoffrey Hayes.
Four Winds Press, 1983. 26 pages.
Colorful, miniature illustrations.
Read-aloud or beginning to intermediate readers.
Out of print but available in libraries and used bookstores.

Patrick and Ted are best friends, "like brothers, and nobody ever thought of one without thinking of the other." During the summer Ted goes away to stay with relatives and Patrick has to figure out what to do with himself. He begins to play with other children and to enjoy being "just Patrick." After Ted returns, they resume their friendship but they no longer do everything together and that's fine too. This little book offers the opportunity to talk about yet another aspect of having a best friend—the idea that sometimes exclusivity isn't always what you want. (Ages 4-8)

Rosie and Michael
by Judith Viorst.
Illustrated by Lorna Tomei.
Aladdin Library, 1998. 40 pages.

Detailed, black-and-white illustrations.
Read-aloud or intermediate to advanced readers.
1974 New York Times Best Illustrated Children's
Books of the Year award winner.

Rosie and Michael are very good friends. But that doesn't mean, that they never tease each other, fight, or disagree. As they explain their friendship, they understand each other, stand up for each other, and trust each other. Rosie likes Michael even when he's dopey. Michael likes Rosie even when she's grouchy. When Michael's parakeet dies, he calls Rosie and when Rosie's dog runs away, she calls Michael. A nice story for exploring the meaning of friendship. (Ages 6-9)

SHARING

Learning to share isn't easy. First, we learn what really belongs to us, and then we learn that we have to share it. Along the way, we also learn that it's more fun when we share our things with others. There's another issue: not everyone will share with us even if we are kind enough to share with him or her. These books add perspective and offer the experiences of many characters in learning this important skill.

The Big Brown Box
by Marisabina Russo.
Greenwillow Books, 2000. 32 pages.
Unusual gouache illustrations.
Read-aloud or intermediate readers.

Sam, a preschooler, takes a big, brown box to his room and makes it into a house, a cave, and a boat. His little brother Ben wants to join in the fun but Sam doesn't want to share the box. He imagines Ben as the big bad wolf, the scary, hairy bear, and the vicious silver shark. Their mother comes to the rescue by giving Ben his own box, a smaller one, and the two children play together. A realistic and humorous story that explores the challenges of sharing as well as sibling interaction. (Ages 3-7)

Group Soup
by Barbara Brenner.
Illustrated by Lynn Munsinger.
Penguin Books, 1992. 25 pages.
Watercolors.
Read-aloud or intermediate readers.
Out of print but available in libraries and used bookstores.

When a family of rabbit children arrive home hungry and tired, they find a note from their mother telling them that they must make dinner for themselves. Everyone pitches in to help except Rhoda, who is too hungry to help. Rhoda complains as she waits for the soup to be ready but when she finally tastes it, she realizes that there is something missing, an ingredient she happens to have. In a side story, her brother plays too roughly with his siblings, gets excluded and then gets the same treatment from his friends. The message is pointed but the story will entertain. (Ages 4-8)

Harriet's Halloween Candy
by Nancy Carlson.
Carolrhoda Books, 2002. 32 pages.
Bright, friendly illustrations.
Read-aloud or intermediate readers.

Harriet gets lots of candy on Halloween and she plans to eat it all. Her little brother, Walter, is too young to go trick-or-treating and her mother reminds Harriet that she should share with him. Harriet hides her Halloween cache but when she runs out of hiding places she begins to eat the remainder. As she feels worse and worse from eating too much candy, she decides to share with Walter. Her mother compliments her and tells her it is dinnertime. We leave a wiser Harriet on the last page, slightly green, too full of candy, and facing her dinner. A funny story about the possible consequences of not sharing. (Ages 4-8)

I Am Sharing
by Mercer Mayer.
Random House, 1995. 19 pages.
Charming illustrations.
Read-aloud or intermediate readers.

A big brother lists everything he does and doesn't share with his little sister. According to him, he would share his toothbrush but his father discourages it. However, it appears that the little sister isn't as good at sharing, for her brother announces that now he needs to teach her to share, too. A chance for siblings to voice their thoughts on the mutuality of sharing in their family. (Ages 3-7)

I Want It
by Elizabeth Crary.
Illustrated by Marina Megale.
Parenting Press, 1996. 32 pages.
Simple black-and-white illustrations.
Read-aloud only due to advice for parents.

Megan and Amy, two good friends, are frustrated by their desire for the same toy and their difficulty in sharing the toy. Various options for resolving their problem are explored. Elizabeth Crary's problem-solving books are unique. They offer an interactive story in which children explore choices they might make in the same circumstances as the fictional characters, as well as the consequences of each choice. (Ages 4-8)

It's Mine!
by Alicia Garcia De Lynam.
E. P. Dutton, 1988. 25 pages.
Bright, humorous watercolors.
Read-aloud or beginning readers.

Out of print but available in libraries and used bookstores.

An older sibling is preparing a tea party for stuffed animals. She (the gender isn't clear) notices that her younger sibling has the stuffed tiger she wants. The older child snatches it back and the younger child cries. The older child is distracted and the younger child retrieves the tiger. The older child notices and a struggle ensues. An adult arrives and says, "Place nicely, then you can have him back," placing the tiger up on the dresser. As the younger child cries, the older child now comforts him by obtaining the tiger and offering to share not only the tiger but also the tea party. A charming and realistic portrayal of siblings and sharing that may feel familiar to your child. (Ages 4-8)

It's MY Birthday!
By Pat Hutchins.
Greenwillow Books, 1999. 32 pages.
Brightly colored illustrations.
Read-aloud or intermediate readers.

It's Billy's birthday. He loves his gifts and he doesn't have to share. After all, it's his birthday. Although he gets a ball, his guests share a balloon since he won't share the ball with them. When he gets a jump rope, they play with a ribbon. When he gets a new red car to ride in, they play in the box. But what will Billy do when he gets a box of games that he can't play alone? A book to read before a birthday party to understand why a friend who usually is willing to share is unlikely to share at his own party. (Ages 4-8)

My New Sandbox
by Donna Jakob.
Illustrated by Julia Gorton.
Hyperion Books, 1996. 30 pages.
Bright, modern designs.
Read-aloud or beginning readers.

A little boy chases away everyone and everything

who tries to enter his new sandbox, including a bug, a bird, a dog, and another child. But when he is alone in his new sandbox, he wants someone to play with. As the story ends, the little boy comments that there is enough room for "all of us" because the new sandbox in his backyard is just "our size." A nice reminder for younger readers about the pleasures of sharing. (Ages 3-7)

That Toad is Mine!
By Barbara Shook Hazen.
Illustrated by Jane Manning.
HarperCollins Children's Books, 1998. 20 pages.
Colorful watercolors.
Read-aloud or beginning readers.

    Two best friends share everything. They divide a candy bar, divvy up toy cars, and share crayons. But what should they do when they find a toad? It can't be cut in half. They discuss the possibilities, including a day with one boy and the next day with the other. While they argue, the toad hops away. Now the friends are mad at each other. They end up kicking a stone back and forth, sharing the anger until it is gone and they are friends again. This simple little book shows how easy it is to get mad at a good friend about sharing and offers a unique solution, too. (Ages 3-7)

We Share Everything
by Robert Munsch.
Illustrated by Michael Martchenko.
Cartwheel Books, 2000. 32 pages.
Bright, detailed, illustrations.
Read-aloud or intermediate readers.
Available in Spanish.

    On the first day of kindergarten, Amanda and Jeremiah have a problem with sharing a book. Their teacher reminds them that in kindergarten "We share everything." The children continue to have problems sharing blocks and paints. Finally they ask each other, "What can we share?" Their discussion of the answer to that question begins with their shoes and continues to a hilarious ending. An opportunity for discussion about the things we do and don't share. (Ages 5-8)

Being a Good Sport

Whether a child excels at something or not, learning to be a good sport is an important skill. It isn't an easy thing to do, as many adults can attest. These books explore the feelings kids have about being good sports.

Molly Gets Mad
by Suzy Kline.
Illustrated by Diana Cain Blumenthal.
G.P. Putnam's Sons, 2001. 71 pages.
Stylized black-and-white drawings.
Read-aloud or advanced readers.

Morty, a third-grade boy, has a friend named Molly who always wants to be the best at everything. The children take a class field trip to an ice-skating rink. When the new girl turns out to be the best figure skater in the class, Molly refuses to skate. Later on, Molly tries to persuade Morty to race, to prove that she's fastest. At first Morty says no, but Molly teases him until he agrees. While they're racing, Molly elbows him out of the way so that she will win and Morty falls and breaks his ankle. Molly learns from this experience that there are things more important than always being the best at everything. A good choice for older children. (Ages 9-12)

BOSSINESS

Someone has to lead the pack, set the tone, and come up with the great ideas. Unfortunately, it's hard to know when being a good leader turns into being bossy. Learning how to moderate one's leadership qualities and learning how to follow without being unduly bossed are growing-up skills your child will want to explore.

Bartholomew the Bossy
by Marjorie Weinman Sharmat.
Illustrated by Normand Chartier.
Atheneum, 1984. 32 pages.
Pleasant tricolor sketches.
Read-aloud or intermediate readers.
Bartholomew is a young skunk who is so popular that he is elected president of the new Block Club. But when he takes advantage and becomes bossy, he soon becomes the least popular animal. Bartholomew is bewildered, until Fabian the owl illustrates what bossiness means. Even though Bartholomew has learned his lesson and wins back his friends, he still feels an impulse to be bossy. The ending has a nice realistic flavor to it, reminding us that even when we learn to control our behavior, it doesn't mean we won't want to behave that way sometimes. (Ages 6-9)

A Weekend with Wendell
by Kevin Henkes.
Mulberry Books, 1995. 32 pages.
Cheerful illustrations.
Read-aloud or intermediate readers.
When Wendell comes to spend the weekend with Sophie, she is noticeably unenthusiastic, and we soon see why. Wendell disparages her toys, insists on making the rules for every game they play, and takes all the best stuff for himself.

Sophie has a miserable time until she gets a chance to turn things around and be the boss sometimes too. A humorous story with a gentle message for all bossy children. (Ages 4-8)

BOASTING

Children often enjoy boasting about their skills and their possessions. This happens particularly during the threes and fours but it can continue into later childhood. A certain amount of boasting is harmless but, when it is a regular pattern, boasting can lead to angry feelings. It's human nature, and most adults have this failing at one time or another as well. Perhaps that explains why the recommended book appeals as much to adults as to children. It reminds us of what we look like when we boast!

Mine's the Best
by Crosby Bonsall.
HarperTrophy, 1997. 28 pages.
Simple, eye-catching illustrations; limited text.
Read-aloud or beginning readers.

Two young boys boast about what their balloons can do, trying to outdo the other. When both balloons pop, they argue about whose fault it is and come to blows until they unite in their dislike of a little girl with a full balloon. The story is realistic for the age of the children shown and its treatment of boasting lets us laugh at ourselves. A good opportunity to discuss the pitfalls of boasting. (Ages 4-8)

Other titles of interest described elsewhere:
Franklin Fibs

SHYNESS

Feeling shy and uncertain in new situations is universal. But some children struggle with this feeling more than others. These books offer solace to the shy by showing both that other children share this feeling and that there are ways to handle the feelings.

Buster, the Very Shy Dog
by Lisze Bechtold.
Sandpiper, 2001. 48 pages.
Ink and watercolors.
Read-aloud or beginning readers.

Buster is a shy dog who lives with Phoebe, a brave and capable ball-catching dog. In a series of vignettes, Buster comes to terms with his shyness and his feelings of competition with Phoebe as he deals with a party and garbage bandits. The message is pointed but many children will enjoy the interaction between the two dogs. (Ages 5-9)

Ellen and Penguin
by Clara Vulliamy.
Candlewick Press, 1995. 24 pages.
Colorful watercolors.
Read-aloud or intermediate readers.
Out of print but available in libraries and used bookstores.

Ellen, a shy young girl, has a special toy penguin through which she expresses her nervous feelings about new experiences. At the park one day Ellen meets Jo who has a scruffy gray monkey named Bill. Bill and Penguin get along well, so the two little girls overcome their mutual shyness and make a date to play at the park the next day. A nice opportunity to talk about things that help us when we are feeling shy. (Ages 4-8)

Emma's Magic Winter
by Jean Little.
Illustrated by Jennifer Plecas.
HarperCollinsChildren's Books, 2000. 64 pages.
Detailed, appealing drawings.

Read-aloud or intermediate readers.
Multicultural.

When new neighbors move into Emma's neighborhood, her mom wants her to take a pie to them and make new friends with Sally who is Emma's age. But Emma is so shy that she reads in a whisper at school. Nevertheless, Emma comes up with the idea that the identical boots she and Sally own have magic and this helps Emma forget her shyness and Sally forget that she is new. A good opportunity to talk about shyness when meeting new friends. (Ages 4-8)

Lucy on the Loose
by Ilene Cooper.
Illustrated by Amanda Harvey.
Golden Books, 2000. 80 pages.
Watercolors.
Read-aloud or intermediate to advanced readers.

Eight-year old Bobby is shy but his lively beagle puppy Lucy helps him overcome his shyness and meet new friends. When Lucy gets lost, Ben must overcome his fear of talking to people in order to find her. An engrossing story for new readers, with a very realistic notion of what it takes to overcome a fear of talking. (Ages 5-9)

Shrinking Violet
by Cari Best.
Illustrated by Giselle Potter.
Farrar, Straus and Giroux, 2001. 40 pages.
Whimsical, detailed illustrations.
Read-aloud or intermediate readers.

Violet is very shy. Attention makes Violet itch and scratch and twirl her hair. She even writes on the inside of her hand, "I am allergic to attention." Like many shy children, Violet becomes the target of a bully's teasing. When her teacher announces that everyone in class will have a part in an upcoming play, Violet panics. But Violet discovers a way to shine through her talents with the help of a sensitive teacher. A good exploration of shyness in school as well as the unwelcome attention it can draw. (Ages 5-9)

Shy Charles
by Rosemary Wells.
Puffin, 2001. 28 pages.
Expressive illustrations.
Read-aloud or intermediate readers.
Available in Spanish.
1989 Boston Globe-Horn Award winner.

Charles is so shy that he embarrasses his mother in public because he won't say thank you or goodbye. His father wants him to join some activities and overcome his shyness. When the babysitter falls down the steps, Charles overcomes his shyness to call the emergency service and get her a blanket and cocoa. Another good opportunity to talk about situations in which one must overcome shyness. (Ages 4-8)

Speak Up, Blanche
by Emily Arnold McCully.
HarperCollins, 1991. 29 pages.
Playful watercolors.
Read-aloud or intermediate to advanced readers.

Blanche, a little lamb who is an only child, has trouble telling others about herself. Although she is eager to be a part of a school play, Blanche is unable to communicate to other people what she really wants to do in the play. As a result, the other animals try to get her to act, to sell tickets, and to assemble props but their efforts fail. In her frustration, Blanche finally finds her voice and tells the others what she can do: make wonderful sets. Blanche realizes that she isn't shy anymore and now defines herself as an artist. Even though the story is humorously told, it offers a gentle reminder to stand up for oneself and take a chance. (Ages 5-9)

Prejudice

At an early age children notice differences, including skin color. It is a normal part of growing up to be concerned with where one fits in, who is part of one's group, and who is different. The key may be learning to be comfortable with differences and to appreciate people as individuals. These aren't easy topics for parents and teachers but good books can help.

Amazing Grace
by Mary Hoffman.
Illustrated by Caroline Binch.
Dial Books, 1991. 24 pages.
Bright, color illustrations.
Read-aloud or intermediate readers.
Multicultural. Available in Spanish.

Grace, an elementary school child, loves to listen to stories and to act them out. So when her teacher announces that the class will perform the play Peter Pan, Grace naturally wants the lead role. Even though her classmate tells her that she can't be Peter because she is a girl and African-American, her grandmother tells her that she can be anything if she puts her mind to it. Her grandmother proves it by taking Grace to a ballet of Romeo and Juliet that features an African-American woman as Juliet. The story can be helpful both to the child experiencing prejudice as well as to children who need to understand how it feels. (Ages 7-11)

Angel Child, Dragon Child
by Michele Maria Surat.
Illustrated by Vo-Dinh Mai.
Scholastic, 1989. 36 pages.

Gentle watercolors.
Read-aloud or advanced readers.
Multicultural.

Ut, a Vietnamese girl who is attending an American school, is overwhelmed by the strangeness of this new place. At her school, the other children tease her about her clothes and her inability to speak perfect English. But she tries to be brave, remembering her mother's words. Her worst tormenter at school, a red-haired boy named Raymond, finally causes her to lose her self-control and they get into a fistfight. The principal assigns Raymond the task of listening to her story about Vietnam and writing it down. In a surprising twist, Ut finds herself comforting Raymond when he is overwhelmed by the task. Together they write her story and Raymond becomes her champion, even helping to organize a fair to earn money for her mother's passage to America. While unduly optimistic, this book fills a niche. (Ages 7-11)

Black like Kyra, White like Me
by Judith Vigna.
Albert Whitman & Company, 1996. 32 pages.
Simple, dreamy illustrations.
Read-aloud or intermediate to advanced readers.
Multicultural.

A young girl describes her best friends, including an African-American child named Kyra. After Kyra's family moves next door to the narrator, some of the other families on the block are uncomfortable. When Kyra's family arrives at the block party at the narrator's house, some of the families leave. The narrator and her father talk about prejudice. They have their own experience with it when someone vandalizes their backyard. The next act of vandalism is directed against Kyra's family but as the story ends, it is another of the narrator's friends who is moving away, not Kyra's family. A realistic look at the anger and fear surrounding prejudice, what each person can do about it, and a great opportunity for discussion. (Ages 7-11)

Bright April
by Marguerite de Angeli.
Doubleday and Company, 1946. 88 pages.
Black-and-white and occasional watercolors.
Read-aloud or advanced readers.
Multicultural.

April, a ten-year-old girl, experiences prejudice for the first time on her birthday. But a wise Girl Scout leader and her supportive mother help her to cope with it. Despite showing its age, this fifty-year-old classic is worth sharing, especially with a daughter who is into Scouting. (Ages 7-11)

Freedom Summer
by Deborah Wiles.
Illustrated by Jerome Lagarrique.
Atheneum Books, 2001. 32 pages.
Powerful, dreamlike illustrations.
Read-aloud or intermediate readers.
Multicultural.
2002 Ezra Jack Keats New Writer and Illustrator Award winner; 2002 Coretta Scott King/John Steptoe Award for New Talent award winner.

Joe and his best friend John Henry, whose mother works as housekeeper for Joe's family, spend many hours swimming together in the creek because John is not allowed in the public pool. On the day the Civil Rights Act is enacted, they visit the town pool together, excited about diving for nickels in the clear water. Instead they find workers filling in the pool with asphalt, in protest of the law. Although the book takes place in another time, the friendship it portrays and the frustration at the impact of racism on the friendship is timeless. As the story ends, the boys prepare to challenge together a whites-only policy in a restaurant. We are left wondering what will happen and that provides opportunities for discussion about the persistence of racism and prejudice today. (Ages 7-12)

Hope
by Isabell Monk.
Illustrated by Janice Lee Porter.
Carolrholda Books, 1999. 32 pages.
Expressive oils.
Read-aloud or advanced readers.
Multicultural.

A young girl of biracial heritage enjoys weekend visits with her Great-aunt Pogee. But one day when she and Aunt Pogee are at the outdoor market, she meets Violet, a friend of her aunt, for the first time. Violet stares at the girl and asks her aunt, "Is the child mixed?" Her words puzzle and trouble the girl. That night as she and her aunt cuddle she hears the story of her name, Hope. She learns that she is the beloved result of her parents' (Jewish and African-American) faith that someday everyone simply will be considered a member of the human race. A touching story with a believable young heroine. (Ages 7-11)

The Jacket
by Andrew Clements.
Illustrated by McDavid Henderson.
Simon & Schuster Books for Young Readers. 89 pages.
Occasional, soft black-and-white sketches.
Read-aloud or advanced readers.
Multicultural.

Sixth-grader Phil mistakenly accuses a younger boy, Daniel, of stealing his brother's jacket. By the time he realizes his mistake the damage is done and Daniel is hurt and angry. Phil is a thoughtful young man who is concerned that his instinct to accuse Daniel was based on Daniel being African American. He sets out to figure out whether he is prejudiced by examining his everyday assumptions. In the course of thinking things through he notices much that he had ignored previously: the all-white composition of his school bus and neighborhood, the difference between his parents in terms of their treatment of the family's housecleaner who is African-American and finally, on a visit to Daniel's neighborhood, how similar their houses are. An insightful contribution on an important topic. (Ages 9-12)

Nina Bonita
by Ana Maria Machado.
Illustrated by Rosana Faria.
Cranky Nell Books, 2001. 24 pages.
Impressionistic, dream-like illustrations.
Read-aloud or intermediate to advanced readers.
Multicultural.
Available in Spanish.

A white rabbit yearns to have a child with beautiful black skin like that of a young girl, Nina Bonita. He asks her for the secret of her beautiful skin and she makes up answers, from having had black ink spilled on her as a baby to drinking lots of coffee to eating lots of blackberries. Finally her mother explains that Nina Bonita has beautiful black skin just like her grandmother. The rabbit realizes that to have a black baby, he must marry a black rabbit, and that's what he does. His babies come in all different colors, including black. For the youngest of children, an opportunity to talk about why people have different skin colors. (Ages 5-9)

The Other Side
by Jacqueline Woodson.
Illustrated by E. B. Lewis.
G. P. Putnam's Sons, 2001. 32 pages.
Exuberant, detailed watercolors.
Read-aloud or intermediate readers.
Multicultural.

Clover, a young African-American girl, lives in a town separated by a fence between the black and the white families. Despite the fence and her mother's warnings not to climb the fence, Clover is drawn to Annie, the little girl who lives just on the other side. Finally, in midsummer Clover and Annie find the courage to meet halfway. By the end, Clover and Annie are playing with Clover's other friends on her side of the fence and look forward to the day when someone knocks the fence down. The story offers an opportunity to talk about past racism as well as the similarities between people.(Ages 5-9)

Play Lady—La Senora Juguetona
by Eric Hoffman.
Illustrated by Suzanne Tornquist.
Redleaf Press, 1999. 32 pages.
Bright, vivid illustrations.
Read-aloud or intermediate readers.
Bilingual book.
Multicultural.

Play Lady is an Asian woman who welcomes all the children of the neighborhood to her garden. She encourages them to write what they feel anywhere in her garden. But one day someone vandalizes her yard, leaving hate messages everywhere. When the Play Lady goes away for a few days, distraught over the hateful words and the vandalism, the children decide not only to fix everything but also to replace all the hateful words with words that describe what they feel for her. The story is contrived but it offers an opportunity to talk about people who commit acts of hate. (Ages 5-9)

BEING DIFFERENT

A child may be "different" because she doesn't wear the "in" clothes, or because of a haircut, or because of a difference that is more profound. Whatever the reason, being different can be painful. These books approach differences and the teasing that often results in a variety of ways. For both the child who is aware and uncomfortable with the "otherness" of children around him and the child who is uncomfortable because he is different, these books offer lots of opportunities for discussion.

The Berenstain Bears' New Neighbors
by Stan and Jan Berenstain.
Random House, 1994. 32 pages.
Familiar Berenstain Bear characters.
Read-aloud or intermediate readers.

The Bear family looks forward to meeting the new occupants of the house across the road. But when Papa Bear sees that they are pandas, he is grumpy about having new neighbors who are different. Even though Mama reminds him of things that are different that he enjoys, Papa is certain that the new fence the neighbors are installing is a "spite fence." The kids make friends anyhow and the "spite fence" turns out to be rows of bamboo. It all turns out happily, which makes this an especially easy story for talking about differences with the youngest of children. (Ages 5-9)

The Big Orange Splot
by Daniel Manus Pinkwater.
Scholastic, 1993. 32 pages.
Colorful, bold illustrations.
Read-aloud or intermediate to advanced readers.
1984 Alabama Emphasis on Reading Award winner.

Mr. Plumbean lives on a street where all the houses are the same. One day, after a seagull drops an orange splot on his house, Mr. Plumbean begins to paint his house and ends up making his house a remarkable sight. After that he builds and paints and changes his house in many creative and ingenious ways, all to the disapproval of his neighbors. To their criticism, Mr. Plumbean always replies,

"My house is me and I am it. My house is where I like to be and it looks like all my dreams." One by one, the neighbors try out his philosophy and by the end the street is filled with original designs and is the most interesting street around. A story that celebrates the joy of expressing one's individuality. (Ages 5-11)

The Brand New Kid
by Katie Couric.
Illustrated by Marjorie Priceman.
Doubleday, 2000. 32 pages.
Colorful, active illustrations.
Read-aloud or intermediate to advanced readers.

Two little girls, Ellie and Carrie, look forward to school starting again but this year there's a new boy in their class with a strange name, Lazlo S. Gadsky. Because he looks and talks differently, the other children alternately tease him and ignore him. One day, after noticing his misery, Ellie decides to be friendly and Lazlo invites her to his house to play. At Lazlo's house Ellie experiences a new world of homemade strudel and chess and she has fun. The next day at school Ellie tells the other kids to give Lazlo a chance and they do. While the message is obvious, there still are opportunities for good discussion with your child about a child he knows who is just a little different (Ages 7-11).

Crow Boy
by Taro Yashima.
Viking Press, 1976 edition. 37 pages.
Exquisite, impressionistic watercolors.
Read-aloud or intermediate readers.
Multicultural. Available in Spanish.
1956 Caldecott Honor Award winner;
1955 Josette Frank Award winner.

Chibi is a shy Japanese boy who is afraid of the other children in the village. He is very different from them and ostracized by them. His story is told by another child who expresses a simple wonder at Chibi's strange behavior, his interest in insects, and his separateness. By sixth grade, a new teacher arrives who recognizes Chibi's knowledge of plants, insects and birds, and his talent in art. The teacher spends time with Chibi and, at the school talent show, the teacher asks Chibi to demonstrate the voices of crows. The other children are astonished by Chibi's skill. They realize how much they have missed in not knowing him all these years. A touching story that conveys a message without preaching and an interesting opportunity for discussing the hidden talents of children your child knows. (Ages 7-12)

It's George!
by Miriam Cohen.
Illustrated by Lillian Hoban.
Yearling Books, 1998. 32 pages.
Soft watercolors.
Read-aloud or intermediate readers.

George and his classmates are aware that he's a little different. When it comes to academic work, George struggles. But he is better than anyone else at taking care of the class pets and it turns out that he has other special qualities too. The class is amazed to learn that George is the subject of a television special about a lonely elderly man and the little boy who visits him every morning. The boy found his friend in need of emergency help one day and had the presence of mind to call 911. Everyone congratulates George and is eager to be identified as his friend. A good discussion about children who are just a little different and how each has his own special skills. (Ages 4-8)

Jack and Jim
by Kitty Crowther.
Hyperion Books, 2000. 32 pages.
Delicate pen-and-ink drawings that occasionally

expand into dreamy full-page color.
Read-aloud or intermediate readers.

Jack, a blackbird who lives in the forest, dreams of seeing the ocean. On his way to fulfill his dream he meets a seagull named Jim who offers to show him his home. The two birds become good friends on their journey but, when they reach Jim's home, the other seagulls do not welcome them. Despite Jim's sharing of his cozy home with Jack, the other seagulls continue to reject this very different bird. It isn't until they discover his special talent for reading that the other birds take a chance and get to know Jack. While the message is emphasized, the story is interesting enough to hold children's interest and offers opportunities for discussion. (Ages 5-9)

Loudmouth George and the New Neighbors
by Nancy Carlson.
Lerner Publications, 2003. 32 pages.
Simple bright illustrations.
Read-aloud or intermediate readers.

George is convinced that pigs make the worst possible neighbors. He believes that they're dirty, they eat garbage, and above all, they're different. So when a family of pigs moves in next door, George doesn't want to get to know them. But when all his friends go over to play with the pigs George is left alone. Finally he goes over, planning to stay just for a moment, and ends up having a lot of fun. At the end, when a family of cats moves in, even though George has his hesitations, he agrees to go meet them. Humor helps convey an important message about being different. (Ages 4-8)

A Pig is Moving in!
by Claudia Fries.
Orchard Books, 2000. 32 pages.
Bright, exciting watercolors.
Read-aloud or intermediate to advanced readers.

In a building full of animals, a new neighbor is anxiously awaited. The animals hope that he will turn out to be a cleanly sort. When they find out that it's a pig they agree that this is not acceptable. After all, pigs are known to be messy, dirty, and sloppy. But even as their expectations seem to be confirmed, the pig also seems to clean up every mess he makes and to make something creative out of the mess. When the neighbors come to the pig's door to confront him, they learn not only how clean and orderly he is but also how thoughtful. A gentle poke at stereotypes and a good opportunity to talk with your child about stereotypes he may have heard. (Ages 4-8)

Spotty
by Margaret Rey.
Illustrated by H. A. Rey.
Houghton Mifflin, 1997. 32 pages.
Cheerful, simple illustrations.
Read-aloud or intermediate readers.

Spotty, a spotted rabbit, is born into a family without spots. The family is so concerned about how Grandpa Bunny will react to Spotty's spots that they decide to leave Spotty at home while they attend Grandpa's birthday party. Spotty decides to run away and meets a family of rabbits who all look just like him, except for one of their children. As in Spotty's family, these rabbits also are concerned about how their relatives will react to the one child who is different. When the two families meet to reunite Spotty with his family, both learn a lot about what is really important. While the preaching is obvious, this may be a good story for the very young who enjoy animals as the main characters. (Ages 4-8)

The Rainbow Tulip
by Pat Mora.
Illustrated by Elizabeth Sayles.

Puffin, 2002. 32 pages.
Soft, luscious illustrations reminiscent of Mexican folk painting.
Read-aloud or intermediate to advanced readers.
Multicultural. Available in Spanish.

A young Mexican girl lives in the United States with her family and experiences the cultural differences between home and school. When it's time for the annual May parade, she needs a tulip costume. Her mother makes a multicolored costume but the girl feels embarrassed to wear it at school and she worries that her mother, who doesn't speak English, will embarrass her. The young girl talks with her mother about how it feels to be different. There is no dramatic conclusion, which makes the story all the more realistic. (Ages 7-12)

Yoko
by Rosemary Wells.
Hyperion Books, 1998. 32 pages.
Gentle ink and watercolors.
Read-aloud or intermediate readers.
Multicultural.

Yoko, a young Asian kitty, brings all her favorite ethnic foods for lunch at school. The other children tease her and Yoko feels bad and doesn't want to go out for recess. Later, at snack time she is teased again about her red bean ice cream. Her teacher organizes International Food Day at school and requests that each child bring and try food from other countries. Each of the children is shown making a special food from his culture but when the big day comes no one will try Yoko's sushi. Then Timothy, a young raccoon from the West Indies, tries Yoko's sushi. Timothy and Yoko become good friends. A gentle reminder about being open to other people's cultures. (Ages 4-8)

SEXISM

When today's adults were growing up, it was commonplace to hear boys called sissies and girls called tomboys. Girls played with dolls and boys played with balls and anything else was odd. Today we understand that there are wide differences among individuals and that there is nothing wrong with enjoying whatever toy or sport you like, even if you're a boy playing with dolls. These books explore the continuing discomfort many people have with behaviors and choices that are just a little different.

Oliver Button is a Sissy
by Tomie de Paola.
Voyager Books, 1990. 48 pages.
Simple illustrations.
Read-aloud or intermediate readers.
Available in Spanish.

When his dance teacher asks him to be in an upcoming talent show, Oliver faces teasing from his classmates. Oliver doesn't win but his parents are proud of his performance and his classmates see him as a star anyhow. It's a powerful story because Oliver remains true to himself despite the teasing of other children and the urging of his father to pursue more traditional boys' sports. For any boy who follows a different road, this book is sure to be a winner. (Ages 5-9)

Tough Eddie
by Elizabeth Winthrop.
Illustrated by Lillian Hoban.
E. P. Dutton, 1985. 32 pages.
Illustrations are dated.
Read-aloud or intermediate readers.
Out of print but available in libraries and used bookstores.

Eddie is a little boy who likes to build spaceships with his friends and engage in imaginary play. He's also a little boy who loves to play with his dollhouse. We know that it's okay with his parents because his father helped him make the furniture. But Eddie keeps it hidden from his friends until one day, when his older sister is irritated, she reveals his secret. His friends tease him and Eddie withdraws but an encounter with a bee gives Eddie a chance to prove how brave he is. Now Eddie feels confident enough to consider bringing his dollhouse for show and tell. A gentle message that a boy can be interested in lots of things, traditional and non-traditional. (Ages 5-8)

William's Doll
by Charlotte Zolotow.
Illustrated by William Pene du Bois.
HarperTrophy, 1985. 32 pages.
Delicate artwork.
Read-aloud or intermediate to advanced readers.
Redbook Children's Picture Book Award winner.

William, a little boy, wants a doll to hug, to take to the park and push in a swing - - in short, all the things that we usually think of little girls doing with their dolls. His brothers and the boy next door tease him. His father then brings home a basketball for him. Although William enjoys the basketball and the electric train that his father gives him, nothing lessens his desire for a doll. When his grandmother visits, he shares his wish with her and she buys him a doll. She explains to his father that William needs a doll so that when he becomes a father he will know just how to care for his child. A gem for any child who defies stereotypes. (Ages 5-8)

TEASING

Being teased can have a humorous and fun element, but the books included here are about the kind of teasing that is unkind and unrelenting. Few children will escape the experience of either teasing or being teased and these books can open discussion about how each of those roles feels.

Ada Potato
by Judith Caseley.
Greenwillow Books, 1989. 24 pages.
Watercolors and colored pencils.
Read-aloud or intermediate readers.

Ada loves playing the violin in the school band but every rehearsal day older kids tease her as she walks to school. Ada stops playing the violin and her mother asks her why. Ada tells her mother that the kids call her Ada Potato, Queen of the Mob, and tease her about having a machine-gun in her violin case. Her mother shares a teasing experience from her childhood and this gives Ada an idea for dealing with the kids who are teasing her. An opportunity to talk about your own experiences with teasing and how you handled them. (Ages 7-10)

The Berenstain Bears and Too Much Teasing
by Stan and Jan Berenstain.
Random House, 1995. 32 pages.
Familiar Berenstain Bear characters.
Read-aloud or intermediate readers.

Brother Bear enjoys teasing at home and at school until the tables are turned and he is the one being teased. He has a chance for a reprieve when the bullies turn their attention to a new kid. But Brother Bear finds himself sticking up for the new kid and even helps the new kid stand up to the teasing. Although the format is predictable and the rhymes may make a parent groan, the Berenstain authors have a winning formula for many children. An opportunity to talk about teasing. (Ages 7-10)

Dancing in the Wings
by Debbie Allen.
Illustrated by Kadir Nelson.
Dial Books for Young Readers, 2000. 32 pages.
Pencils and oil paint.
Read-aloud or intermediate readers.
Multicultural.
2001 Children's Literature Council of Southern
California Award winner.

Sassy, an aspiring ballerina, worries about her awkwardness, her big feet, and her height. At an audition Sassy does everything she can to be noticed, including wearing a bright yellow leotard and standing in the front row. Despite the teasing of other girls, Sassy's determination wins her a place in the festival. A good book for discussion about self-confidence, teasing, and belief in oneself. (Ages 7-10)

Fat, Fat Rose Marie
by Lisa Passen.
Henry Holt and Company, 1991. 32 pages.
Eye-catching cartoon characters.
Read-aloud or intermediate readers.

Claire, the narrator, has been teased at school but now her tormenters have turned their attention to Rose Marie, the new girl in class, teasing her about her weight. Claire doesn't like the way the other girls tease Rose Marie but she remains silent until a crisis at the amusement park forces her to choose between standing up for Rose Marie or being accepted by the kids who do the teasing. Claire initially makes a choice that hurts Rose Marie but soon regrets it and makes it clear where she stands. A realistic look at some of the choices children have to make. (Ages 7-10)

Honey Bunny Funnybunny
by Marilyn Sadler.
Illustrated by Roger Bollen.

Beginner Books, a Division of Random House, 1997. 48 pages.
Bright cartoon illustrations.
Read-aloud or beginning reader.

Honey Bunny has a brother who loves to tease her. Every morning P.J. pulls the covers off her bed. He changes the heads on her dolls and one night he even paints her face green. P.J. gets in trouble and stops teasing but, to Honey Bunny's surprise, she misses his teasing and begins to wonder if he really loves her anymore. The final trick shows that he still does. The story can spark discussion of the difference between bothersome teasing and affection. (Ages 7-10)

The Meanest Thing to Say
by Bill Cosby.
Illustrated by Varnette P. Honeywood.
Cartwheel Books, 1997. 40 pages.
Bright primary colors.
Read-aloud or intermediate to advanced readers.
Multicultural.

Little Bill, a young African-American boy, learns a game, "Playing the Dozens," from a new boy at school. In the game, each person has twelve chances to say something mean to someone and the person who says the meanest thing wins. After experiencing a round of the game, Little Bill is furious and awaits his own turn. But his father suggests to Little Bill that the most effective response is simply to say "So?" to every mean thing that is said. Little Bill tries it and finds that the technique works. A useful approach to a problem that is worth introducing to a child. (Ages 7-10)

Phoebe's Parade
by Claudia Mills.
Illustrated by Carolyn Ewing.
Macmillan Publishing Company, 1994.

Colorful, painted illustrations.
Read-aloud or intermediate readers.

Phoebe alerts the entire neighborhood that she will be in the 4th of July parade carrying her baton, following the high school majorettes with the school marching band. Her two brothers are the only ones who don't share in the excitement. Her older brother David teases her that she isn't actually throwing the baton, just carrying it in the parade "like a dumb old stick." Phoebe throws her baton high to impress her family as she marches by, but it lands in the crowd. Phoebe is embarrassed and fears that her brothers will tease her but they surprise her by finding the baton and returning it to her. Phoebe returns the favor by inviting them to join her on the fire engine after the firemen offer her a ride. As the sirens blare triumphantly, the three share the honor of being in the parade. This book shows a win-win ending as the siblings stop teasing and help each other out. (Ages 7-10)

Other titles of interest, described elsewhere:
The Last Noo-Noo
Teeth Week
Arthur's First Sleepover
Swimming Lessons
Last One in is a Rotten Egg
Timothy Goes to School
Marvin One Too Many
Today Was a Terrible Day
The Flunking of Joshua T. Bates
Kelly's Creek
Thank you, Mr. Falker
Mary Marony, Mummy Girl
Mary Marony and the Chocolate Surprise
Shrinking Violet
Angel Child, Dragon Child
The Brand New Kid

Yoko
Tough Eddie
Oliver Button is a Sissy
William's Doll
Buster Gets Braces
Hue Boy
The Best Fight
Jim Meets the Thing
Jorah's Journal
Going with the Flow

BULLIES

Bullies are a problem for which the solution may not be within a child's control. Many books reflect that fact by featuring a hero who gains the upper hand through some magical or fantastic solution. Yet even reading those stories offers the opportunity for discussion and reflection about this upsetting and all too frequent problem.

Amelia Takes Command
by Marissa Moss.
Pleasant Company Publications. 1999. 40 pages.
Journal format; illustrations portrayed as the main character's drawings.
Read-aloud or intermediate to advanced readers.

Amelia, a fifth-grade girl, confides in her journal about being the target for the class bully, another fifth-grade girl. When Amelia attends Space Camp she is the student commander of the Space Shuttle and gains self-confidence when she leads her group in the most successful mission at camp. When Amelia comes home she faces her bully with new confidence. A good choice for a girl dealing with a bully. (Ages 9-12)

The Berenstain Bears and the Bully
by Stan and Jan Berenstain.
Random House, 1993. 32 pages.

**Familiar Berenstain Bear characters; limited text.
Read-aloud or intermediate readers.**

The Bear Family is dismayed when Sister Bear comes home scratched and dirty and tells them that a bully beat her up. Brother Bear discovers that the bully is another girl bear cub who tries to goad him into a fight too. He decides to teach Sister Bear self-defense, although the Bear family cautions Sister Bear to avoid a fight if possible. But when Sister Bear sees the bully throwing stones at a baby bird, she takes on the bully and they both wind up in the Principal's office. While waiting, she learns that the bully's parents sometimes hit her. There aren't any consequences for Sister, but the bully loses a week of recess and has to visit the school psychologist. The series, noteworthy for its attempts to offer real-life solutions, makes it seem a little too easy in this book. Despite that shortcoming, for the child who enjoys the Berenstain bears, it can be useful for discussion. (Ages 5-9)

Bully on the Bus
**by Carl W. Bosch.
Illustrated by Rebekah J. Strecker.
Parenting Press, 1988. 58 pages.
Simple black-and-white drawings.
Read-aloud or advanced readers.**

A young boy faces the problem of being bullied on the school bus. In a problem-solving format, the reader has the opportunity to make choices, such as talking to the bus driver, asking advice from a teacher, fighting the bully, or ignoring the bully. The consequences of each choice are explored. A useful book for children who respond to this format because it offers solutions and probable consequences. (Ages 5-11)

Herbie's Troubles
**by Carol Chapman.
Illustrated by Kelly Oechsli.**

E.P. Dutton, 1981. 32 pages.
Cartoon illustrations.
Read-aloud or intermediate to advanced readers.

Herbie, age six, is a happy kid who likes school until he begins having problems with a bully named Jimmy John. Since they are both young, the bullying takes the form of messing up paintings, stomping on granola bars, and holding the door shut to the boys' bathroom. But it's enough to make Herbie dread school. After getting advice from friends, Herbie tries standing up to Jimmy John and punching him, but it doesn't seem to help. Finally Herbie tries his own idea, ignoring Jimmy John. To his delight, he finds that it works. A practical suggestion, particularly at the early elementary-school stage of bullying. (Ages 5-9)

I Sure Am Glad to See You Blackboard Bear
by Martha Alexander.
Candlewick Press, 1969. 40 pages.
Color-washed illustrations.
Read-aloud or intermediate readers.

Anthony, a young boy, has a friend in a bear that has come to life from a drawing on the blackboard. The Bear helps when he needs it, such as when kids tease him. When Anthony buys Bear's favorite ice cream cone, a bully is waiting for him as he comes out of the store. The bully is about to take Anthony's ice cream cone when Bear picks the bully up by his suspenders. No practical suggestions but children will enjoy the fantasy of power over a bully and may want to talk about how that might feel. (Ages 4-8)

Just a Bully
by Gina and Mercer Mayer.
Golden Books, 1999. 24 pages.
Quirky characters and illustrations.
Read-aloud or intermediate readers.

Little Monster explains that his parents have told Little Sister and him to stick up for each other. So when a large alligator picks on Little Sister, Little Monster sticks up for her and draws the attention of the bully to himself. After that, the bully makes life miserable for Little Monster until Little Monster fakes illness to avoid school. When he returns to school and the bullying begins again, Little Monster tries physical force. Unfortunately, he is out-matched and it isn't until Little Sister tries force against the bully that the bullying stops, at least for awhile. Sibling loyalty and charming characters make this a worthy entry for encouraging discussion. (Ages 5-9)

King of the Kooties
by Debbie Dadey.
Illustrated by Kevin O'Malley.
Walker & Co, 1999. 112 pages.
Pencil drawings.
Read-aloud or intermediate to advanced readers.

On the first day of fourth grade, Nate and his new neighbor, Donald, are noticed by Louisa, the school bully. When Donald makes the mistake of smiling at Louisa, she starts in on him. Nate thinks of ways to get Louisa to ignore them but he wishes that his father were home to offer advice. He remembers his father's suggestion that sometimes you have to kill someone with kindness. The boys set out to be nice to Louisa and end up becoming friends. An opportunity to talk about an alternative approach to bullies. (Ages 9-12)

King of the Playground
by Phyllis Reynolds Naylor.
Illustrated by Nola Langner Malone.
Aladdin Paperbacks, 1994. 32 pages.
Watercolors.
Read-aloud or intermediate readers.

Kevin, a young boy, is bullied on the playground by Sammy, a boy who calls himself King of the Playground. Sammy threatens Kevin with fantastical and unlikely consequences if he plays on the playground. After Kevin talks to his father, he begins to see that Sammy's threats are not real and he gains the courage to respond to Sammy with an invitation to play together. A good book for talking with your young child about the difference between real and empty threats and creative ways of responding. (Ages 4-8)

Louise Takes Charge
by Stephen Krensky.
Illustrated by Susanna Natti.
Dial Books for Young Readers, 1998. 80 pages.
Stylized black-and-white drawings.
Read-aloud or intermediate to advanced readers.

When Louise starts school, she discovers that Jasper, a former class outcast, is now the class bully. Among other things, Jasper takes the best parts of everyone's lunches. Louise comes up with an idea. She suggests that each of the children apprentice themselves to Jasper, helping him find the best lunches. As everyone becomes a part of Jasper's team, no one is left for him to bully. Then the children join together to tell Jasper that he can't bully them anymore. A creative solution in an entertaining story. (Ages 9-12)

Pinky and Rex and the Bully
by James Howe.
Illustrated by Melissa Sweet.
Simon & Schuster, 1996. 48 pages.
Color illustrations.
Read-aloud or intermediate readers.
1996 Parenting Best Books of the Year Award winner.

Pinky, a younger elementary school boy, is bullied by a third-grader because of his unusual name and his friendship with a girl. The teasing includes telling Pinky that he's not a boy, he's a girl. Initially Pinky reacts by giving up his nickname and avoiding his friend but a conversation with a wise neighbor helps him to see that he has to be true to himself. The story offers a chance to ponder together the questions the book raises: who makes the "rules" that say a boy can't like pink or be friends with a girl, and what do you do if you're different? (Ages 7-10)

Who's Afraid of the Big Bad Bully?
by Teddy Slater.
Illustrated by Pat Porter.
Scholastic Press, 1995. 45 pages.
Illustrations are dated.
Read-aloud or intermediate readers.
Out of print but available at libraries and used bookstores.

Big Bertha, a young girl, is large and mean. The other children, including a little boy named Max, are afraid of her. Max tries to avoid Bertha. He studies karate and gives his new dog a fierce name, Fang. But when Bertha is mean to Fang, Max finds the courage to stand up to her. When the other children see Max's action, they too find the courage to refuse to put up with her bullying. The story ends on a happy note as Bertha becomes part of the crowd instead of a bullying outsider. Useful both for discussion about being bullied and being a bully. (Ages 5-9)

Other titles of interest, described elsewhere:
Last One in is a Rotten Egg
The Flunking of Joshua T. Bates
Shrinking Violet
Angel Child, Dragon Child
Tough Beans
Furlie Cat

Appearance

Most children aren't preoccupied with their appearance until the preteen years unless they've been teased. But sooner or later, children may become concerned about some aspect of their appearance. They may be late bloomers and small for their age. They may be sporting a mouthful of silver braces. Learning to accept how you look is a goal many adults never reach so it's a good idea to begin exploring it when your child voices a concern.

Glasses

Arthur's Eyes
by Marc Brown.
Little, Brown and Company, 1986. 32 pages.
Familiar characters from the series.
Read-aloud or intermediate readers.

Arthur, the familiar and beloved aardvark, needs glasses. Otherwise, he has to hold his book so close when he reads that his nose gets in the way. But Arthur dislikes his glasses and tries to lose them. Unfortunately, he then stumbles into the girls' bathroom and ends up in the principal's office. After Arthur's teacher talks with him about glasses, Arthur feels better. To his surprise, Francine decides to copy him by wearing glasses too. A good story for children adjusting to glasses. (Ages 4-8)

Baby Duck and the Bad Eyeglasses
by Amy Hest.
Illustrated by Jill Barton.
Candlewick Press, 1999. 32 pages.
Full-page pencil and watercolors.
Read-aloud or intermediate readers.

Baby Duck isn't happy about her new glasses. It's time to go to the park but Baby Duck is afraid to hop or dance for fear that her glasses will fall off. Grampa encourages her to splash in the lake and to twirl around and Baby Duck is happy to find that her glasses stay on. Then Grampa shows her how easy it is for her to read with glasses and Baby Duck feels better. A gentle tale for the very young who aren't happy about glasses. (Ages 4-8)

Glasses...Who Needs 'Em?
by Lane Smith.
Puffin, 1995. 32 pages.
Unusual oil illustrations.
Read-aloud or advanced readers.
Available in Spanish.

A young boy and his doctor talk about needing glasses. As the doctor tries to persuade the boy that lots of folks wear glasses, his examples become increasingly hilarious. The little boy reacts with sarcasm that strikes a realistic note for a smart little guy of this age group. By the end, the little boy is specifying the kind of frames he wants and you know that he has come to accept the inevitable. A good choice for a boy facing glasses. (Ages 5-9)

Spectacles
by Ellen Raskin.
Aladdin Library, 1988. 47 pages.
Bright illustrations.
Read-aloud or intermediate readers.
Out of print but available in libraries and used bookstores.
1968 New York Times Best Illustrated Children's Books of the Year Award winner.

Iris Fogel didn't always wear glasses. As a result, she saw the world in a different way. Her Great-Aunt Fanny appeared to be a fire-breathing dragon and her good friend Chester looked like a giant pygmy nuthatch. When the doctor (who looks to her like a blue elephant) prescribes glasses, Iris is entirely opposed. But the new glasses help her in lots of ways and she still holds onto some of her more imaginative ways of viewing the world. If your little girl needs glasses, she will find Iris a sympathetic character.(Ages 5-9)

Braces

Buster Gets Braces
by Jane Breskin Zalben.
Henry Holt and Company, 1992.
Realistic, detailed pictures.
Read-aloud or intermediate readers.

Buster is a young dinosaur who needs braces. Mom and Dad are sympathetic but his little sister Sally teases him. She calls him Metal Mouth and at school she points out bits of his lunch that stick in his new braces. When Sally has cavities and has to eat soft food like Buster, she finally realizes how difficult it is for him. A good combination of sibling interaction and braces. (Ages 9-12)

Hair

Franny B. Kranny, There's a Bird in Your Hair!
by Harriet Lerner and Susan Goldhor.
Illustrated by Helen Oxenbury.
HarperCollins Children's Books, 2001.
Humorous and expressive watercolors.
Read-aloud or intermediate to advanced readers.
Parents' Choice Award winner.

Franny insists on wearing her hair as she likes it, no matter how others feel about it or what happens as a result (such as a bird nesting in it). When she finally gets her hair cut, it's clear that she cut it because she decided to and not because anyone else said it was time. For every child who insists on the right to wear her hair the way she wants, here's a good book to spark discussion. (Ages 5-9)

Hairs/Pelitos
by Sandra Cisneros.
Illustrated by Terry Ybanez.
Random House, 1997. 32 pages.
Colorful, humorous illustrations.
Read-aloud or beginning to intermediate readers.
Multicultural. Bilingual.

More a lyrical description than a story, this simple story celebrates the differences in the hair of each of the members of a young girl's family. The narrator, a young girl, tells us that her father's hair is "like a broom, all up in the air." She describes each family member's hair, concluding with her mother's hair. Here, she adds the way her mother's hair makes her feel and how it reminds her of cozy and safe feelings. A loving look at differences. (Ages 5-9)

Happy to Be Nappy
by Bell Hooks.
Illustrated by Chris Raschka.
Hyperion, 1999. 32 pages.
Bold, childlike paints on colorwash; text in cursive.
Read-aloud or advanced readers.
Multicultural.

A happy, rhythmic ode to nappy hair, but no actual story. Offers opportunities to talk about hair differences and other ways that individuals' appearances differ. (Ages 5-9)

I Love My Hair!
by Natasha Anastasia Tarpley.
Illustrated by E. B. Lewis.
Little Brown & Company, 2001. 32 pages.
Exuberant illustrations.
Read-aloud or intermediate readers.
Multicultural.

A little girl, Keyana, narrates a celebration of her

hair as a source of delight, play, and pride in her heritage. No story but good for a child who has questions about his hair and why it may be different from other children's hair. (Ages 5-9)

Other titles of interest, discussed elsewhere:
Mike's First Haircut
Katy's First Haircut
Will Gets a Haircut
Jeremy's First Haircut
The Day of the Bad Haircut

HEIGHT

The Biggest Boy
by Kevin Henkes.
Illustrated by Nancy Tafuri.
Greenwillow Books, 1995. 32 pages.
Big bright watercolors.
Read-aloud or intermediate readers.

Billy is a preschooler who can do all sorts of things, including eating with a fork and reaching some of the cupboards in the kitchen. But like any child he dreams of being bigger. In fact he wants to be the biggest boy in the world. In this sweet story, he and his parents imagine him as a huge boy, so big that he drinks from lakes and moves the clouds by blowing on them. In the meantime, he's just the right size for a boy his age. Reassurance for a child longing to grow bigger. (Ages 3-7)

Hue Boy
by Rita Phillips Mitchell.
Illustrated by Caroline Binch.
Penguin UK, 1999. 24 pages.
Realistic, color illustrations.
Read-aloud or intermediate to advanced readers.
Multicultural.

1993 Nestle Smarties Book Prize winner; 1993 New York Times Best Illustrated Children's Books of the Year Award winner; 1993 Parenting Best Books of the Year Award winner.

Little Hue Boy gets advice from everyone in his village about how to grow taller. His mother serves him fresh vegetables and fruit every day; his grandmother gives him new clothes, and his neighbor teaches him stretching exercises. Still, Little Hue Boy doesn't grow and he is teased by other children. Finally, when his father returns to the village, Little Hue walks proudly through the village with his father and his happiness makes him feel tall. No practical suggestions but a message of the importance of accepting who you are, while realizing that you will grow. (Ages 5-9)

Roller Coaster
by Kevin O'Malley.
Lothrop, Lee & Shepard, 1995. 21 pages.
Bold, bright illustrations.
Read-aloud or intermediate readers.
Out of print but available in libraries and used bookstores.

A young girl tells about the wonderful day she had at an amusement park last year, with the exception of the roller coaster. When she tried to go on that ride the attendant told her she was too short. But this year, she reports with delight, she is now tall enough to ride the roller coaster. No practical suggestions for coping with being short but recognition both of its frustration and the fact that children do eventually grow. (Ages 5-9)

The Shortest Kid in the World
by Corinne Demas Bliss.
Illustrated by Nancy Poydar.
Random House, 1995. 48 pages.
Conventional illustrations.

Read-aloud or intermediate readers.

Emily is smaller than everyone in her family and her class and she hates it. No matter how hard she tries she doesn't seem to grow any taller. One day a new girl joins her class, Marietta Fairchild, who is shorter than Emily but takes pride in her size. In fact, Marietta insists on special privileges because of her small size. Seeing Marietta's example, Emily decides that being short isn't so bad after all and she becomes best friends with Marietta. Eventually both girls grow and someone else has a turn being the shortest. A good reminder that everyone grows eventually. (Ages 5-9)

Titch
by Pat Hutchins.
Aladdin Library, 1993. 32 pages.
Simple watercolors.
Read-aloud or beginning to intermediate readers.

Titch is the youngest of three children so it's no surprise that he's also the smallest. In this charming tale Titch is the one with the smallest bicycle (a tricycle), a pinwheel instead of a kite, a wooden whistle instead of a real musical instrument, and so on. Titch's feelings of frustration are evident until we come to the final comparison. His older siblings have the gardening tools but it's Titch who has the tiny little seed that grows and grows. A satisfying conclusion that will cheer your smallest child. (Ages 5-9)

The Very Little Boy
by Phyllis Krasilovsky.
Illustrated by Karen Gundersheimer.
Scholastic, 1992. 28 pages.
Delicate watercolors.
Read-aloud or beginning readers.

An unnamed little boy is "smaller than a cornstalk, smaller than a baseball bat, and too small to ride his bicycle." As time passes he can reach the pedals on his bicycle and do many other things he has looked forward to doing. As he continues to grow, he becomes big enough to be a big brother to a new sister who's very, very little. A gentle look at the feelings of frustration with being small and the feelings of achievement as one grows. (Ages 4-8)

You'll Grow Soon, Alex
by Andrea Shavick.
Illustrated by Russell Ayto.
Walker & Company, 2000. 24 pages.
Zany illustrations.
Read-aloud or advanced readers.
Alex is a small boy and he doesn't like it. When wishing doesn't work, he solicits ideas from everyone and follows each idea faithfully. From eating healthy food to stretching to sleeping more, Alex tries everything but nothing helps. Then one day his Uncle Danny, the tallest person Alex knows, lets him in on a secret. Sometimes being tall isn't fun either. Uncle Danny tells him that what's important is growing on the inside. A cheerful take on an issue many children experience. (Ages 5-9)

Other titles of interest, described elsewhere:
The Worry Stone

GROWING UP

FEELINGS

Everyone has feelings that are uncomfortable, from anger to envy, from anxiety to embarrassment. Children may not understand their feelings or be able to put them into words. These wise and funny books talk about all kinds of feelings and offer lots of good ideas for handling feelings.

Anger

Angry Arthur
by Hiawyn Oram.
Illustrated by Satoshi Kitamura.
Random House of Canada, 1993. 28 pages.
Distinctive watercolors.
Read-aloud or intermediate readers.
Available in Spanish.

Arthur threatens to get angry if his mother won't let him stay up to watch television but she is unmoved by his threat. Arthur's anger is enormous. It literally becomes a dark cloud, then a full-scale storm. Even after his mother, his father and his grandfather tell him, "That's enough," Arthur's anger escalates into a hurricane, a typhoon, and an earth tremor. Eventually his anger splits the earth and becomes a universe-sized quake. As Arthur sits on a piece of Mars, he realizes that he cannot remember why he was angry. A delightful story that acknowledges the power of feelings. (Ages 4-9)

Come Home Wilma
by Mitchell Sharmat.
Illustrated by Rosekrans Hoffman.
Albert Whitman & Company, 1980. 32 pages.
Exquisite, imaginative drawings.
Read-aloud or intermediate readers.

An angry little girl, in "time out" for hitting her brother, imagines running away from home to punish her mother. In her imagination she draws a horse that comes to life and carries her away despite her mother's pleas. But when she imagines her mother missing her, she imagines that she will return home laden with gifts for her mother and that she will apologize then to her mother. A story that accepts the power of a child's angry feelings and provides opportunities for discussion of your child's anger. (Ages 4-9)

Danny, the Angry Lion
by Dorothy Lachner.
Illustrated by Gusti.
Translated by J. Alison James.
North South Books, 2000. 26 pages.
Colorful watercolors.
Read-aloud or intermediate readers.

Danny is angry when he doesn't get what he wants for dinner. He put on his lion costume, "sharpened his claws, shook his mane and twitched the tip of his tail back and forth." Since he's still hungry, he decides to eat anything he can get his paws on, including a man with a bike, a newspaper lady, and a boy with a ball. But as each person seems to welcome him and ask for his help in some way, he begins to calm down. The boy with a ball invites him to play and after they have lots of fun together, they go to the boy's house where his mom offers Danny just what he wants to eat. It's reassuring to hear how another little boy's very angry feelings go away without actually harming anyone. (Ages 4-8)

Dinah's Mad, Bad Wishes
by Barbara M. Joose.
Illustrated by Emily Arnold McCully.
Harper & Row, 1989. 32 pages.
Impressionistic drawings.
Read-aloud or intermediate readers.
Out of print but available in libraries and used bookstores.

Dinah and her mother are angry at each other about the colored marks Dinah drew on a newly painted wall. While her mother cleans off the marks, Dinah goes to her room. Both of them have a chance to think about their angry feelings. Dinah wishes bad things would happen to Mama; Mama works out her angry feelings by scrubbing vigorously and riding her exercise bicycle. Then Mama begins to reflect on her own mischievous exploits as a child and Dinah's fearsome wishes begin to worry her. Mama and Dinah hug each other--"they had whizzed and bumped and wished their angry feelings away. Now only the loving was left." A story that accepts angry feelings and offers practical solutions. It's also refreshing to see that the parent has feelings too. (Ages 4-9)

Goldie Is Mad
by Margie Palatini.
Hyperion Books, 2001. 32 pages.
Bold, primary colors.
Read-aloud or beginning readers.

A little girl named Goldie is very angry with her toddler brother because he drooled on her doll. As Goldie talks about her anger, she realizes that there are things she likes about having a little brother. A tale that focuses on the angry feelings that come with having younger siblings. (Ages 4-8)

I'm Mad at You!
by Louise Gikow.
Illustrated by Manhar Chauhan.
Checkerboard Press, 1989.
Familiar Sesame Street illustrations.
Read-aloud or intermediate to advanced readers.
Out of print but available in libraries and used bookstores.

Fozzie Bear and Kermit are supposed to go to the Museum of Natural History and Fozzie is very excited at the prospect. But Kermit forgets their date. Fozzie is angry but he doesn't know how to handle it. After several days go by, his mother gently inquires about his mood and he confides his feelings to her. She suggests he tell Kermit and, with her encouragement, he confronts Kermit who finally apologizes. Fozzie realizes that when he is angry, the anger won't go away unless he deals with it directly. While the story openly preaches, it offers opportunities for discussion with younger children and fans of Sesame Street. (Ages 4-8)

I Was So Mad
by Mercer Mayer.
Golden Books Publishing, 2000. 24 pages.
Whimsical illustrations.
Read-aloud or intermediate readers.

A young monster of indeterminate gender is mad at his parents and grandparents who all seem to be telling him that he can't do what he wants to do. He rejects angrily all of their suggestions and decides to run away. He makes all his preparations but just when he is ready to go, his friends invite him to play ball in the park. He asks his mom for permission and this time she says yes. So he decides he will run away tomorrow. A delightful story, especially for younger readers who will identify with being told "no." (Ages 4-8)

I Was So Mad!
by Norma Simon.
Illustrated by Dora Leder.
Albert Whitman & Company, 1991. 32 pages.
Simple, tricolor illustrations.
Read-aloud or intermediate to advanced readers.

A young girl talks about the situations that make her mad, including being left out because she's a girl, being told what to do, being blamed for something she didn't do, and being teased. Her father offers her an image of anger from his own experience, saying that he feels like a firecracker going off, a balloon popping or a volcano exploding. Although this is a problem-solving book, many children enjoy its recitation of reasons for feeling angry (with such a long list, it's easy to identify). Useful for exploring things that anger your child as well as ways to deal with anger. (Ages 5-9)

Mean Soup
by Betsy Everitt.
Voyager, 1995. 32 pages.
Bold, distinctive watercolors.
Read-aloud or intermediate readers.

Horace, a little boy, has had a bad day. He forgot the answer to a question in class, a girl gave him a love note, and the babysitter nearly hit three poodles when she was driving him home. Fortunately Horace's mother understands. She suggests making soup and, although Horace resists, she makes the soup and then screams into the pot. "Your turn," she tells Horace, and he screams into the soup too. Together they scream and growl, stick out their tongues and bang the pot with spoons, until they both smile. "What's the name of this recipe?" Horace asks, and the answer is Mean Soup. A wonderful tale with a charming solution for angry feelings. (Ages 5-9)

Sometimes I'm Bombaloo
by Rachel Val.
Illustrated by Yumi Heo.
Scholastic Press, 2002. 24 pages.
Distinctive collage, pencil and paint illustrations.
Read-aloud or intermediate readers.

Katie, a little girl, tells us about herself both when she's happy and when she's angry, which she describes as being Bombaloo. When she is Bombaloo, Katie shows her teeth, makes fierce noises, uses her fists instead of her words, and wants to smash stuff. In those moments, often brought on by her younger sibling's actions, she realizes she needs to calm herself, but when she is Bombaloo she doesn't want to think about it or say she is sorry. Her mother understands and accepts her anger and enforces some cool-down time. A reassuring story that acknowledges the reality of angry feelings and explores ways to cope with those feelings. (Ages 5-9)

Spence and the Mean Old Bear
by Christa Chevalier.
Albert Whitman & Company. 1987. 32 pages.
Simple two-color ink drawings.
Read-aloud or intermediate readers.

When Spence, a little boy, is told by his mother that he must clean up his room before he watches television, he is angry. He imagines a mean old bear that would take his mother away and free him from her rules. He draws a picture of the bear, imagines it coming to life, and has a conversation with the bear. But when the imaginary bear's plans for Spence's mother begin to worry Spence, he rushes to his mother's defense. She reassures him that she is a match for any bear and Spence sees that his angry feelings will not hurt her. Reassurance that children need not fear the power of their feelings. (Ages 4-8)

When Sophie Gets Angry—Really, Really Angry
by Molly Bang.
Scholastic Press, 1999. 33 pages.
Bright color illustrations.
Read-aloud or intermediate readers.
Available in Spanish.
2000 Caldecott Honor Award winner; 2000 Jane Addams Book Award winner; 2000 Charlotte Zolotow Award winner; 1999 Parenting Best Books of the Year Award winner.

A little girl named Sophie is angry when her mother tells her to share a toy truck with her sister. Sophie feels like she "wants to smash the world to smithereens." So she runs, cries a little, and climbs a tree. Up high in the tree, the feeling of nature and the sights she sees comfort her and she returns home feeling better. Sophie's success at calming herself makes this a good choice. (Ages 4-9)

ANXIETY

Don't Worry, Grandpa
by Nick Ward.
Barron's Juveniles, 1995. 24 pages.
Soft watercolors.
Read-aloud or intermediate to advanced readers.

Grandpa is about to tell a story to his young grandson, Charlie, when a storm distracts them. Although Grandpa is the storyteller, he also is the one who needs reassurance about the storm and Charlie is good at providing that, in a most imaginative way. When Grandpa falls asleep, Charlie warns the giants from the imaginary tale to be quiet and let Grandpa sleep. A loving inter-generational story reminding us that it isn't just children who worry. (Ages 4-8)

Sam's Worries
by Maryann MacDonald.
Illustrated by Judith Riches.
Hyperion Books, 1994. 32 pages.
Dreamy watercolors.
Read-aloud or intermediate readers.
Available in Spanish.
Out of print but available in libraries and used bookstores.

Sam has trouble sleeping because his fears overwhelm him. Although his mother reassures him, her reassurances fail to soothe him because he hasn't told her about taking cookies from the cookie jar. He talks to his stuffed bear about how his mother might be wrong and his bear offers to share worrying with him. If Sam will worry in the daytime, his bear will do the nighttime worrying. Sam agrees and his bear stays up worrying while Sam sleeps. In the daytime when it's Sam's turn, he finds the worries easier to cope with. A gentle message about the persistence of nighttime worries and how daytime brings relief. (Ages 4-8)

The Secret Life of Bethany Barrett
by Claudia Mills.
Simon & Schuster, 1995. 163 pages.
No illustrations.
Read-aloud or advanced readers.

A sensitive, realistic tale of a middle-school girl named Bethany shows us her anxieties about her younger brother who is slow to speak, her older sister who may be distracted from her college goals by a boy, her mother, and her own imperfections. Well-told with believable situations faced by the young heroine. A good book for a mature child. (Ages 9-12)

Timothy Twinge
by Florence Parry Heide and Roxanne Heide Pierce.
Illustrated by Barbara Lehman.
Lothrop, Lee & Shepard Books, 1993. 32 pages.
Bright, distinctive illustrations; rhyming verse.
Read-aloud or intermediate readers.
Out of print but available in libraries and used bookstores.

Tim worries a lot. In fact, Tim worries all through his day about all sorts of improbable things. But in a surprise and humorous ending, his before-bed worry about aliens actually comes true except that the aliens turn out to be friendly. The aliens congratulate Tim on his imagination and his bravery. They offer him the opportunity to be Ruler of the Galaxy and Tim decides that he'd better begin being brave. A humorous story that offers an opportunity to talk with your imaginative child about his fears. (Ages 5-9)

What If It Never Stops Raining?
by Nancy Carlson.
Puffin, 1994. 32 pages.
Brightly colored, detailed illustrations.
Read-aloud or intermediate readers.

Tim, an older elementary school child, worries about everything. His parents try to reassure him but Tim is a master at finding the holes in their reassurances. As it turns out, while some of his fears do come true, Tim sees that the consequences are not as dire as he had feared. A nice depiction of the comforting difference between what we worry about and what actually happens. (Ages 7-11)

Will It Be Okay?
by Crescent Dragonwagon.
Illustrated by Ben Shecter.
HarperCollins Children's Books, 1977. 32 pages.
Sweet, if dated, watercolors.
Read-aloud or intermediate to advanced readers.
Out of print but available in libraries and used bookstores.

A young girl confides her worries to her mother, including big dogs, thunderstorms, snakes, angry feelings, forgetting her lines in a school play, and her mother's death. To each of these, her mother responds lovingly and lyrically. For a child who is not put off by the touchy-feely quality of the book, this can spark good discussion. (Ages 5-9)

The Worry Stone
by Marianna Dengler.
Illustrated by Sibyl Graber Gerig.
Rising Moon, 1996. 40 pages.
Watercolor and pencils.
Read-aloud or intermediate to advanced readers.

An old woman and a little boy are sitting on a park bench. As they talk, the old woman realizes that the boy is worried about his small size. She tells him a story about

RECOMMENDED BOOKS — EMBARASSMENT — 129

a magical "worry stone." The idea of a "magic" talisman offers a surprisingly practical approach to handling worry (Ages 7-9).

Other titles of interest, listed elsewhere:
Wemberly Worried

EMBARRASSMENT

Oh, I Am So Embarrassed
by Anna H. Dickson.
Illustrated by Tom Cooke.
Western Publishing Company, 1988. 25 pages.
Familiar Sesame Street character illustrations.
Read-aloud or intermediate readers.
Out of print but available in libraries and used bookstores.

When Grover comes over for lunch at Herry Monster's house, he accidentally spills milk on the table. He is so embarrassed that he loses his appetite. The next day Grover fumbles a ball and when his baseball cap falls off, he is embarrassed to have the other kids see his short haircut. But his friends share their embarrassing moments and secrets: not being able to swim, having to wear rain boots and a slicker, and sleeping with a nightlight. The knowledge that everyone sometimes is embarrassed helps Grover get past his uncomfortable feelings. For Sesame Street fans, a helpful starting place for discussion about a recent incident in which your child was embarrassed. (Ages 5-9)

Top Secret! My Worst Days Diary
by Suzanne Altman.
Illustrated by Diane Allison.
Gareth Stevens Publishing, 1996. 48 pages.
Soft watercolors.
Read-aloud or intermediate readers.

Maureen Murphy is starting a new school and when she is asked to say her name to the class, she burps. A succession of incidents bring further embarrassment (coming to a party on the wrong day, dog poop on her shoe, forgetting her lines in a school play, spinach stuck to her teeth, toilet paper stuck to her shoe). But despite these events, which she handles in good humor, she makes friends and learns to cope with the ordinary embarrassments of everyday life. A nice portrayal of a girl who is just a little bit different, and only occasionally embarrassed by it. (Ages 7-10)

Other titles of interest, described elsewhere:
The Rainbow Tulip

ENVY

The Berenstain Bears and the
Green-Eyed Monster
by Stan and Jan Berenstain.
Random House, 1995. 29 pages.
Familiar Berenstain Bear characters; limited text.
Read-aloud or intermediate readers.

Sister Bear watches with envy as Brother Bear enjoys his birthday, including a beautiful new racing bicycle. Her envy leads her to try out the new bike without permission and she crashes it. Luckily this part of the story turns out to be a bad dream from which she learns. As the story ends, Sister is enjoying Brother's old bike but Papa is beginning to show his own signs of envy, of the neighbor's new car. Even though the Berenstain Bears series is tedious at times, kids love them. Perhaps the reason for their success is that Sister and Brother Bear are believable characters and Papa Bear is an adult with whom we can all enjoy laughing. (Ages 4-8)

I Wish I Was Sick, Too!
by Franz Brandenberg.
Illustrated by Aliki.
Puffin, 1978. 32 pages.
Expressive, appealing sketches.
Read-aloud or beginning to intermediate readers.
Out of print but available in libraries and used
bookstores.

Edward, a little boy cat, is sick and receives lots of attention. Elizabeth, his sister, notices and comments on all the ways that Edward seems to be luckier than she is. But the tables turn when Elizabeth gets sick and Edward is well. Now Elizabeth envies all the things her brother can do. Finally they are both well and they agree that the best part of getting sick is getting well. A simple story that doesn't attempt to persuade its readers out of their feelings. (Ages 4-8)

It's Not Fair!
by Anita Harper.
Illustrated by Susan Hellard.
Putnam Publishing Group, 1986. 24 pages.
Simple watercolors.
Read-aloud or beginning to intermediate readers.
Out of print but available in libraries and used
bookstores.

A little girl kangaroo talks about how unfair everything is for her now that her parents have a new baby. But as she lists all the ways life is unfair for her, she notices a few ways that life isn't so very fair for her baby brother either. By the end of the story, her baby brother has begun to talk and when he isn't allowed to accompany her to a party, he says, "It isn't fair." A deft look at the pros and cons of being the older and the younger child. (Ages 4-8)

It's Not Fair!
by Deborah Hautzig.
Illustrated by Tom Leigh.
Random House, 1986. 36 pages.
Familiar Sesame Street character illustrations.
Read-aloud or beginning to intermediate readers.
Out of print but available in libraries and used
bookstores.

Ernie and Bert decide to sell lemonade but Ernie
makes a mistake by buying oranges instead of lemons.
When Bert returns home, he finds Ernie making a mess.
Later Ernie makes yet another mess that Bert has to clean
up. Once they set up the lemonade stand, their friends
compliment Ernie on his good ideas. Bert explodes with
frustration that he always does the work while Ernie has
all the fun. His friends empathize and Ernie spends his
lemonade money on a gift for Bert. Bert realizes that he
actually likes his role, at least some of the time. Especially
for fans of Sesame Street, the characters illustrate different
skills and personalities, and the feelings that can result.
(Ages 4-8)

Jane, Wishing
by Tobi Tobias.
Illustrated by Trina Schart Hyman.
Viking Press, 1977. 48 pages.
Fanciful illustrations.
Read-aloud or advanced readers.
Out of print but available in libraries and used
bookstores.

This story about a young girl named Jane alternates
between Jane's thoughts and wishes, which are shown in
color, and the reality of her family's likely reactions to her
wishes, shown in black-and-white. Thus, when she wishes
she had long flowing red hair, her mother comments that
she should wash and brush her hair, her grandmother
observes that red hair doesn't run in the family, her little

brother scoffs at caring about hair, and her older sister remarks that blond curly hair like her own is better. Jane has many wishes, about her appearance, her name, her friends and her talents. But by the end she decides to be happy regardless of whether her wishes are fulfilled. This story will appeal particularly to girls. (Ages 8-11)

Pinky and Rex and the School Play
by James Howe.
Illustrated by Melissa Sweet.
Aladdin Library, 1998. 48 pages.
Simple watercolor illustrations.
Read-aloud or advanced readers.

Pinky and Rex, a boy and a girl, are best friends. Pinky confides to Rex that he hopes to be an actor when he grows up and he wants to get the lead in the upcoming school play. Pinky pleads with Rex to come with him to the tryouts and she agrees. But Pinky is aghast and jealous when the cast list is posted and Rex has been chosen for the lead! When he tries to persuade Rex to drop out, she is furious. But the children make up and when the play is presented, Pinky saves the day in a way that he had not anticipated. An opportunity to talk about jealousy of a friend's good fortune. (Ages 6-9)

Twitchell the Wishful
by Marjorie Weinman Sharmat.
Illustrated by Janet Stevens.
Holiday House, 1981. 40 pages.
Detailed and droll black-and-white drawings.
Read-aloud or intermediate readers.

Twitchell, a charming little boy mouse, "liked anything that belonged to anyone else." Each of his friends has something that Twitchell enjoys and covets, such as Claudette Hedgehog's fireplace and Jacqueline Chicken's new shoes. Twitchell's desire for his friends' possessions makes him so unhappy that his friends decide to give him everything he wants. Predictably, reality is nothing like Twitchell's fond imaginings about how he would enjoy each thing. He doesn't fit in Jacqueline Chicken's shoes and his house is already snug and warm without a fireplace. By the end of the story, he returns everything to his friends, and continues enjoying these things at their houses. While the message is obvious, the charming illustrations bring humor to it and there is room for discussion about what your child enjoys at friends' houses. (Ages 4-8)

FRUSTRATION

I'm Frustrated
by Elizabeth Crary.
Illustrated by Jean Whitney.
Parenting Press, 1992. 32 pages.
Simple black-and-white illustrations.
Read-aloud only due to advice for parents.

Alex is frustrated that his attempts to roller-skate with his older siblings meet with repeated failure. Alex talks to his mother and considers eight ideas for what he can do. Each of the consequences can be explored and discussed. Elizabeth Crary's problem-solving books offer an interactive story in which children can consider choices they might make in the same circumstances as the fictional hero, and the consequences of each choice as well. They are generally well-written and realistic enough to engage even an older child. (Ages 7-10)

Other titles of interest, described elsewhere:
Today Was a Terrible Day

FEARS

Sometimes it's hard for a child to put into words what scares him. Perhaps many things scare him, both real and imagined. The books in this section explore many different things that cause fear, including those too fearsome to be named.

GENERAL

A Cool Kid—like Me!
by Hans Wilhelm.
Random House, 1991. 32 pages.
Gentle, blurred watercolors.
Read-aloud or intermediate readers.
Available in Spanish.
Out of print but available in libraries and used bookstores.

As a young boy tells us about his skills, he confides that his coolness is only on the outside. Inside, he's afraid of lots of things. Only his grandmother knows how he really feels. When she goes on a vacation, he's worried about how he will do without her. She gives him a present, a teddy bear, which his parents deride as too young for him. But his grandmother insists, and at night he confides his fears to his bear. He finds comfort in the bear until his grandmother returns. A story about the scared kid in cool kids as well as the special relationship between grandparents and kids. (Ages 7-10)

Furlie Cat
by Berniece Freschet.
Illustrated by Betsy Lewin.
William Morrow & Company, 1986. 32 pages.
Humorous watercolors.
Read-aloud or intermediate readers.

Furlie Cat is a tough-looking cat whose secret is that he is afraid of everything. He spends his time indoors longing to be outside but too afraid to go out. Then one day he begins practicing being brave, including growls. When he finally gets the courage to try out his new growl, the results are promising. Oscar the dog is totally scared. But Furlie's newfound courage leads him to become a bully toward the other animals until he meets up with a bear cub who scares him into a tree. When Oscar helps him, Furlie decides to stop being a bully and use his courage wisely. Although preachy, this story offers an opportunity not only to talk about your child's fears but also to talk about some of the things that motivate bullies. (Ages 4-8)

Jim Meets The Thing
by Miriam Cohen.
Illustrated by Lillian Hoban.
Greenwillow Books, 1981. 32 pages.
Whimsical, expressive drawings.
Read-aloud or intermediate readers.

Jim watches a program on television and is scared by it but when he goes to school he discovers that the other children are talking enthusiastically about it. Jim doesn't even want to hear about it and the other kids tease him. But when the other kids are scared by a praying mantis, it's Jim who has the courage to lift the bug off his friend and set it free. This small event leads other kids to talk about things that scare them and Jim realizes that he isn't the only kid in first grade with fears. A good choice to help children understand that fear is universal. (Ages 4-8)

Other titles of interest, described elsewhere:
My Own Big Bed
Sheila Rae, the Brave

OF THE DARK

Big Scary Wolf
by Harvey Stevenson.
Clarion Books, 1997. 32 pages.
Moody, acrylic paint illustrations.

Read-aloud or intermediate readers.

A little girl, Rose, can't sleep because of her fear that a scary wolf is in her room. Her wise father doesn't dismiss her fears but rather talks to her about how the wolf wouldn't want to be in her room because "in his warm furry coat, he'd want to be outside playing with his friends, under the stars." As they talk, the illustrations subtly convey a change in the wolf. He's no longer the frightening apparition Rose first imagined but instead something cuddly and vulnerable. By the end of their loving conversation, Rose no longer is afraid of the wolf. A charming way to work through fears. (Ages 4-8)

Can't Sleep
by Chris Raschka.
Orchard Books, 1995. 32 pages.
Unique, striking illustrations.
Read-aloud or beginning to intermediate readers.

An unseen voice explains to a young dog that the moon will watch over him during the night and keep him safe. The repetition of the lines, the reassuring voice of the narrator, and the charming illustrations work together to convey the message that we're never really alone at night. (Ages 4-8)

Can't You Sleep Little Bear?
by Martin Waddell.
Illustrated by Barbara Firth.
Candlewick Press, 2002. 32 pages.
Tender and sensitive illustrations.
Read-aloud or intermediate readers.
Available in Spanish.
1988 Nestle Smarties Award winner; Kate
Greenaway Award winner.

Little Bear is afraid of the dark and he repeatedly calls for Big Bear. No matter what Big Bear does, Little Bear is still afraid until Big Bear takes Little Bear outside to face the biggest dark of all. Outside in the night, Big Bear offers the moon and stars to light the way. A reassuring way to think about darkness. (Ages 4-8)

Clyde Monster
by Robert L. Crowe.
Illustrated by Kay Chorao.
E. P. Dutton Children's Books, 1993. 32 pages.
Wonderful, appealing illustrations.
Read-aloud or advanced readers.

Clyde Monster is an adorable little monster whose fears of the dark and people amaze and distress his parents. His parents try to reason with him and to reassure him, and Clyde Monster is persuaded, somewhat. But in the end, he still wants the door to his cave bedroom left open, just a little. The idea of monsters as friendly creatures with fears of their own may be reassuring. (Ages 4-8)

Faraway Drums
by Virginia Kroll.
Illustrated by Floyd Cooper.
Little, Brown and Company, 1998. 32 pages.
Blurry, soft oil illustrations.
Read-aloud or advanced readers.
Multicultural.
1998 Parents Choice Award.

Two sisters are home alone at night in a new neighborhood because their mother works nights. The older sister, Jamila, is both proud and abashed by the fact that she is in charge. When they are frightened by the noises that they hear, Jamila recounts stories that her great-grandmother told her about Africa and their ancestors. Jamila turns banging on the thin walls of the apartment into a drummer beating out a message. Angry voices are translated as hyenas fighting over scraps and car horns are elephants showing off at the water hole. A powerful story that speaks not only of conquering fear but also of sibling affection. (Ages 7-10)

Flashlight
by Betsy James.
Illustrated by Stacey Schuett.
Alfred A. Knopf, 1997. 32 pages.
Dark atmospheric illustrations.
Read-aloud or intermediate readers.
Out of print but available in libraries and used
bookstores.

When Marie stays at her grandfather's house it isn't easy to fall asleep. Even though her sister is there, Marnie feels alone because her sister quickly falls asleep. When Marnie calls her grandfather he brings a flashlight to illuminate the room. Marnie even shines the flashlight through her fingers so "fire glows right through my bones." She calls grandpa once more just to make sure and then the flashlight reassures her so that she is able to go to sleep. In an unfamiliar, dark place, a flashlight might be a big help to anyone afraid of the dark. (Ages 5-9)

Franklin in the Dark
by Paulette Bourgeois.
Illustrated by Brenda Clark.
Scholastic, 1987. 30 pages.
Colorful cartoon illustrations.
Read-aloud or intermediate readers.
Available in Spanish.

Franklin is afraid of small, dark places. That's a problem since he is a turtle too afraid to get into his shell so he has to drag it around behind him. When he asks for help he finds that everyone, even his mom, is afraid of something. And how does he face the dark? One night he just climbs bravely into his shell and turns on a little night-light. Franklin might help someone who is just about ready to sleep in a small dark room with just a little night-light. (Ages 4-8)

Ghost's Hour, Spook's Hour
by Eve Bunting.
Illustrated by Donald Carrick.
Clarion Books, 1989. 32 pages.
Dark painting illustrations.
Read-aloud or intermediate readers.

A little boy wakes up after hearing a scary noise. He tells himself that it was just the wind. Then he feels a cold wetness and he knows it's just Biff, his dog, who sleeps at the end of his bed. He tries to turn on the light but finds that it isn't working. So he and Biff walk through his dark house to find out what is happening. He calms himself on the way by explaining out loud all the scary things he encounters but ultimately he's relieved to find his parents sleeping downstairs with candlelight. Useful suggestions for calming one's fears. (Ages 4-8)

Go Away, Bad Dreams!
by Susan Hill
Illustrated by Vanessa Julian-Ottie.
Random House, 1985. 32 pages.
Old-fashioned watercolors.
Read-aloud or intermediate to advanced readers.
Out of print but available in libraries and used bookstores.

A little boy named Tom who has a good imagination is scared by a book he reads, by a television program he watches, and even by his neighbor's hedge clippers. Each time, his mom gets rid of the item that causes the fear but when it comes to the ordinary household items, she takes a different approach. She carries out a small ritual of telling him she has made some good dreams for him, touching his eyelids while saying so. Her method succeeds and Tom concludes that he doesn't even need it any more but, just the same, he'd like her to do it for one more night. Perhaps you and your imaginative child will develop your own ritual for chasing away bad dreams after you read this story. (Ages 4-8)

Kate's Giants
by Valiska Gregory.
Illustrated by Virginia Austin.
Candlewick Press, 1995. 32 pages.
Pencil and watercolors.
Read-aloud or intermediate readers.

Kate is sleeping in her new room and she's afraid because there is a door to the attic in her room. When she calls for her parents, they offer her a way to think about it, "If you can think them up, then you can think them out." Putting the mantra into practice isn't easy and Kate needs more advice, such as, "Just take a deep breath before you think." This time the mantra works for Kate as she takes a deep breath and says out loud, "STOP! If I can think you up, then I can think you out!" There's an unexpected benefit as Kate figures out that the reverse must be true. She has the power also to "think in" friendly visitors. Some children will benefit from a ritual or mantra for those times when they are scared in the dark, and this book offers a handy one. (Ages 4-8)

The Night-Light
by Jane Feder.
Illustrated by Lady McCrady.
Dial Books for Young Readers, 1980. 32 pages.
Pencil, ink and color-wash illustrations.
Read-aloud or advanced readers.

Kate struggles with her fear of the dark as she lies in bed. The next morning she tells her mother that she wants a night-light. But in the dark the next night her night-light isn't comforting, it's scary. She tries the overhead light but it's too bright. Her reading lamp casts funny shadows and her flashlight doesn't stay in place. With all the lights out, she notices the moon and the lights from the apartment across the street and she realizes that the glow in her window is just right. A nice story about alternatives to night-lights. (Ages 4-8)

Scared of the Dark
by Liza Alexander.
Illustrated by Tom Cooke.
Golden Press, 1986. 25 pages.
Familiar Sesame Street characters.
Read-aloud or advanced readers.

Ernie is afraid of the dark and Bert has advice and practical suggestions. In this story the message is that we can overcome our nighttime fears by imagining nice things instead of scary things. For Sesame Street fans, the use of familiar characters helps convey the message. (Ages 4-8)

Shadow Night
by Kay Chorao.
Dutton Children's Books, 2001. 32 pages.
Detailed, color drawings.
Read-aloud or intermediate readers.

When James sees shadows on his bedroom wall he's certain they are monsters and he calls for his parents. His parents show him that it was only curtain shadows, then they have fun making their own shadow animals with their hands and telling a story to go along with their shadow show. An original idea for taking the scariness out of shadows. (Ages 4-8)

The Something
by Natalie Babbitt.
Farrar, Straus and Giroux, 1987. 32 pages.
Zany, humorous pencil drawings.
Read-aloud or intermediate readers.

Mylo, a hairy monster child, has trouble explaining his fears. He tells his mother that he's afraid of the dark because he thinks that something will come in through the window. His monster mother tries to explain away his fears and apply logic to the situation. But Mylo, like any child, is unconvinced. His wise mother buys him modeling clay and he works diligently with the clay, trying to figure out just what the Something looks like. When he finally produces a figure that satisfies him, he puts it by his bed and that night he has a good dream about the Something (which in a humorous ending, looks just like a little girl). A good story for those times when it's hard to describe what we fear. (Ages 4-8)

Tell Me Something Happy before I Go to Sleep
by Joyce Dunbar.
Illustrated by Debi Gliori.
Harcourt, 1998. 32 pages.
Full-color illustrations.
Read-aloud or intermediate to advanced readers.

Willa, a little rabbit girl, can't fall asleep because she's afraid that she might have a bad dream. Her older brother Willoughby suggests that she think of something happy. But Willa can't figure out what to think about so her brother gives her ideas: her slippers are waiting for her feet, her clothes are longing to be on her, the food on the shelves is waiting to be made into breakfast, and so on. By the end, Willoughby has thought of lots of good ideas and Willa has fallen asleep. A gentle tale for younger readers who may find Willoughby's suggestions useful. (Ages 4-8)

There's a Monster Under My Bed
by James Howe.
Illustrated by David Rose.
Aladdin Library, 1990. 32 pages.
Delightful, evocative watercolors.
Read-aloud or intermediate readers.

A little boy wishes that he hadn't told his mom that he's too old for a night-light like the one his younger brother Alex has. He draws us immediately into the story, "There's a monster under my bed. I can hear him breathing. Listen. I told you…" Not surprisingly, he can't sleep for fear of what's hiding under his bed. As his fear grows he finds at last the flashlight his wise mother left for him. When he gets the courage to shine it on the monster under his bed, we get a surprise. It's his brother Alex hiding under his bed because he's afraid of the monster under his bed. The two boys snuggle up together and the story ends happily. An entertaining story with a subtle message that it's not likely that anything truly scary is under the bed. (Ages 4-8)

There's a Nightmare in My Closet
by Mercer Mayer.
E. P Dutton, 1992. 28 pages.
Evocative, humorous illustrations.
Read-aloud or intermediate readers.
Available in Spanish.

A little boy is determined to do something about the monster he's certain is in his closet at night. Armed with his helmet, toy soldiers and a gun, the little boy traps the monster and shoots it. But he sees things differently when the monster begins to cry and needs comforting. In the end, the little boy lets the monster sleep in his bed. No solutions but the pleasure of watching the little boy turn the tables on his fears makes this book a good choice for a child who is willing to laugh (a little) about what scares him. (Ages 4-8)

There's an Alligator Under My Bed
by Mercer Mayer.
E.P. Dutton, 1987. 32 pages.
Delightful humorous illustrations.
Read-aloud or intermediate readers.

In this sequel to *There's a Nightmare in My Closet*, the hero returns, older, wiser, braver and star of an even funnier nighttime adventure. He tries to be proactive about the alligator under the bed and uses a plank in order to get into bed safely. Of course, the alligator hides every time he calls his parents. Finally he decides to take action. The fridge is full of alligator bait that he spreads from his bedroom down to the garage. Sure enough, the beast can't resist and is soon locked in the garage. Back in bed, our hero thinks of his dad getting into the car in the morning. What about the alligator? No worries here; he leaves a note offering to help. After all, he has dealt with alligators before. A humorous approach to nighttime fears. (Ages 4-8)

Who's Afraid of the Dark?
by Crosby Bonsall.
HarperTrophy, 2002. 32 pages.
Cartoon illustrations.
Read-aloud or beginning readers.
Multicultural.

A little boy talks over a big problem with his older friend. He has a stuffed dog, Stella, who is so afraid of the shapes she sees in the dark that she shivers and shakes. The friend tells the little boy that Stella is silly and that he must protect her, hug her, and hold onto her in the dark. The little boy tries it and it works. Stella is asleep and the boy is not afraid at all. A conversational tone makes this a good book for having your own conversation about what works. (Ages 4-8)

A World Full of Monsters
by John Troy McQueen.
Illustrated by Marc Brown.
HarperCollins Children's Books, 2001. 32 pages.
Bright, appealing, and humorous illustrations.
Read-aloud or beginning to intermediate readers.

In a "once-upon-a-time" style, this story begins a long time ago when monsters were everywhere. As the cheerful illustrations show us, monsters and humans lived together in perfect harmony and monsters were most human in their attributes and good deeds. For reasons left unspecified, there aren't many monsters left anymore. The little boy to whom the story is told concludes that at night when he hears sounds it's just friendly monsters doing ordinary chores. A useful approach for an imaginative child. (Ages 4-8)

Other titles of interest, listed elsewhere:
The Tapping Tale
Sarah's Sleepover
Sam's Worries
My Best Friend
Arthur's First Sleepover

OF THE OUTDOORS AT NIGHT

Once When I Was Scared
by Helena Clare Pittman.
Illustrated by Ted Rand.
E.P. Dutton, 1988.
Vivid, dreamlike illustrations.
Read-aloud or advanced readers.

The narrator tells a story about his grandfather, Daniel, who as a boy had to go to a neighbor's house during a storm. Exciting illustrations help us feel Daniel's fears as he hurries through the woods. In a remarkable sequence, as Daniel seems to stumble he turns into a fox and bounds through the woods. Later, he becomes a bobcat when faced with another obstacle and when he encounters a bear he turns into an eagle. As the story ends, the narrator asks his grandfather whether it really happened and his grandfather gives him the eagle feathers he found in his pocket the next morning. When the narrator faces his own fears, he tells us that he takes out the feathers and holds them in his hands, remembering his grandfather's face. A lovely, imaginative way of handling fears. (Ages 4-9)

Scrabble Creek
by Patricia Wittmann.
Illustrated by Nancy Poydar.
Atheneum, 1993. Watercolors. 32 pages.
Read-aloud or intermediate readers.

During a family camping trip, a young girl and her family experiences a wilderness that is beautiful by day but feels scary to her as darkness descends. The family fantasizes with her about all the things that might be making scary sounds in the woods, including elephants, baboons, and wild tigers. Their humor helps her handle her fears. An entertaining story with a practical suggestion. (Ages 4-8)

OF STORMS

Franklin and the Thunderstorm
by Paulette Bourgeois.
Illustrated by Brenda Clark.
Scholastic, 1998. 32 pages.
Colorful detailed watercolors.
Read-aloud or advanced readers.

Franklin the turtle is an engaging little fellow. He can count, name the seasons, and read the thermometer. But Franklin worries about the weather because he is afraid of storms. He shares his fear with his animal friends who try to reassure him. When Franklin hides during a storm his understanding friends divert him with entertaining stories about the thunder, such as that the noise is "cloud giants playing drums in the sky." No message about how to conquer fear but a nice portrayal of friends who understand. (Ages 4-8)

Just a Thunderstorm
by Gina and Mercer Mayer.
Golden Books, 2003. 24 pages.
Cheerful, zany illustrations.

Read-aloud or intermediate to advanced readers.

The little monsters are scared by a power outage until parents turn it into a camp-out. Then they're scared by the thunder until Mom and Dad let them crawl into their bed to sleep. By morning the sun is shining again and if the little monsters don't agree with their mom's cheerful statement that thunderstorms are nothing to be afraid of, they do see a bright side -- thunderstorms make great mud puddles. An entertaining look at storms. (Ages 4-8)

Storms in the Night
by Mary Stolz.
Illustrated by Pat Cummings.
HarperTrophy, 1990. 32 pages.
Dark, atmospheric illustrations.
Read-aloud or advanced readers.
Multicultural.

Thomas and his grandfather are alone in the dark during a storm. Although Thomas repeatedly declares that he isn't afraid of anything, Grandfather tells him a story about his childhood when he was afraid of storms. Through Grandfather's story and his calm acceptance of Thomas' feelings, Thomas is able to admit that if he had been alone in the storm, he might have been afraid. Not merely a story that ably deals with children's fears of storms, this lovely book also celebrates the role of grandparents. (Ages 4-8)

Thunderstorm
by Mary Szilagyi.
Atheneum, 1985. 32 pages.
Colored pencil drawings.
Read-aloud or intermediate readers.
Out of print but available in libraries and used bookstores.

A young girl and her dog are enjoying the outdoors. But the air is very still, the sky changes color, the thunder begins, and the little girl is afraid and runs home.

Her mother understands her fear and comforts her. In turn, the girl comforts her frightened dog. As the story ends, the storm quiets and the sun comes out. A simple and reassuring way to talk about weather changes especially appropriate for young children. (Ages 4-8)

Thunderstorm!
by Nathaniel Tripp.
Illustrated by Juan Wijngaard.
Dial Books for Young Readers, 1994. 47 pages.
Realistic, detailed watercolors.
Read-aloud or advanced readers.

A farm child's work continues even as a storm approaches. The careful prose gives us a full picture of the storm and its effect on the place and its inhabitants. Realistic illustrations assist in giving a complete sense of what is occurring. Some children handle fears best by understanding the nature of the thing that scares them. If that describes your child, he will appreciate the factual material presented in this story. (Ages 4-8)

OF DOGS

I'm Scared
by Elizabeth Crary.
Illustrated by Jean Whitney.
Parenting Press, 1996. 32 pages.
Black-and-white illustrations.
Read-aloud only due to advice for parents.

Tracy is eager to meet her new neighbors but when she sees that they have a large dog, her fear of dogs becomes an issue. The story invites the reader to make choices along with Tracy and to see the probable outcome of each choice. The author offers help to the adult reader on how to approach a discussion. An excellent choice, filled with practical suggestions. (Ages 4-8)

Scared Stiff
by Katie Davis.
Harcourt, 2001. 32 pages.
Bright, eye-catching cartoons.
Read-aloud or intermediate to advanced readers.
1994 California Young Readers Medal winner.

The heroine of this charming tale is scared of many things, including the neighborhood dog. She calls her Ono, because whenever she sees her she says, "Oh, no." She has strategies for handling her fears from singing a slimy eyeball song to wearing a witch's hat. But when she has a real confrontation with Ono she finds to her surprise that there hasn't been anything to be afraid of--it's just that Ono is protective of her puppies. A cheerful way to accept your child's fears while encouraging her to find her own strategies for facing them. (Ages 4-8)

OF FLYING
See titles listed under New Experiences
OF DOCTORS AND DENTISTS
See titles listed under New Experiences
OF SWIMMING
See titles listed under New Skills
OF RIDING A BICYCLE
See titles listed under New Skills

BEDWETTING

Most children experience this problem at some point in childhood. In fact, up to twenty percent of 5- to 6-year-old children have problems with bedwetting. Bedwetting is considered so common at this age that experts don't suggest any special treatment at all. If the problem persists, it may be more serious. Understandably, most children think that they are the only ones in their class who wet the bed. Reading books can open up discussion, as well as reassure your child that he isn't alone.

Accidental Lily
by Sally Warner.
Illustrated by Jacqueline Rogers.
Alfred A. Knopf, 2000. 96 pages.
Limited black-and-white illustrations.
Read-aloud or intermediate to advanced readers.
Out of print but available in libraries and used
bookstores.

Six-year-old Lily, who narrates her story, has a problem with bedwetting. Her older brother Casey teases her but her mother is supportive and reassuring. Lily believes that it is happening because of their recent move and blames her mother for making that decision. Everyone in the family has a theory about what causes Lily's problem and how to solve it. Then a boy in Lily's class reveals that another boy has the problem and Lily's friends invite her to a sleepover. This time, her brother comes up with a solution that enables Lily to go to the party. A warm, realistic look at bedwetting with good ideas for you and your child. (Ages 4-8)

Dry Days, Wet Nights
by Maribeth Boelts.
Illustrated by Kathy Parkinson.
Albert Whitman & Company, 1996. 32 pages.
Warm, reassuring watercolors.
Read-aloud or intermediate to advanced readers.

Little Bunny wants to stop wearing diapers at night but he can't seem to stay dry through the night. Even when he tries sleeping next to the toilet he just can't stay dry. His father reassures him that lots of bunnies have had this problem, even his father. Time passes and Little Bunny grows up in lots of other ways. One morning he awakens to find that he is dry. The whole family celebrates. Reassuring treatment because of the parents' calm acceptance, this gentle story also includes a note for parents. (Ages 3-5)

HONESTY

Honesty is a concept children understand better as they grow up. For very young children, it may not feel like a fib to boast of one's prowess or possessions. For an older child, there is a growing realization of the line between truth and lies, and also of the meaning of "white lies." These books explore all kinds of lies, with all kinds of consequences.

Arnie and the Stolen Markers
by Nancy L. Carlson.
Viking Press, 1987. 32 pages.
Colorful illustrations; limited text.
Read-aloud or intermediate readers.

Arnie spends his allowance as soon as he gets it and always on candy. One day, after Arnie has spent all his money, he sees a set of color markers that he yearns to possess. In a moment of weakness, he steals the markers. Arnie is unable to enjoy them even after he gets home because he is so nervous about being caught. Yet he also leaves the stolen markers prominently in view and is caught by his mother. She insists that he return them immediately. Arnie dreads the store owner's likely reaction. The storeowner gives Arnie the opportunity to work off what he owes and after a week of hard work he feels better about himself and his new markers. A realistic story about temptation and consequences. (Ages 5-9)

Edwurd Fudwupper Fibbed Big Explained by Fannie Fudwupper
by Berkeley Breathed.
Little, Brown and Company, 2000. 48 pages.
Unique and humorous illustrations.
Read-aloud or intermediate readers.

Edwurd Fudwupper is an accomplished liar, as his

admiring younger sister tells us in rhyming text reminiscent of Dr. Seuss. But when Edwurd accidentally smashes Mom's porcelain pig his lie brings unexpected consequences, including the arrival of angry aliens. The aliens demand to have the liar and threaten to swallow him. But with unexpected heroism, Edwurd's little sister takes the blame in a fib of her own. Although the story is zany, the sibling interaction is believable, as is the urge to lie. (Ages 5-9)

Finders Keepers
by Elizabeth Crary.
Illustrated by Rebecca Striker.
Parenting Press, 1987. 64 pages.
Simple black-and-white illustrations.
Read-aloud only due to advice for parents.

Two children find a lost wallet. Both they and the reader are offered the choice between turning it into Lost and Found and looking inside to see if there is money. Despite an explicitly problem-solving format, Crary's approach can be helpful. In this book, written for older readers or children mature enough to articulate choices, the book presents situations in which some action must be taken. Depending upon the reader's choice of actions, he then is directed to different sections of the book to discuss the probable consequences. Good for children who enjoy discussing their opinions. (Ages 4-9)

Franklin Fibs
by Paulette Bourgeois.
Illustrated by Brenda Clark.
Scholastic, 1992. 30 pages.
Colorful detailed watercolors.
Read-aloud or intermediate to advanced readers.
Available in Spanish.

Franklin, a little boy turtle, can do many things but he boasts to his friends that he can do something he cannot--swallow seventy-six flies in the blink of an eye.

When Franklin's friends demand that he prove it, he makes up an excuse. Later, he tries to think up other ways to avoid telling the truth. Finally he realizes that he has to admit the truth but he comes up with an ingenious way to do something close to what he had bragged about. That tempts him to lie again but this time Franklin has learned his lesson and resists. A pleasant little story that explores the motivation and the consequences of bragging and lying. (Ages 4-8)

Harriet and the Garden
by Nancy Carlson.
Carolrhoda Books, 1999. 32 pages.
Simple, childlike drawings; limited text.
Read-aloud or intermediate readers.

Harriet, a young dog, is enjoying a baseball game with her friends. When a fly ball comes her way, she's determined to catch it and doesn't notice that she has trampled Mrs. Hoozit's garden in the process. Rather than staying to admit it, she runs home and hides in her room. That night she can't enjoy dinner or television and it is hard to fall asleep. When she finally does, she has nightmares of being attacked by the garden. In the morning, Harriet realizes that she must take responsibility and make amends. She does just that and feels much better. A simple, sensitive story about how we feel when we evade responsibility and how much better we feel after we tell the truth. (Ages 4-8)

The Honest-to-Goodness Truth
by Patricia McKissack.
Illustrated by Giselle Potter.
Atheneum, 2000. 40 pages.
Distinctive watercolors, pencils and ink.
Read-aloud or intermediate readers.
Multicultural.

Libby's mother has taught her to "speak the truth and shame the devil" but it's still easy to lie sometimes. After she tells a lie to Mama, Libby decides to tell the truth from then on. So she tells her best friend that she has a hole in her sock and is surprised by her friend's angry and hurt reaction. She tells her teacher that another child has not done his homework and she tells the whole class that another child didn't have lunch money and had to borrow it. By the time school is out, most of the children aren't speaking to her. When she goes to Mama with her confusion, Mama tells her that "sometimes the truth is told at the wrong time, or in the wrong way or for the wrong reasons. But the honest-to-goodness truth is never wrong." When Libby gets a dose of her own truth telling, she begins to understand. A lovely, understanding treatment of an issue that baffles many children and adults. (Ages 5-9)

Mary Marony and the Chocolate Surprise
by Suzy Kline.
Illustrated by Blanche Sims.
G.P. Putnam's Sons, 1995. 85 pages.
Occasional black-and-white drawings.
Read-aloud or intermediate to advanced readers.

Mary Marony, a second-grader who loves her teacher, yields to a momentary impulse to take a chocolate that contains a golden ticket entitling the holder to a special lunch with her teacher. It doesn't help that the rightful owner is Marvin, a boy who teases both the teacher and Mary. But after the teacher announces the winners and Marvin accuses Mary of taking the ticket, Mary feels miserable. One lie leads to another and Mary also lies to her best friend and her mother. Mary finally tells the truth and her teacher and friends reassure her that they understand how she felt. In an enjoyable ending, it turns out that Marvin also lied. He had switched the chocolates before Mary did because he noticed that Mary's chocolate had the golden ticket. A warm and empathetic tale. (Ages 7-10)

My Big Lie
by Bill Cosby.
Illustrated by Varnette P. Honeywood.
Cartwheel Books, 1999. 40 pages.
Bright and expressive illustrations.
Read-aloud only due to advice for parents.
Multicultural.

Little Bill comes home late for dinner to find his parents worried. Hastily, he makes up a story to cover up his failure to remember to come home on time. His story involves getting into a car with a stranger. When his parents call the police, Little Bill recants and as a consequence he is sent to his room to copy the story The Boy Who Cried Wolf. Little Bill fears that his parents won't ever trust him again but they reassure him that they still have confidence in him. Told in a young boy's voice, this story is one of a series featuring Little Bill's experiences growing up that include a letter to parents from a psychiatrist. Although the story is explicitly problem-solving, it can spark discussion. (Ages 7-10)

Nina, Nina Star Ballerina
by Jane O'Connor.
Illustrated by Dyanne DiSalvo-Ryan.
Grosset & Dunlap, 1997. 48 pages.
Soft, appealing illustrations; limited text.
Read-aloud or beginning readers.

Nina is excited about an upcoming dance show in which she will play a twinkling star. But when Nina tells her friend Ann about her role, Ann misunderstands and tells everyone else that Nina is the star of the show. Because Nina enjoys the fuss, she doesn't correct the misunderstanding. But when Ann asks to come to the show,

Nina worries that Ann will find out she wasn't honest. So Nina makes up the lie that she isn't feeling well to get out of being in the show. When Nina admits her lie to her mother, her mother counsels her to tell the truth to Ann. Ann is very accepting and tells Nina she just wants to see Nina dance. A warm and gentle portrayal of Nina's lie and her feelings. (Ages 7-10)

That's Mine, Horace
by Holly Keller.
Greenwillow Books, 2000. 24 pages.
Striking watercolors.
Read-aloud or intermediate readers.

Horace finds a little yellow truck at the schoolyard. In vivid detail, Horace describes exactly why he thought it was the best truck he had ever seen. When no one is watching, Horace pockets the truck. But when Horace takes the truck out later to play with, Walter claims it. Horace claims the truck is his and sticks to his story even after his teacher tells him she trusts him and even after his mother says the same. But that night, Horace has a night-mare and in the morning he doesn't feel well enough to go to school. Even get-well letters from school fail to cheer him until he opens a letter from Walter, giving him permission to keep the truck until Horace returns to school. Children can relate to Horace's ambivalence about returning a prized possession. (Ages 4-8)

Winners Take All
by Fred Bowen.
Illustrated by Paul Casale.
Peachtree Publishers, 2000. 112 pages.
Soft charcoal drawings.
Read-aloud or advanced readers.

Kyle, an eleven-year-old boy on a baseball team, is playing in a tough game against a rival team, the Cubs, when he makes what the umpire calls a game-winning catch. The catch is that he didn't really catch the ball. At first it appears that Kyle will get away with the lie until an older Cub tells Kyle he knows Kyle cheated. Kyle grows more and more uncomfortable with his lie. Finally, the older Cub tells everyone that Kyle lied about the catch and the league calls a meeting. At the meeting Kyle admits he lied. A predictable ending, with Kyle's team winning a playoff game, but still a good, solid story of a boy who admits he has lied.(Ages 9-12)

Other titles of interest, described elsewhere:
Arthur in a Pickle

SELF-ESTEEM

What makes children feel good about themselves? What can we adults do to help a child's self-esteem? As these wise and caring books show, sometimes we have a role to play, but much of the time self-esteem comes from a child's own experiences.

I Never Win!
by Judy Delton.
Illustrated by Cathy Gilchrist.
Dell Publishing, 1991. 32 pages.
Dated illustrations.
Read-aloud or intermediate to advanced readers.

A little boy explains that no matter what he does, he never wins. Whether he's playing Monopoly or baseball, he always seems to lose. He expresses his frustration through his piano practice and he even works harder at it just so he won't make any mistakes. But his sense that he always loses continues as he goes through his week. Then one night, his piano teacher calls him and asks him to play at her house for her guests. He performs without a single mistake and as the story ends, he confides that he felt like he was at "Little

League and won." He realizes then that "not every prize is one you can see." A good way to begin a discussion with your child about the things at which he excels. (Ages 4-8)

Loretta, Ace Pinky Scout
by Keith Graves.
Scholastic Press, 2002. 40 pages.
Full-color, wacky illustrations.
Read-aloud or intermediate to advanced readers.

Loretta is a larger-than-life little girl who is just about perfect. She comes from a long line of perfect people and she works hard to be just like them, especially her grandmother. She even saves the world every Thursday. Of course she has earned every merit badge as a Scout except one, the Gold Marshmallow Badge. Although Loretta has trained for months to earn it, her marshmallows burst into flame and she fails to earn her badge. Shown through her eyes, the consequences are huge as she imagines front page headlines about her failure. But when she despairs about her lack of absolute perfection her grandmother's portrait reminds her that every one of her ancestors had some way in which he or she was not perfect. A charming, silly, and fun way to talk about the impossibility of perfection. (Ages 5-9)

The Best Fight
by Anne Schlieper.
Illustrated by Mary Beth Schwark.
Albert Whitman & Company, 1994. 63 pages.
Soft charcoal illustrations.
Read-aloud or intermediate to advanced readers.

Jamie is in fifth grade but he can barely read because of a learning disability. He gets into fights with the other boys when they tease him about not being able to read. He gets detention for fighting and as a result, he must spend time meeting with the principal after school for a week.

His principal's support and suggestions help Jamie to believe in himself. A good story about trusting in yourself. (Ages 9-12)

The Carrot Seed
by Ruth Krauss.
Illustrated by Crockett Johnson.
HarperFestival, 1993. 24 pages.
Simple, evocative line drawings.
Read-aloud or beginning readers.
Available in Spanish.

A little boy is convinced that his carrot seed will grow despite the kind and not-so-kind discouragement of his parents and older sibling. And in the end, he's right. What's the definition of a classic? How about an utterly simple story with words that practically beg to be memorized, a message any and every child can relate to, and an ending that affirms a child's belief in himself? (Ages 4-8)

The One in the Middle Is the Green Kangaroo
by Judy Blume.
Illustrated by Irene Trivas.
Yearling Books, 1991. 32 pages.
Blurry watercolors.
Read-aloud or advanced readers.

Freddy Dissel is a middle kid and that means hand-me-down clothes, giving up his room, not being invited to play with his older brother and being expected to be kind to his annoying younger sister. But when Freddy gets a part in the school play, his family applauds his accomplishment and he feels, at last, that he has a real role in the family. A nice exploration of sibling issues as well as discovering one's talents. (Ages 4-8)

Wrongway Applebaum
by Marjorie Lewis.
Illustrated by Margot Apple.
Putnam Publishing Group, 1984. 63 pages.
Limited black-and-white illustrations.
Read-aloud or advanced readers.

Fifth-grader Stanley Applebaum comes from a sports-playing, sports-loving family. But for Stanley, sports don't come naturally. He's afraid of getting hit, uncomfortable with other kids, and has difficulty remembering directions, locations, and rules. Still, he wants desperately to be part of the local baseball league and he convinces his grandmother to sponsor the team. By the end of the season, his team is in the championship, although Stanley hasn't helped get them there. In the championship game, Stanley tries desperately to hit the ball and he succeeds. But when he runs the bases, he mistakenly runs them in reverse. Because of his fast running, he makes it to home base and the umpire declares the game a tie. But Stanley is miserable about his mistake and confides in his father. His father has some wise things to say about strengths and weaknesses and about winners and losers. A very good book for your less-than-perfect athlete. (Ages 9-12)

Other titles of interest, described elsewhere:
Billy's Big-Boy Bed
My Own Big Bed
I Have to Go
Koko Bear's New Potty
On Your Potty
Leo the Late Bloomer
Archibald Frisby
Dancing in the Wings
Amazing Grace

Family Life

Chores

What parent hasn't argued with her child about chores? Some children resist cleanup in every room of the house; others hate the chore of cleaning their own room. In these books, messy rooms find a way of getting cleaned up and children find that there are benefits to an orderly room in a clean house.

Clean Your Room Harvey Moon
by Pat Cummings.
Scott Foresman, 1994. 32 pages.
Bright full color illustrations; rhyming text.
Read-aloud or intermediate readers.
Multicultural.

An older elementary school boy is watching television when his mother reminds him that today is the day he must clean his room. He marches angrily to his room and puts most of his things under his bed covers. He realizes that he's hungry and tired and that he has missed his favorite television shows. His mother says he can take a lunch break but after lunch, she says, they will both get started on all the lumps in his bed. An understanding look at the difference between a child and a parent's view of cleanliness, with the recognition that sometimes parental assistance may be required. (Ages 4-8)

Maisy Cleans Up
by Lucy Cousins.
Candlewick Press, 2002. 24 pages.
Bright gouache illustrations.
Read-aloud or beginning to intermediate readers.

Maisy, a young mouse, has just baked cupcakes and is mopping the floor when Charley the Crocodile comes over. He'd love a cupcake but the floors are still wet and there's housework to be done. Charley pitches in and together they put away toys, vacuum the living room, and wash windows. When they're done, the floor is dry and it's time to relax with treats. For young children, a simple tale about doing chores first and enjoying a treat afterwards. (Ages 4-8)

More or Less a Mess
by Sheila Keenan.
Illustrated by Patrick Girouard.
Cartwheel Books, 1997. 32 pages.
Detailed drawings; rhyming verse.
Read-aloud or intermediate readers.

A little girl faces her extraordinarily messy room and wonders how to clean it. She tries a big pile but when it falls down around her, she comes up with a plan to sort things by category. At first it's tough but she's almost done when she realizes that there is still more to do. So she comes up with the idea of a flea market for the things she doesn't want. In the end, she shoves it all under her bed when her mom shows up. While the ending isn't inspiring, there are good ideas here to help your child get started cleaning. (Ages 4-8)

Pigsty
by Mark Teague.
Scholastic, 1994. 32 pages.
Visually striking and humorous color illustrations.
Read-aloud or beginning to intermediate readers.
Available in Spanish.

Wendell Fultz's mom tells him it's time to clean his room because "it's turning into a pigsty." From there, the story takes a humorous and unexpected turn when Wendell goes upstairs and finds a pig sitting on his bed. When his mother comes to check his work, she reluctantly concludes that it's up to him if he wants to live in a pigsty. Soon more and more pigs come to live in his room and he has lots of fun with them, further messing up his room. Although Wendell tries to ignore the mess, when he finds hoof prints on his comics he complains to his mother. But she puts the responsibility squarely on him and he decides to make use of his guests as a cleanup crew. The pigs are startled but compliant and by afternoon, Wendell's room is clean. Too clean, in fact, for pigs and so they all go home and Wendell keeps his room clean except for every now and then when the pigs come to visit. An amusing take on the problem; no new ideas but the mother puts the responsibility for cleanup right where it belongs. (Ages 4-8)

Sally's Room
by M.K. Brown.
Scholastic, 1993. 32 pages.
Watercolors.
Read-aloud or advanced readers.

Sally's room is so disgusted by how messy it is that it follows her to school one day, marching through town. Sally insists that she likes her room that way and even argues with her room about it. But to her room's surprise, Sally's desk at school is very neat. When Sally arrives home before her room does, she is impressed by all the space left by the exit of all of her stuff. She realizes the potential for dancing in her very own room and decides that she likes a clean room. Any parent, and most kids for that matter, will enjoy this humorous story of a girl's room taking revenge. A nice, defused way of talking about cleanliness and order. (Ages 4-8)

The Berenstain Bears and the Messy Room
by Stan and Jan Berenstain.
Random House, 1983. 32 pages.

Familiar illustrations and characters.
Read-aloud or intermediate readers.
Available in Spanish.

The Bear Family keeps a tidy house except in Brother and Sister Bear's room. Brother and Sister Bear argue about whose job it is to clean up. Although Mama Bear usually ends up doing the cleanup, one day she gets fed up and brings the cubs a big box. As the cubs watch in horror, Mama begins to load all of their mess into the box to give away. Then Papa suggests that he help the cubs organize their room, using lots of boxes for different things, and even a pegboard. The whole family joins in organizing their room and when they're done it's a much more enjoyable room in which to live and play. The familiar morals of this series always seem more palatable to kids because they come from the experiences of the Bear Family. (Ages 4-8)

Tidy Titch
by Pat Hutchins.
Mulberry Books, 1995. 32 pages.
Bright full-page watercolors.
Read-aloud or beginning to intermediate readers.

Peter and Mary, the older children in the family, are surprised when their mother points out how messy their rooms are in comparison to Titch's, their younger sibling. As they clean their rooms, they find many things that they've outgrown or lost interest in and they give all of it to Titch. When Mother comes to check their rooms, she praises the job they've done but expresses surprise that Titch hasn't helped. Then she sees his room, now a complete mess. A humorous reminder that one way to clean up is to pass things on to siblings or other children. (Ages 4-8)

When the Fly Flew In...
by Lisa Westberg Peters.
Illustrated by Brad Sneed.
Dial Books for Young Readers, 1994. 32 pages.
Watercolors with humorous details.
Read-aloud or intermediate readers.

A young child offers an unusual excuse for not cleaning his room—all the animals in it are sleeping. Just then, a fly flies in the window, causing mayhem among the animals that eventually results in the whole room being cleaned up. A humorous and delightful story that might cause your child to wish for such a solution to his room cleanup problem. (Ages 4-8)

Other titles of interest, described elsewhere:
The Ornery Morning

PICKY EATERS

Is there a picky eater in your household? How does a child become a more adventurous eater? As the children in these charming books discover, there's more than one way to make spinach palatable.

Bread and Jam for Frances
by Russell Hoban.
Illustrated by Lillian Hoban.
HarperTrophy, 1993.
Cheerful drawings. 32 pages.
Read-aloud or advanced readers.
Available in Spanish.

When Frances, a young badger, declares that bread and jam is all she wants to eat, her wise parents do not argue. They simply continue to serve bread and jam to her until Frances is tired of eating the same food over and over. Lots of opportunities to talk with your picky eater. (Ages 4-8)

D. W. the Picky Eater
by Marc Brown.
Little, Brown and Company, 1995. 32 pages.
Familiar, colorful characters from the Arthur series.
Read-aloud or intermediate readers.
Available in Spanish.

Arthur's little sister D. W. has her own interesting quirks, among them a picky appetite. Whether she's at home or out, she finds lots of familiar ways to avoid eating foods that she thinks she doesn't like. But even D. W. can be fooled into eating something new, as she is when she orders a potpie and enjoys it, only to find out later that between the crusts was spinach. A humorous look at a common childhood phenomena with a subtle hint at how to get around the problem. (Ages 4-8)

Eat Up, Gemma
by Sarah Hayes.
Illustrated by Jan Ormerod.
Lothrop Lee & Shepard Books, 1988.
Colorful, distinctive illustrations.
Read-aloud or intermediate to advanced readers.
Multicultural.

The narrator, a young boy, observes the picky eating habits of his toddler sister, Gemma. Then one day in church his sister reaches for the artificial fruit on a lady's hat, with predictable results. That gives the narrator an idea. When they get home, he arranges fruit on top of an upside-down bowl to simulate the look of the lady's hat. Sure enough, Gemma falls for the trick and eats all the fruit, to the great relief of his parents. A simple story that will appeal to any child. (Ages 4-8)

I Will Never Not Ever Eat a Tomato
by Lauren Child.
Candlewick Press, 2003. 32 pages.
Wild, wacky, eye-catching mixed media.
Read-aloud or advanced readers.
2003 Kate Greenaway Award winner; California
Young Reader Medal winner.

Lola is an exceptionally picky eater. But Lola hasn't counted on the stratagems of her older brother Charlie who has the job of getting her to eat one evening. Charlie inventively uses everything from reverse psychology to enticing new names for familiar foods to get Lola to eat. In the end, Charlie's ideas work. A humorous story to use when talking about picky eating. (Ages 4-8)

BAD DAYS

We have all had bad days, days we'd like to forget, days we can't wait to see end. Most adults understand that a bad day doesn't last forever and doesn't mean that the next day will be bad too. But for a child who's had a bad day, it can feel like tomorrow will never come.

Alexander and the Terrible, Horrible, No Good, Very Bad Day
by Judith Viorst.
Illustrated by Ray Cruz.
Aladdin Library, 1987. 32 pages.
Distinctive, humorous drawings.
Read-aloud or intermediate readers.
Available in Spanish.
1988 George G. Stone Center for Children's Book
Recognition of Merit Award winner; 1977 Georgia
Children's Book Award winner.

Alexander's day begins with gum in his hair and it doesn't get any better. As he recites the awful things that have happened that day, he resolves several times to move to Australia. Every tribulation is funny and believable and, by the end, we are rooting for a better day tomorrow for Alexander. Fortunately, his wise mother consoles him by offering hope for tomorrow and the reassurance that bad days happen to everyone. (Ages 4-9)

Fortunately
by Remy Charlip.
Aladdin Paperbacks, 1993. 48 pages.
Bright cheerful color illustrations alternate with black-and-white renderings to emphasize the contrast between good and bad.
Read-aloud or intermediate readers.

Ned, a little boy, receives an invitation to a surprise party. In a "fortunately, unfortunately" format on alternating pages, Ned ultimately finds his way to the party, which turns out to be for him. Not only is the rhythm of the story fun, but it offers a good way to look at the ups and downs of a day. You may want to consider crafting your own fortunately/unfortunately story. (Ages 4-8)

Grover's Bad, Awful Day
by Anna H. Dickson.
Illustrated by Tom Brannon.
Goldencraft, 1986. 25 pages.
Familiar Sesame Street characters and settings.
Read-aloud or intermediate to advanced readers.

Grover's bad day begins with stubbing his toe. From then on it gets worse with difficulties getting ready for school, in the classroom, and on the playground. When Grover comes home, he tells his mother all about his bad day and she consoles him with the reassurance that bad days happen to everyone but they don't last forever. For any child who loves the Sesame Street characters this is a good choice. (Ages 4-8)

I Should Have Stayed in Bed
by Joan M. Lexau.
Illustrated by Sydney Hoff.
HarperCollins Children's Books, 1965.
Cheerful, lively illustrations.
Read-aloud or intermediate readers.

Sam's day begins with a blue sky and sunshine but it rapidly deteriorates in arguments with his mother and troubles at school. He observes that "some days it doesn't pay to get up...some days you can't do anything right." Sam winds up sick and at home but he realizes what he needs to do–start the day over again. And that's just what he does. This charming story offers both a chance to empathize with Sam and a practical idea—picking oneself up and starting all over again. (Ages 5-9)

No! No! No!
by Anne Rockwell.
Macmillan Books for Young Readers, 1995. 22 pages.
Bright childlike illustrations; limited text.
Read-aloud or beginning to intermediate readers.

The narrator (unspecified gender) doesn't like the way the day is going, from the cereal he's served to the clothes he has to wear. To everything that happens he responds "No! No! No!" Despite his protests he has to do some of these unwanted things. By the time he falls asleep he realizes that tomorrow will be a fresh new day. A lovely reminder that a bad day doesn't last. (Ages 3-5)

OOOPS!
by Suzy Kline.
Illustrated by Dora Leder.
Albert Whitman & Company, 1988. 27 pages.
Colorful illustrations; limited text.
Read-aloud or beginning to intermediate readers.

This cheerful book portrays a variety of situations in

which things go wrong for a young girl, from spilling break-fast juice on her Dad to tripping on her cat to her coat falling off the hook. She doesn't seem to mind too much but just the same it reassures her that she isn't the only one "who does an ooops." Mom drops the phone while talking to her boss and Dad drops the bag of groceries, breaking all the eggs. Her parents seem calm about their mishaps and the lit-tle girl concludes that most of the time she does just fine. A simple reassuring tale for little ones who are feeling clumsy or incompetent. Reassuring for moms, too. (Ages 4-8)

The Ornery Morning
by Patricia Brennan Demuth.
Illustrated by Craig McFarland Brown.
Dutton Children's Books, 1991.
Full-page smudgy illustrations.
Read-aloud or intermediate readers.

Farmer Bill awakens to a farm full of animals that refuse to do their jobs, beginning with a rooster who just doesn't feel like crowing. But Farmer Bill's daughter has a good idea. If the animals won't do their jobs, then Farmer Bill won't do his job, feed them. What's more, Farmer Bill and his daughter talk in loud voices guaranteed to reach the ears of the animals. Suddenly the animals spring into action and everything is running smoothly again. A nice reminder about the interrelatedness of all that we do. (Ages 4-8)

Other titles of interest, described elsewhere:
Mean Soup

Siblings

Brothers and sisters are the source of joy, fun, anger and competition for every child. Whether a child has older or younger siblings or even a new baby in the family, there are good fiction books that deal with sibling issues. Among these recommended books you're certain to find a book that fits your child.

New Baby in the Family

A Baby Sister for Frances
by Russell Hoban.
Illustrated by Lillian Hoban.
HarperTrophy, 1993. 32 pages.
Gentle, childlike illustrations.
Read-aloud or intermediate to advanced readers.
Available in Spanish.

Frances, the well-loved raccoon of these stories, is irritated when her mother doesn't have her dress ready in the morning or her favorite breakfast foods prepared because she has been busy with Gloria, the new baby. Frances decides to run away—to underneath the dining-room table. From her spot under the table Frances listens to her parents talk about how they miss her and how baby Gloria is crying because she misses her big sister. Her parents continue to talk about how the family just isn't the same without Frances. Frances "telephones" her parents from beneath the table and announces her plan to return home. A loving reassurance to children that baby doesn't replace them and a way to start a discussion about how your child is feeling about a new baby. (Ages 4-8)

Baby Brother Blues
by Maria Polushkin.
Illustrated by Ellen Weiss.

Atheneum, 1987. 20 pages.
Cartoon illustrations.
Read-aloud or intermediate readers.
Out of print but available in libraries and used
bookstores.

The narrator, a young girl, is adjusting to a new baby brother. While she notices all the things about him that she doesn't like, she also notices her special effect on him when he is cranky. Her relatives say it's because he likes her, and so she concludes that she likes him too. A good story about the power of the older sibling. (Ages 4-8)

Dilly's Big Sister Diary
by Cynthia Copeland Lewis.
Millbrook Press, 1998. 32 pages.
Fictional diary with sketches, comics, and
photographs.
Read-aloud or advanced readers.
Out of print but available in libraries and used
bookstores.

Eight-year-old Dilly fills her new diary with her feelings about her baby brother Matthew. In a unique approach to a new sibling, Dilly initially thinks of Matthew as a science experiment. But as she fills her diary with confessions, cartoons, drawings, and photographs, Dilly also records her brother's growth. She begins to feel that having a younger brother might not be so bad after all. Dilly's voice is believable, as are her feelings and experiences. (Ages 7-10)

Julius, the Baby of the World
by Kevin Henkes.
Mulberry Books, 1995. 32 pages.
Watercolors and black pen.
Read-aloud or intermediate to advanced readers.
Available in Spanish.

1992 Alabama Emphasis on Reading Award winner; 1993 California Young Reader Medal winner.

Lily, an imperious little girl, eagerly awaits the birth of her brother Julius. Before he is born, she is "the best big sister in the world," but after he arrives, Lily feels differently. Her parent's attention to Julius annoys her, as do the sacrifices, such as sharing her room, which her brother's arrival means for her. Lily tries everything to make Julius disappear and her parents try everything to help her accept the new baby. Nothing works until one afternoon when the relatives have come to a celebration in Julius's honor. Lily is annoyed by the focus on Julius until her cousin Garland voices his negative feelings about Julius. Lily immediately comes to Julius's defense and insists that Garland admire Julius and acknowledge him as the baby of the world. That seems to mark a turning point in her opinion of her baby brother as well. Great characters and a realistic story make this a good book for talking about feelings regarding the new baby. (Ages 4-8)

When the New Baby Comes, I'm Moving Out
and
Nobody Asked Me if I Wanted a Baby Sister
by Martha Alexander.
Dial Books for Young Readers, 1988. 32 pages.
Small, humorous illustrations.
Read-aloud or intermediate readers.

These two charming stories are companion books that can be enjoyed separately as well. In *When the New Baby Comes, I'm Moving Out*, a young boy, Oliver, must come to terms with some of the consequences of the impending arrival of his sibling. His old crib and high chair must be passed on. Oliver expresses all of his angry feelings to his mother, including his thoughts about leaving his mother at the dump and about running away. But in the end, his mother's wise and calm reactions convince him that there may be good consequences to the new baby as well.

In *Nobody Asked Me if I Wanted a Baby Sister*, we encounter Oliver as a big brother who is fed up with all the compliments his baby sister is receiving. In the end, the baby rejects everyone else for him and he changes his mind about her. A lovely pair of books to help your older child talk about the positive and negative aspects of being an older sibling. (Ages 4-8)

Oonga Boonga
by Frieda Wishinsky.
Illustrated by Carol Thompson.
Dutton Books, 1999. 32 pages.
Squiggly cartoon illustrations.
Read-aloud or intermediate to advanced readers.
Out of print but available in libraries and used bookstores.

Baby Louise cries enough to rattle pictures off the walls and make neighborhood pets howl. Unfortunately, nothing seems to console her, not her mother's singing, her father's rocking or a warm bottle. But when her older brother Daniel consoles her with a nonsense phrase, "Oonga boonga," Louise stops crying. His success doesn't mean that anyone else in the family can use the magic words with Louise. When Daniel goes out to play and others try to cheer her with the words, it doesn't work. But when Daniel comes home again and whispers "bunka wunka," Louise is happy again. A charming take on siblings that reminds your child of the important role he plays in the baby's life. (Ages 4-8)

Peter's Chair
by Ezra Jack Keats.
Puffin Books, 1998. 32 pages.
Stunning, unusual illustrations.

Read-aloud or intermediate readers.
Multicultural.
Available in Spanish.

A young boy, Peter, is building a tower when it crashes to the floor. His mother chides him to be quiet because of the new baby. Peter notices that his old cradle has been given to his baby sister and it has even been painted pink. Then his father invites him to help paint his old high chair for his baby sister. But Peter is determined that this is one thing of his that will not belong to his baby sister. He plans to run away with it but first he sits down in his old chair to plan his escape. That's when he notices that he doesn't fit in the chair anymore and decides to paint his chair pink for his new baby sister. An honest and believable portrait of ambivalent feelings as well as pride in growing up. (Ages 4-8)

The Lapsnatcher
by Bruce Coville.
Illustrated by Marissa Moss.
Bridgewater Books, 1997. 32 pages.
Bright cheerful illustrations.
Read-aloud or intermediate to advanced readers.
Multicultural.

Jacob has a new baby sister and he doesn't like her very much. He expected the new baby to be a boy and to be fun. Instead, he got a "lapsnatcher" who keeps his parents from playing with him. Jacob tries to persuade the mailman to mail his sister to Alaska, the garbage man to take her to the dump, and the diaper service to take her away with them. Although no one will take her, he does learn that others have had his problem too and that he would have had the same problems if the baby had been a boy. Although everyone tries to convince him that he will like the baby someday, he remains skeptical. In a lovely, realistic ending he snuggles with his parents and asks to hear about his own babyhood. A good book to help your child express his less-than-enthusiastic feelings about a new baby in the family. (Ages 4-8)

Worse Than Willy
by James Stevenson.
Greenwillow Books, 1987. 32 pages.
Cheerful cartoon illustrations.
Read-aloud or advanced readers.
Out of print but available in libraries and used bookstores.

There's nothing like commiserating with someone who knows what you feel. In this charming tale, it's Mary Ann and Louie's grandfather who understands their complaints about the new baby brother in their family. The kids are amazed when Grandpa tells them that his baby brother, their beloved Uncle Wainey, was terrible as a baby. He regales them with stories about how everyone gushed over Wainey while ignoring poor Grandpa. As Wainey grew he began blaming Grandpa for everything and even wrecking his toys. But the tale becomes more fanciful (and fun) when Grandpa tells about the one time Wainey saved his life during a great storm. By the time he's done, the children are ready to consider the possibility that there are worse kids than their new baby brother and that he might grow up to be as nice as Uncle Wainey. (Ages 4-8)

Other titles of interest, described elsewhere:
Alvin Webster's Surefire Plan for Success
(and How It Failed)
It's Not Fair!

The Same Old Brother/Sister

Annie Rose is my Little Sister
by Shirley Hughes.
Candlewick Press, 2003. 32 pages.

Old-fashioned watercolors.
Read-aloud or intermediate readers.

A loving and mostly tolerant older brother tells about his little sister, Annie Rose. His descriptions of her antics are affectionate but we believe him because he also expresses irritation at some of her behavior, such as her preference for his toys and her occasional tantrums. There aren't any big surprises in this gentle tale but it's a good choice for siblings who generally enjoy each other and suffer through occasionally difficult times. (Ages 4-8)

Hard to be Six
by Arnold Adoff.
Illustrated by Cheryl Hanna.
Lothrop Lee & Shepard, 1991. 24 pages.
Realistic watercolors.
Read-aloud or intermediate readers.
Multicultural.

A young boy talks about how hard it is to be six years old, particularly when you have a sister who is ten. No matter how hard he tries, he comes in last in races, he spills his food, and he crashes his sister's big bike. But both his sister and his parents encourage him. His sister suggests that he think about the best things he can do right now. His mother comments on how big he is growing and his father muses on how all things grow. A very loving observation about a child's eagerness to grow up and the ways his family can reassure him that it will happen someday. (Ages 4-8)

I Hate My Brother Harry
by Crescent Dragonwagon.
Illustrated by Dick Gackenbach.
HarperTrophy, 1989. 32 pages.
Humorous if somewhat dated illustrations.
Read-aloud or intermediate to advanced readers.

Harry's little sister is certain that she hates her brother. No one believes her when she says so but she shares lots of reasons why she might hate him. He won't share his toys, he calls her mean names, and he tries to trick her into leaving desserts. She wishes that he would be like the nice brothers on television and in books, and she knows that sometimes he is. But why can't he stay that way? Her parents share stories from the past about when she was small and Harry did special things for her. They also tell her that this is something all siblings experience but that when they grow up she and her brother will be friends. A wise and reassuring book about angry feelings toward a sibling. (Ages 4-8)

I'll Fix Anthony
by Judith Viorst.
Illustrated by Arnold Lobel.
Aladdin Library, 1988.
Humorous illustrations. 32 pages.
Read-aloud or intermediate to advanced readers.

Alexander, the little boy who had a bad day in Viorst's *Alexander and the Terrible Horrible, No Good, Very Bad Day*, is back in a tale of brothers who don't get along. Although his mother tells him that deep down Anthony does love him, Alexander knows better. He knows because Anthony has told him what he feels deep down, and it isn't love. So Alexander, who feels bullied by his brother, can only wait until he's older to get the better of the situation. A satisfying tale but no practical suggestions. (Ages 4-8)

Katie Couldn't
by Becky Bring McDaniel.
Illustrated by Lois Axeman.
Children's Book Press, 1985. 32 pages.
Simple, uninspiring illustrations.

**Read-aloud or beginning to intermediate readers.
Multicultural.**

Katie, a young girl, is frustrated by all the things she can't do, like riding a two-wheel bike, staying up late, and walking to the park. But when her father comes home from work, only Katie is small enough for him to lift high in his arms, throw up in the air, and be caught in a big hug. A nice way to open a conversation about your child's frustrations and about the special perks of being the youngest. (Ages 4-8)

Much Bigger Than Martin
**by Steven Kellogg.
Dial Books for Young Readers, 1992. 32 pages.
Simple tricolor illustrations.
Read-aloud or intermediate to advanced readers.**

As told by Martin's younger brother, Martin can be a real pain. He lines up other kids by size, bosses his brother around, takes the biggest piece of cake, and makes fun of his brother for being too short to reach the basketball hoop. Martin's brother, like so many younger siblings, dreams of being bigger than Martin--much bigger. In fact, in this humorous and imaginative tale, Martin's brother tries all kinds of ideas to grow bigger, including watering himself and eating lots of apples. He fantasizes about what he would do if he were giant-size. His parents create a basketball hoop just the right size for him and Martin confides that when he was his brother's age he couldn't reach the high basket either. But in a most realistic ending, the next day Martin reverts to his usual self and this time his little brother has the last laugh. A good opener for talking to your younger child about his feelings. (Ages 4-8)

My Brother, Ant
**by Betsy Byars.
Illustrated by Marc Simont.
Viking Children's Books, New York. 1996. 32 pages.**

Gentle, soft watercolors.
Read-aloud or intermediate readers.
1996 Parenting Best Books of the Year Award winner.

In this short chapter book, an older brother tells about his younger brother Anthony (Ant) with some exasperation in his voice. But the older brother also shows love when he reassures Ant that the monster under his bed is gone. He tells Ant the story of the three little Figs and composes a letter to Santa for him. A loving reminder of the friendship between brothers. (Ages 4-8)

That Bothered Kate
by Sally Noll.
Puffin, 1993. 32 pages.
Gouache paint and colored pencil illustrations.
Read-aloud or beginning to intermediate readers.
Out of print but available in libraries and used bookstores.

Kate and Tory are sisters. Like many siblings, Tory, the younger girl, tries to copy Kate. Kate is irritated by Tory's persistent imitation even though her mother assures her that it's just a part of growing up. But when Tory begins to have her own friends, that bothers Kate too. Now Kate wonders if her little sister needs her at all and her mother reassures her that Tory still does because there are still things only an older sister can do with a younger one. You may find that your oldest child has similar ambivalent feelings about the way her sibling imitates her. (Ages 4-8)

The Pain and the Great One
by Judy Blume.
Illustrated by Irene Trivas.
Yearling Books, 1985. 32 pages.
Humorous pen and ink drawings.
Read-aloud or intermediate to advanced readers.
1986 Alabama Emphasis on Reading Award winner.

Narrated in the realistic voices of an older sister and

a younger brother, this two-chapter story reveals their conflicting emotions about each other and the question of who Mom and Dad love best. But, somewhere in the middle of their complaints about each other, each one admits that it's not much fun playing without the other. Believable and funny too. Your children will be able to relate to this story. (Ages 4-8)

Why Couldn't I Be an Only Kid Like You, Wigger?
by Barbara Shook Hazen.
Illustrated by Leigh Grant.
Atheneum, New York. 1975. 27 pages.
Black-and-white illustrations.
Read-aloud or intermediate readers.
Out of print but available in libraries and used bookstores.

The narrator is a middle child and he complains loudly to his friend Wigger, an only child, about the downside of having siblings. Hand-me-downs, waiting to use the bathroom, getting stuck taking care of the baby, and being blamed for a sibling's misconduct all are part of his day, he tells his friend. In contrast, his image of Wigger's life as an only child is glamorous and filled with parental attention. In fact, he can't understand why Wigger wants to spend so much time at his house until Wigger tells him the one thing he hasn't thought of--that it can be lonely sometimes without siblings. For a child feeling overwhelmed by his siblings, this may be a helpful book. (Ages 4-8)

If It Weren't for Benjamin, I'd Always Get to Lick the Icing Spoon
by Barbara Shook Hazen.
Illustrated by Laura Hartman.
Human Sciences Press, 1988. 30 pages.
Somewhat dated but still appealing tricolor

watercolor illustrations.
Picture Book for read-aloud or intermediate to advanced readers.

  A young boy talks about his angry and envious feelings toward his older brother Benjamin to both his mother and father. Neither of them try to talk him out of his feelings or judge him. They focus on the things he can do and make an effort to praise his accomplishments. This book is more difficult to find but well worth the effort because the narrator's voice is believable and his frustrations are universal. (Ages 4-8)

Other titles of interest, described elsewhere:
Dogger
Arthur's First Sleepover
The Big Brown Box
I Am Sharing
It's Mine!
Phoebe's Parade
Honey Bunny Funnybunny
Just a Bully
Buster Gets Braces
Titch
Sometimes I'm Bombaloo
When Sophie Gets Angry—Really, Really Angry
Goldie is Mad
Come Home, Wilma
I Was So Mad!
I Wish I Was Sick, Too!
The Berenstain Bears and the Green-Eyed Monster
I'm Frustrated
The One in the Middle is the Green Kangaroo
Tidy Titch
Brian's Bird
Alexander and the Terrible, Horrible, No Good,
 Very Bad Day

TWINS

The issues for twins include problems that all siblings face--problems unique to twins alone. Twins experience sibling rivalry of course but they also feel a connection unique to their situation. Twins may enjoy being similar but they may need the opportunity to be their own unique selves.

Harry and Tuck
by Holly Keller.
Greenwillow Books, 1993. 21 pages.
Simple line drawings with watercolors.
Read-aloud or intermediate readers.
Out of print but available in libraries and used bookstores.

Harry and Tuck are twin boys who have always done everything together. They understand each other, although that doesn't mean that they never get angry with each other. But when kindergarten begins they are placed in separate classrooms and for the very first time they are apart. At first it's scary but Harry and Tuck also welcome the opportunity to be different from each other. A good story to encourage twins to enjoy their differences as well as their togetherness. (Ages 3-5)

Twinnies
by Eve Bunting.
Illustrated by Nancy Carpenter.
Voyager Books, 2001. 32 pages.
Oil painting illustrations.
Read-aloud or intermediate to advanced readers.

As the narrator, a young girl, ruefully tells us, "Last June I got twin baby sisters. The worst thing is that there are two of them." With that charming introduction, we understand immediately that the twins dominate life in her family. Not only does her mother pay attention only to the twins, even passersby don't seem to notice her now that there are twins to coo over. But the narrator confides her feelings to her father and he reassures her. When a neighbor complains about the babies making noise with their crying, the narrator rushes to their defense. As the story ends with the whole family sleeping in bed together, she feels overwhelmed with love for the twins. An honest look at the ups and downs of being an older sibling to multiples. (Ages 4-8)

ADOPTION

Adding another person to a family affects the entire family. But what if a child is adopted? How do the other children in the family view her? How does she see herself? What if she is from another country or has a different racial background so that people recognize right away that she is adopted? What if she is adopted as an older child? These and other thought-provoking issues are explored in good books.

Abby
by Jeannette Caines.
Illustrated by Steven Kellogg.
HarperTrophy, 1984. 32 pages.
Black-and-white sketches may seem dated.
Read-aloud or intermediate readers.
Multicultural.
Out of print but available in libraries and used bookstores.

Told entirely in a conversation, this little book is about a cheerful toddler whose older brother, unlike her, is not adopted. The older brother reacts to her as any older brother might, with a mixture of annoyance and pride. A nice portrait of the feelings of an older child about a younger, adopted sibling. (Ages 4-8)

Adoption is for Always
by Linda Walvoord Girard.
Illustrated by Judith Friedman.
Albert Whitman & Company, 1991. 32 pages.
Expressive pencil drawings.
Read-aloud or advanced readers.

Celia has always known that she is adopted but one day she feels angry. Even after her parents reassure her, she has questions and bad feelings. Her teacher and her parents encourage her to express her feelings. The story covers many basic issues that children cope with when they learn or comprehend the meaning of their adoption. (Ages 4-8)

Allison
by Allen Say.
Houghton Mifflin, 1997. 32 pages.
Expressive watercolors.
Read-aloud or intermediate readers.
Multicultural.
1998 NAPPA Award winner.

Allison is an Asian preschooler adopted by a Caucasian family. One day while looking in the mirror with her doll, Mei Mei, Allison realizes that she looks like her doll but not like her parents. They explain that she and Mei Mei came from a country far away and that they brought Allison and her doll home to be part of their family. The book follows Allison's changing feelings of sadness and anger as she observes other families at her preschool and tries to understand her own. Finally, when Allison takes in a stray cat and realizes how much she cares about it she begins to accept her own adoption and to realize the love her parents have for her. A realistic and loving book. (Ages 3-7)

Emma's Yucky Brother
by Jean Little.
Illustrated by Jennifer Plecas.
HarperCollins Children's Books, 2001. 64 pages.
Simple, expressive drawings.
Read-aloud or beginning readers.
Multicultural.
2001 Parenting Best Books of the Year Award
winner.

Emma has waited forever for a brother. Now four-year-old Max is available for adoption. The social worker brings him for a first visit. But he isn't the little brother Emma has been dreaming about. He calls the cookies she made for him "yucky" and likes her best friend Sally better than her. When Max misses his foster mother, the book briefly describes foster care. Emma learns about brothers from Sally and keeps working to be the sister that Max needs. Eventually and with hard work a bond develops between Emma and Max. A nice portrayal of the feelings of an older child toward a new brother or sister who is adopted. (Ages 4-8)

Horace
by Holly Keller.
Greenwillow, 1991. 32 pages.
Endearing cartoon illustrations.
Read-aloud or intermediate readers.

Horace is a spotted cat with striped parents. Every night his mother tells him the story of his adoption. "We chose you when you were a tiny baby because you had lost your first family and needed a new one. We liked your spots, and we wanted you to be our child." At a large family birthday party for Horace it bothers him that he is spotty while everyone else in the family has stripes. He runs away and finds a family "all spotted just like him." But at the end of the day, Horace is ready to return to his own mother and father. For children who prefer to discuss family situations in an indirect way, discussing an issue illustrated by animal characters is a great choice. (Ages 4-8)

Jin Woo
by Eve Bunting.
Illustrated by Chris Soentpiet.
Clarion Books, 2001. 32 pages.
Realistic illustrations.
Read-aloud or intermediate to advanced readers.
Multicultural.

David isn't sure that he wants to share his parents with his newly adopted Asian brother, Jin Woo. In a twist, it turns out that David also is adopted. David worries whether his parents were as happy when they adopted him. But through the sensitivity of neighbors and his mother he is reassured of their love for him and joins in welcoming his new brother. A useful book for helping with a similar situation. (Ages 6-9)

A Koala for Katie: An Adoption Story
by Jonathan London.
Illustrated by Cynthia Jabar.
Albert Whitman & Company, 1997. 24 pages.
Ink, watercolors and colored pencils.
Read-aloud or intermediate to advanced readers.

This simple story portrays a little girl and her questions about adoption and families. No negative emotions are shown, just the reassurance that whether or not a child grows in her mother's body, she is greatly loved by her mother. For very young children. (Ages 4-8)

The Little Green Goose
by Adele Sansone.
Illustrated by Alan Marks.
North-South Books, 1999. 32 pages.

Expressive pencil drawings and watercolors.
Read-aloud or intermediate readers.

Here is an adoption story with a twist. It's told by a loving goose who wants to be a dad. When none of the barnyard hens will give him an egg to hatch, Mr. Goose adopts a large unusual egg, builds a nest, and sits patiently day after day. The chick hatches and it has short paws, glossy green skin, and a long tail. Mr. Goose loves his "wonderful green goose" and cares for him like any proud father. When the baby is introduced to the barnyard animals they tell him that he couldn't belong to Mr. Goose. The baby goes in search of his real mother but finally comes home to Mr. Goose who tells him, "I'm not your mother, I'm your father." A gentle reminder that every loving family can be different. (Ages 4-8)

Lucy's Family Tree
by Karen Halvorsen Schreck.
Illustrated by Stephen Gassler III.
Harpswell Press, 2003. 40 pages, including
author's suggestions for family tree projects.
Soft watercolors.
Read-aloud or advanced readers.

Lucy, an older elementary school child, dreads her class assignment to create a family tree because she feels that her adoption from Mexico makes her family very different. But her parents refuse to write an excuse for her, challenging her instead to name three families she knows that really are all the same. Lucy accepts the challenge and thinks about her friends. Each time she thinks that she has found the "perfect" family, she learns something about them that is different, from a stay-at-home dad to gay parents to different religions. Eventually Lucy begins to reject the idea of sameness and to embrace the idea of diversity in families. Her teacher warmly accepts her version of a family tree. (Ages 7-10)

Mommy Far, Mommy Near: An Adoption Story
by Carol Antoinette Peacock.
Illustrated by Shawn Costello Brownell.
Albert Whitman & Company, 2000. 32 pages.
Soft impressionistic drawings.
Read-aloud or advanced readers.
Multicultural.

A young Chinese girl, Elizabeth, lives with her adopted family who are not Chinese. Elizabeth shares how she felt when she began to comprehend that she was adopted. Like many adopted children, she has questions about why her biological mother didn't keep her and how it would feel to have a Chinese mother. Her feelings are portrayed sensitively, including her sense of loss about her biological mother. Her adoptive mother reassures her that she is loved and wanted, and together they have a very special adoption ceremony. A warm and realistic look at a child's feelings that offers many opportunities to talk with your child. (Ages 4-8)

A Mother For Choco
by Keiko Kasza.
Scott Foresman, 1996. 32 pages.
Playful watercolors.
Read-aloud or intermediate readers.
Available in Spanish.

Choco, a little bird, lives all alone and wishes he had a mother. On a search for a mother who looks like him, Choco meets many animals but doesn't find his mother. But he does find Mrs. Bear, who holds him, kisses him, and dances with him just as he imagined his mother would. Mrs. Bear offers to be his mother and takes Choco home where he sees that her other children also do not look like her. Choco realizes that with Mrs. Bear he can have the mother he has longed for. Best for younger children, this cheerful book offers the message that mothers come in all shapes and sizes. (Ages 4-8)

Pablo's Tree
by Pat Mora
Illustrated by Cecily Lang.
Simon & Schuster, 1994. 32 pages.
Bright collages.
Read-aloud or intermediate readers.
Multicultural.

When Pablo is adopted, his adoptive grandfather plants a small tree. Every year on his grandson's birthday, he decorates the tree in a new way. Pablo remembers every year's decorations and wonders what next year will bring. A wonderful story for discussion of an extended family and adoption issues. (Ages 4-8)

Pinky and Rex and the New Baby
by James Howe.
Illustrated by Melissa Sweet.
Aladdin Library, 1999. 48 pages.
Detailed colorful illustrations.
Read-aloud or strong beginning readers.

Pinky and Rex are next-door neighbors and best friends. When Rex's mother and father adopt a baby, Rex is afraid that her parents will forget about her. Pinky is lonely for Rex because she spends all her time trying to be a perfect sister. Finally Pinky steps in with a special gift that helps Rex get back to normal. This book in the Pinky and Rex series is a realistic and serious look at adoption. It is appropriate for young school age kids and includes a discussion in Pinky's family about the baby's birth mother and her possible reasons for giving the baby up for adoption. A helpful look at an infrequently discussed question. (Ages 7-10)

Seeds of Love: For Brothers and Sisters of International Adoption
by Mary E. Petertyl
Illustrated by Jill Chambers.

Folio One Publishing, 1997. 32 pages.
Bright drawings.
Read-aloud or intermediate readers.

Carly's parents are flying abroad to adopt a new baby sister. Carly worries about her parents' extended absence and about the adoption. The story offers good ideas, such as including a picture of Carly to show to her new sister, a calendar with stickers to mark off the days they will be gone, and a little pot of seeds to water. When the seeds start to grow, Carly's parents will be home with the baby. Carly is happy when her parents arrive with the baby whom she describes "as even softer and sweeter than I had imagined." A helpful story for children facing the extended absence of parents. (Ages 4-8)

Tall Boy's Journey
by Joanna Halpert Kraus.
Illustrated by Karen Ritz.
Carolrhoda Books, 1992. 47 pages.
Realistic watercolors.
Read-aloud or intermediate to advanced readers.
Multicultural.
Out of print but available in libraries and used bookstores.

This book chronicles the adoption of an eight-year-old orphan from Korea. It offers a very different view of adoption since Tall Boy remembers his birth family and country and wishes fervently to return. The excellent description of a child's immersion in a new and strange culture helps us to understand Tall Boy's mounting frustration as he attempts to communicate with his adoptive family. A Korean co-worker from his father's company comes and talks with Tall Boy. He explains many of the confusing aspects of American life to the child and helps with some of Tall Boy's misconceptions. When a neighbor boy arrives to take him sledding, Tall Boy begins to accept his place in his new life in America. This book could open conversation about adoption of an older child. (Ages 8-11)

Through Moon and Stars and Night Skies
by Ann Turner
Illustrated by James Graham Hale.
HarperTrophy, 1992. 32 pages.
Gentle, restrained watercolors.
Read-aloud or intermediate readers.

In a lyrical and touching story, a young Asian boy retells the well-known family story of his adoption into his American family. He tells about the pictures he received from his new parents of themselves, their red dog, and a teddy bear quilt. He relates his memories of flying through a day and moon and stars and night skies. When he arrived, his parents from the pictures were there to greet him. When he arrived home, he met the red dog, and at night he slept under the teddy bear quilt. A lovely book to help discussion about an adopted child's early memories. (Ages 7-10)

We Adopted You, Benjamin Koo
by Linda Walvoord Girard.
Illustrated by Linda Shute.
Albert Whitman & Company, 1992. 32 pages.
Watercolors.
Read-aloud or advanced readers.
Multicultural.

Benjamin Koo narrates a story about his adoption by American parents from a Korean orphanage. The weakness of this otherwise helpful book is that Benjamin's voice does not sound like a nine year-old. Other than this shortcoming, the story offers lots of opportunities to talk about the feelings a child may have. Benjamin has known always that he was adopted but as he points out, "When I was little, I didn't think about who I was." As he grows he notices the differences between himself and his family and he copes with prejudice. Finally he is involved in his parent's adoption of another child. Despite the lack of realism in Benjamin's voice, this book still may be helpful to a family with an older adopted child. (Ages 7-10)

FOSTER HOME

A child who enters a home as a foster child already has experienced difficult things. Whether she is placed in foster care because of family problems or her own issues, it is a challenging situation for all concerned. These books may help explore the feelings that fostering raises.

Mama One, Mama Two
by Patricia MacLachlan.
Illustrated by Ruth Lercher Bornstein.
HarperCollins Children's Books, 1987. 32 pages.
Gentle, evocative pastels.
Read-aloud or advanced readers.

Maudie is a foster child in Katherine's home. One night, as both Maudie and her foster mother Katherine are caring for Katherine's baby, Maudie asks Katherine to tell her again the story of Mama One and Mama Two, which turns out to be Maudie's own story. Maudie's mother was depressed and unable to care for Maudie so she sought help. As a result, Maudie now lives with Katherine and will stay with her until her mother becomes well enough to care for her. A warm story that shows the foster mother managing the difficult balance between loving Maudie and reassuring her that her own mother is trying hard to come back to her. (Ages 7-10)

Zachary's New Home
by Geraldine Blomquist and Paul Blomquist
Illustrated by Margo Lemieux.

Magination Press, 1991. 32 pages.
Black-and-white drawings.
Read-aloud or advanced readers.

Zachary is a young cat that goes to a foster home because of parental abuse. Zachary is angry, confused, and scared as he goes through separation, court proceedings, and assignment to "new" parents. Eventually, Zachary accepts his situation. Unabashedly bibliotherapeutic, this story is best for the youngest of children. (Ages 7-10)

PARENTS LEAVING ON A TRIP

Some children seem relaxed about having a parent go away while others are distressed both by the prospect of a parent's absence and the disruption in the usual routines. There are good ideas in these stories as well as opportunities to talk about an upcoming trip and all the feelings it raises.

I'll See You When the Moon is Full
by Susi Gregg Fowler.
Illustrated by Jim Fowler.
Greenwillow Books, 1994. 20 pages.
Soft, gentle, watercolors.
Read-aloud or intermediate readers.

Abe, a young boy, helps his father pack for an upcoming trip and asks him how much he will miss Abe. When his father gives imaginative answers, Abe responds in kind. Then his questions turn to how soon his father will return. When the answer "in two weeks" doesn't satisfy Abe, his father finds a way to help him count the time and to reassure Abe that, like the certain cycles of the moon, his father will return from his trip. Especially good for younger children, this sweet story provides a concrete way to help them measure the passage of time. (Ages 4-8)

Mommy, Don't Go
by Elizabeth Crary.
Illustrated by Marina Megale.
Parenting Press, 1996. 32 pages.
Black-and-white illustrations; extensive text.
Read-aloud only due to advice for parents.
Multicultural.

Matthew is coping with his mother's impending travel. Matthew explores his feelings as well as his options, including seeking the help of a grownup (here, his babysitter), and other steps to cope. For each choice, Matthew and the reader can see the probable consequences. Crary's problem-solving books offer an interactive story in which children can explore choices they might make in the same circumstances as the fictional hero and the consequences of each choice. An excellent vehicle for good discussion. (Ages 4-8)

My Mom Travels a Lot
by Caroline Feller Bauer.
Illustrated by Nancy Winslow Parker.
Scott Foresman, 1985. 43 pages.
Childlike watercolors; limited text.
Read-aloud or intermediate readers.
1982 Christopher Award winner; 1981 New York Times Best Illustrated Children's Books of the Year Award winner.

The narrator, a little girl, tells us that there are good and bad things about having her mom travel so much. She lists some of each and her examples seem realistic and well-chosen for the most part. She concludes with the predictable, that the best part is having her mom return. Good for young children who view parents' comings and goings exclusively through the lens of what it means for them. (Ages 4-8)

You Go Away
by Dorothy Corey.
Illustrated by Diane Paterson.
Albert Whitman & Company. 1999. 32 pages.
Childlike, simple watercolors; limited text.
Read-aloud or beginning readers.
Multicultural

In a story for very young children, various children experience the comings and goings of their parents and caregivers and are reassured by the predictability of it. A nice way to talk about departures with the very young. (Ages 3-5)

WORKING MOTHERS

Working mothers are not a recent phenomenon but for children, having mom go back to work is a big adjustment. A child may be sad about facing an empty house or about going to daycare after school, and she may wonder who will care for her if she needs help. In addition, her mother may have her own ambivalent feelings about choosing or having to work. These books will help defuse the situation.

By the Dawn's Early Light
by Karen Ackerman.
Illustrated by Catherine Stock.
Aladdin Library, 1999. 32 pages.
Soft watercolors.
Read-aloud or intermediate to advanced readers.
Multicultural.

In this gentle story about a mother who works the swing shift, the only discordant note is the misleading title that may lead readers to assume that the story has something to do with American history. Rachel, the older sister, and her little brother Josh are on a different schedule from their mother, who leaves for work at dinnertime. Through the evening Rachel imagines what her mother must be doing and empathizes with her mother's probable fatigue. She also shows maturity as she recognizes both that she is a little angry that her mother works at night and that her mother has no choice. In the end, Rachel matter-of-factly states that at least they have time together in the very early morning when her mother comes home and they prepare to leave for school. A warm and reassuring acceptance of the necessary reality of mother working is the strong feature of this story. (Ages 7-10)

The Terrible Thing that Happened at Our House
by Marge Blaine.
Illustrated by John C. Wallner.
Scholastic, 1986. 32 pages.
Humorous illustrations.
Read-aloud or intermediate to advanced readers.
Out of print but available in libraries and used bookstores.

Narrated by the daughter, this story contrasts what life was like before her mother went back to her work and now. As the daughter sees it, her mother used to be "a real mother," someone who made delicious lunches and always had time to listen, to read, and to take trips to the park. But now that her mother has returned to work, everyone rushes in the morning, has responsibility for themselves, and has to eat awful cafeteria lunches. What's more, not only the mother but apparently the father too has changed. The daughter's frustration grows until she explodes at dinner and shares her grievances. Her parents listen and together they discuss possible solutions. Realistic and helpful. (Ages 7-10)

MOVING

WHEN YOUR OWN FAMILY MOVES

For an adult or a child, moving is one of life's greatest stresses. But an adult can look ahead, draw on past experience and feel some confidence that life will regain a familiar routine. For a child, it's an upheaval that seemingly has no end. Sometimes it can be a good idea to talk about and read about other children's experiences and feelings about a move.

Alexander, Who's Not (Do You Hear Me? I Mean It!) Going to Move
by Judith Viorst.
Illustrated by Robin Glasser.
Aladdin Library, 1998. 32 pages.
Simple but humorous drawings.
Read-aloud or advanced readers.
Available in Spanish.

Alexander is determined not to move. He is sad about leaving his best friend, his favorite babysitter, his soccer team and everyone he knows. He daydreams about staying and living with other families or even by himself. Although he continues to maintain that he won't go, he says goodbye to favorite places and people. Finally he accepts the move by announcing that his parents "better not try to move anymore when we get to where we're going to go." A good perspective on all the reasons that moving is difficult. (Ages 4-8)

Amelia's Notebook
by Marissa Moss.
Pleasant Company Publications, 1999. 32 pages.
Unique detailed drawings purport to be the
heroine's own illustrations in her notebook.

Read-aloud or advanced readers.

Nine-year-old Amelia is moving, an event that she describes both as to the tasks involved and her feelings. She shares her thoughts about her new school and remains close to the best friend she left behind. A good choice for a young girl hoping to hold onto a long-distance friendship. (Ages 8-11)

Amelia's Road
by Linda Jacobs Altman.
Illustrated by Enrique O. Sanchez.
Lee and Low Books, 1995. 32 pages.
Richly colored folk-art illustrations.
Read-aloud or intermediate to advanced readers.
Multicultural.
Available in Spanish.

Amelia is a child of migrant workers who remember the time and place that she was born by the crop they were picking at that time. Amelia hates the constant moving that is a part of her family's life. She dreams of living in a house and staying there, of feeling a sense of belonging. The place where her family currently lives has a wonderful school and Amelia longs to stay. Although her wish does not come true, she does find a special tree in the area where she spends happy afternoons. When the time comes to move, Amelia makes a map to remember the place and buries her valuables there. From these small acts, Amelia feels that she now has a place where she belongs and to which she will return someday. Warm and touching. (Ages 8-11)

I'm Not Moving, Mama!
by Nancy White Carlstrom.
Illustrated by Thor Wickstrom.
Aladdin Library, 1999. 32 pages.
Lively, humorous illustrations.
Read-aloud or advanced readers.

In this charming tale, a mouse mother and son talk about their impending move. The son repeatedly voices his determination not to go and the mother responds gently and with humor. By the end, he acknowledges that he is going to have to move but tells her that he doesn't like it. Her response is loving: "I don't either. But the best part is not leaving you behind. Someday we'll say, 'Remember how good it was to live in that old place.' But it's better being all together in someplace new." The honest discussion between mother and son is a highlight of this story. (Ages 3-7)

I Want to Go Home
by Alice McLerran.
Illustrated by Jill Kastner.
William Morrow & Company, 1992. 32 pages.
Vivid illustrations.
Read-aloud or intermediate readers.
Multicultural.
Out of print but available in libraries and used bookstores.

Marta, a young girl, isn't happy in her new house. Her new cat Sammy seems to feel the same way because he disappears shortly after Marta gets him. While Marta searches for Sammy she empathizes with what she assumes is his homesickness for his old home. When Marta finally finds her cat, who is hiding in her closet, she comforts him. As Sammy adjusts and Marta reassures him, she finds that the new house has become home for both of them. A lovely way to start a talk about your child's new home and how he feels about missing his old one. (Ages 6-9)

Jorah's Journal
by Judith Caseley.
Greenwillow Books, 1997. 64 pages.
Soft illustrations in shades of black, blue, and grey.

Read-aloud or intermediate readers.
Out of print but available in libraries and used
bookstores.

Jorah, a little girl, has to move because of her father's new job. During her first day at school a girl teases Jorah about her new green shoes with feathers. But eventually Jorah finds a new friend to sit with on the bus, the very same girl who made fun of her shoes. A reassuring message that even if it's tough in the beginning, moving can turn out okay. (Ages 4-8)

Maggie Doesn't Want to Move
by Elizabeth Lee O'Donnell.
Illustrated by Amy Schwartz.
Aladdin Library, 1990. 32 pages.
Whimsical, distinctive watercolors.
Read-aloud or intermediate readers.

Simon's family is moving and he isn't happy about it. In a believable way, Simon expresses all of his feelings by attributing them to his toddler sister, Maggie. As he takes Maggie with him to all the familiar places in the neighborhood, he tells everyone how Maggie feels. He even suggests to his mom that Maggie should remain behind and live with his best friend's family and, of course, Simon would stay to help out. Fortunately, his sympathetic mom catches on and proposes that they show Maggie the new house and neighborhood first. As they tour, Simon's mom helps him see all that is good in the new place and, by the end of the tour, he's confident that Maggie won't mind moving. A nice, indirect way to talk about difficult feelings. (Ages 4-8)

My Diary from Here to There;
Mi diario de aqui hasta alla
by Amada Irma Perez.
Illustrated by Maya Christina Gonzalez.

Childrens Book Press, 2002. 32 pages.
Vivid, colorful illustrations.
Read-aloud or advanced readers.
Bilingual, in English and Spanish.
Multicultural.
Americas award winner; 2004 Pura Belpre Honor Award Winner.

In journal format, a young girl, Amada, recounts preparations for her family's move from a small Mexican town to Los Angeles. Some of her concerns are universal, such as leaving behind good friends, worrying about a new school and making new friends. She also has fears that are unique to her situation, including whether she will be able to learn English and if she will ever return home. As we read her diary, we experience her growing confidence in her ability to survive the changes. A good opener for discussion with any child about a move. (Ages 9-12)

The Leaving Morning
by Angela Johnson.
Illustrated by David Soman.
Orchard Books, 1992. 26 pages.
Full-color watercolor paintings; limited text.
Read-aloud or beginning to intermediate readers.
Multicultural.
Out of print but available in libraries and used bookstores.

This gentle book portrays moving day--saying good-bye and visiting old favorite places. There are hints of other changes as the mother is visibly pregnant. The parents offer warm reassurance to the children that soon they will be someplace they will love. The children are young enough to find that sufficient. A good way simply to talk about what moving day may feel like. (Ages 4-8)

The Lost and Found House
by Michael Cadnum.
Illustrated by Steve Johnson and Lou Fancher.
Viking Children's Books, 1997. 32 pages.
Dreamy, exquisite illustrations.
Read-aloud or advanced readers.
Out of print but available in libraries and used
bookstores.

In rich lyrical language, a young boy describes the
experience of leaving his old house and coming to the
new house. We sense his wonder and his feelings of dis-
placement in both settings. The old house feels empty
and the new house has no curtains and no pictures hung.
Yet the ending is optimistic. The new kitchen is filled
with sunlight, his parents are hanging pictures, the air
smells like the ocean, and the neighbor children are waiting outside to play. A lovely, positive take on the experience while acknowledging the tougher feelings it raises.
(Ages 6-9)

Time to Go
by Beverly and David Fida
Illustrated by Thomas B. Allen.
Harcourt Young Classics, 1990. 32 pages.
Soft, blurry charcoal and colored pencil drawings.
Read-aloud or intermediate to advanced readers.

A young boy describes his family's impending
move away from the family farm. As the young boy talks
of everything he will remember and miss, we sense his
feelings of loss. He knows what he is leaving and the only
consolation is his determination, expressed at the end,
that "I'll be back someday. I know I will. But for now, it's
time to go." For a more mature child, this story acknowledges the pain of leaving a very special home. (Ages 7-12)

What You Know First
by Patricia MacLachlan.
Illustrated by Barry Moser.
HarperCollins Children's Books, 1998. 32 pages.
Unusual, engraved wood block illustrations.
Read-aloud or advanced readers.

In this lyrical narration, a child tells how he doesn't want to leave his home on the prairie in the Midwest. Not even the promise of an ocean is enough to make him want to go. He thinks of the people and the land that he will miss so much. In the end, he takes with him a twig of the cottonwood tree and a little bag of prairie dirt so that neither he nor the new baby in the family will ever forget what they knew first. A good choice for an older child. (Ages 7-12)

WHEN YOUR BEST FRIEND MOVES

Even if a child himself isn't moving, having a best friend move away, even if only across town, is a great loss. It is entirely understandable that a child would grieve the loss, both in advance and afterwards. Words of reassurance about new friends, no matter how well-meant, won't ease the pain of such a change. Books can help.

Andrew Jessup
by Nette Hilton.
Illustrated by Cathy Wilcox.
Ticknor and Fields, 1993. 30 pages.
Bright humorous watercolors.
Read-aloud or advanced readers.

A little girl tells us about her friend Andrew Jessup who was her best friend until last year when he moved away. After his house sits vacant for awhile, a new family moves in. Their daughter Madeleine Havenblower doesn't like the same things that Andrew Jessup and the narrator liked. But she's a great football kicker and she likes to bathe dogs. The two girls enjoy each other's company and the narrator says that while Madeleine Havenblower is her new friend, "Andrew Jessup is still my very best faraway friend." Although the new friend moving into the old friend's house feels contrived, the narrator's feelings and reactions are believable and well-portrayed. (Ages 4-8)

Ira Says Goodbye
by Bernard Waber.
Houghton Mifflin, 1991. 40 pages.
Cartoon illustrations.
Read-aloud or advanced readers.

Ira first learns that his best friend Reggie is moving away when his unsympathetic sister teasingly tells him so. His parents understand his feelings but then something unexpected happens. Reggie acts as though he's glad about the move. For most of the story, Ira feels angry and alienated from Reggie because Reggie doesn't appear to share his feelings about the move. It's only on moving day that Reggie demonstrates how sad he feels and the two boys are reconciled. As the story ends, they are planning their first get-together since Reggie moved. Useful for a child facing a best friend's move in the near future. (Ages 4-8)

Janey
by Charlotte Zolotow.
Illustrated by Ronald Himler.
Harper and Row, New York. 1973. 24 pages.
Very soft, blurry drawings.
Read-aloud or advanced readers.

Narrated in the voice of a lonely little girl, we hear how much she misses her best friend who has moved. This little book offers no cheerful solutions. There aren't any new friends waiting in the wings to replace the best friend who moved away. Instead, it honestly acknowledges the feelings of pain and loss occasioned by the departure of a best friend. This is a story that may encourage your child to share her feelings of loss. (Ages 4-8)

Lee Henry's Best Friend
by Judy Delton.
Illustrated by John Faulkner.
Albert Whitman & Company, 1980. 32 pages.
Somewhat dated illustrations.
Read-aloud or intermediate to advanced readers.
Out of print but available in libraries and used bookstores.

Lee Henry's best friend is Blair Andrew because Blair Andrew knows how to take turns, to share, and to be loyal to his best friend. So when Blair Andrew moves away, Lee Henry misses him terribly. His parents' assurances that he will make new friends don't comfort Lee Henry. Instead, he feels angry. He does meet a new friend but he remains loyal to Blair Andrew. He even lets the new friend know that he already has a best friend. With that established, Lee Henry feels comfortable getting to know the new friend. Although the book is over twenty years old, the story feels fresh and realistic. (Ages 4-8)

My Best Friend Moved Away
by Nancy Carlson.
Viking Books, New York. 2001. 29 pages.
Bright, cheerful, illustrations.
Read-aloud or beginning to intermediate readers.
Multicultural.

A little girl narrates the story, which begins with her best friend's move and her heartfelt question, "Will I ever have a best friend again?" As it turns out, the new family moving into her best friend's house also has a girl her age. Best for younger children who will not resent the cheery confidence and convenient resolution. (Ages 4-8)

My Best Friend Moved Away
by Joy Zelonky.
Illustrated by Angela Adams.
Chariot Family Publications, 1991. 32 pages plus a note from a psychologist.
Colorful illustrations.
Read-aloud or advanced readers.
Out of print but available in libraries and used bookstores.

Brian's best friend Nick is about to move across town and go to a different school. The two boys spend a lot of time together just before the move. Once Nick moves, Brian feels bereft. His father's reassurance that he will make new friends doesn't make him feel better, it just makes him feel that his father doesn't understand. When Brian visits Nick at his new house he feels alienated and uncomfortable. His father helps him to see that this is a hard time for Nick too and that because things have changed for Nick, Nick may change as well. Some parents may not agree with the implied message that Brian should move on and forget about Nick. However, this book may resonate with kids who experience a change in a good friend after he moves away. (Ages 4-8)

CHANGES AND CHALLENGES IN FAMILY LIFE

DIVORCE

In a divorce, a family literally is divided. For children, who desire security and predictability, the change is staggering. Most often, it means dad is moving out and the loss of his regular presence can be felt as a kind of death. Sometimes, it also means that a child moves to another home or spends time at more than one home. However it happens, it's a huge adjustment that deserves many discussions.

As the Crow Flies
by Elizabeth Winthrop.
Illustrated by Joan Sandin.
Clarion Books, 1998. 32 pages.
Detailed, colorful watercolors.
Read-aloud or intermediate readers.

Michael, a second-grader, tells how his parents live in different states and don't speak to each other except when they have to make plans. He hates the physical and emotional distance between his parents and how infrequently he sees his father. Since their visits occur only once a year, Michael treasures the time he has with his father, who is portrayed as a loving parent. But when Michael stays with his father he misses his mother and his life with her. By the end, his parents have some good news for him. He is old enough to travel by plane to visit his father and he will get to see his father in the summers as well. There are no happy endings but rather a picture of life with divorced parents that will help begin discussions. (Ages 4-8)

At Daddy's on Saturdays
by Linda Walvoord Girard.
Illustrated by Judith Friedman.
Albert Whitman and Company, 1987. 32 pages.
Muted watercolors.
Read-aloud or intermediate to advanced readers.

Katie's story begins on the day her father moves out. Katie's sadness and confusion are palpable and small details make this sensitive portrayal even more moving. Saturday arrives, the day that Katie will stay over at her father's new apartment. Katie's father lets her decide where the furniture should go and encourages her to share her feelings. As the weeks pass her father's apartment becomes familiar and homey to her and new routines replace the old ones. Katie notices that now when she is with her father he has time for her, where before he often seemed busy or was arguing with her mother. The story ends on a positive note. Best suited for younger children for whom the loss of familiar routines looms large. Older children may not accept the positive slant to the divorce presented in the final pages. (Ages 5-8)

Charlie Anderson
by Barbara Abercrombie.
Illustrated by Mark Graham.
Aladdin Library, 1995. 32 pages.
Soft realistic illustrations.
Read-aloud or intermediate readers.

Two sisters find a stray cat that they name Charlie. Although Charlie leaves every morning, he returns every night to eat his dinner and sleep on their beds. On weekends, when the sisters stay with their father and stepmother in the city, Charlie stays behind with their mom. One night Charlie doesn't appear and the sisters are distraught. Their search for Charlie brings them to a new neighbor's house. There, the sisters learn that their Charlie is also Anderson, beloved cat of their neighbor, and they realize that just like them Charlie has two homes. A gentle loving way to reassure that having two homes doesn't mean less love. (Ages 4-8)

The Days of Summer
by Eve Bunting.
Illustrated by William Low.
Harcourt, 2001. 40 pages.
Colorful illustrations.
Read-aloud or intermediate readers.

When a family hears that the grandparents are getting a divorce, the two girls who are very close to their grandparents can't believe the news. The fourth-grade sister explains many of the confusing aspects of divorce to her younger sister. As they leave for their first visit to grandma's house since the news, their father reminds them that it's a difficult situation for everyone. A complicated, emotional situation handled well in an age-appropriate story. (Ages 7-12)

Ginger Brown: Too Many Houses
by Sharon Dennis Wyeth.
Illustrated by Cornelius Van Wright and Ying-Hwa Hu.
Random House, 1996. 69 pages.
Occasional black-and-white sketches.
Read-aloud or advanced readers.
Multicultural.
Out of print but available in libraries and used
bookstores.

Ginger Brown, a biracial girl, must leave her familiar home and even her beloved kitten when her parents divorce. For a while she has to live with her grandparents and it feels to her that she has too many places to live and none that's really home. By the end of the year that the book chronicles, Ginger feels more stable and her kitten is returned to her. A gentle way to talk about the changes that divorce brings. (Ages 4-8)

I Don't Want to Talk About It
by Jeanie Franz Ransom
Illustrated by Kathryn Kunz Finney.
Magination Press, 2000. 32 pages.
Illustrations are not the strong point in this otherwise good book.
Read-aloud or advanced readers.

Narrated by a little girl, this story covers a very short but important time when her parents tell her about their pending divorce. By imagining she is different animals, the little girl conveys her feelings, including loneliness, anger, and confusion. A good choice for a young child. (Ages 4-8)

I Wish I Had My Father
by Norma Simon.
Illustrated by Arieh Zeldich.
Albert Whitman & Company, 1987. 32 pages.
Somewhat dated illustrations.
Read-aloud or intermediate readers.

A young boy talks about how much he hates Father's Day. It is a difficult for him because not only are his parents divorced, he never sees his dad. He is filled with questions about why his dad never calls or comes to see him. Many things remind him of the emptiness in his life without a father. There are hints in the conversations he has with his mother that his father may have been abusive but the story focuses more on the other adult men in his life. The ending is realistic; he still wishes he knew his father. Well-suited for a child in this situation. (Ages 4-8)

It's Not Your Fault Koko Bear
by Vicki Lansky
Illustrated by Jane Prince.
Book Peddlers, 2003. 32 pages.
Simple line drawings.
Read-aloud only due to advice for parents.
Available in Spanish.

Koko Bear's feelings, from the moment she learns of her parents' pending divorce to later when she has adjusted to the change, are the focus of this story. Vicki Lansky's books about difficult issues present a story with suggestions for discussion. In addition, Lansky's books contain advice for parents on each page in smaller print that clearly is not meant for the child reader. A helpful book except for the unfortunate marketing of a Koko Bear stuffed animal on the last page. (Ages 4-8)

Loon Summer
by Barbara Santucci.
Illustrated by Andrea Shine.
Eerdmans Books for Young Readers, 2001. 32 pages.
Soft watercolors with cut papers.
Read-aloud or intermediate readers.

It is the first summer at the lake for Rainie, a young girl, and her dad. As they watch for the return of the loons they see each summer, Rainie reminds her father, "You told me loons stayed together for life. Why can't you and mom?" As the summer passes they watch the loons build a nest and care for their young and Rainie begins to believe again in the love both of her parents feel for her. This story chronicles the successful struggle of a young girl to accept the change in her family situation soon after her parents' divorce. (Ages 5-9)

Mama and Daddy Bear's Divorce
by Cornelia Maude Spelman.
Illustrated by Kathy Parkinson.
Albert Whitman & Company, 1998. 24 pages.
Colored pencil and watercolors.
Read-aloud or intermediate readers.

This simple story describes Dinah, a bear cub, and her life before and after Mama and Papa Bear get a divorce. This gentle story emphasizes that although Dinah's life will change, many of her favorite routines and toys will remain the same. Especially appropriate for younger children. (Ages 4-8)

Missing Rabbit
by Roni Schotter.
Illustrated by Cyd Moore.
Clarion Books, 2002. 32 pages.
Whimsical and colorful pictures.
Read-aloud or intermediate readers.

Kara takes Rabbit to Papa's house to eat "oodles of

noodles" and to Mama's house to dance and eat chicken. When Rabbit asks her one day, "Where do I live?" Kara can't answer. She decides to leave Rabbit to live at her father's house but ends up missing her stuffed toy too much. But when she leaves him at her mother's house she has the same problem. Kara's parents explain that she lives part of the time with Mama and part of the time with Papa but all of the time in both of their hearts. Kara is able to reassure Rabbit and herself about where they live. For a very young child faced with spending time at each parent's house, this book sets a positive tone. (Ages 3-7)

Mom and Dad Break Up
by Joan Singleton Prestine.
Illustrated by Virginia Kylberg.
McGraw Hill, 2001. 32 pages, including suggested discussion questions.
Eye-catching color illustrations.
Read-aloud or intermediate readers.
Multicultural.

The narrator of this simple but poignant story is a young Asian boy who begins by observing, "Some things belong together. Peanut butter and jelly. Bees and honey. Mom and Dad." But that's not how it works out in his life. He talks about his angry and sad feelings and how he sometimes takes his feelings out on his friends. The young boy wishes that his parents would reunite and worries that it is his fault. He begins to accept the reality that he can't fix the problem and that, most importantly, both of his parents still love him. A very good book for exploring the feelings that many children experience and for initiating discussion. (Ages 4-8)

Mom and Dad Don't Live Together Anymore
by Kathy Stinson.
Illustrated by Nancy Lou Reynolds.

Firefly Books, 1988. 26 pages.
Soft, watercolors.
Read-aloud or beginning to intermediate readers.
A little girl's face shows her different feelings, including sadness and bewilderment, about her parents' divorce. But we hear increasing acceptance of the fact that she has a life with each of her parents and that despite their separation, both of them still love her very much. There isn't any sugarcoated ending; it's clear that she wishes that her parents were still married. A good choice to reassure younger children that some things won't change. (Ages 4-8)

Mommy and Me by Ourselves Again
by Judith Vigna.
Albert Whitman & Company, 1987. 32 pages.
Gentle, blurry watercolors.
Read-aloud or intermediate readers.
Amy is six years old and sad about the breakup of her mother with her mother's boyfriend Gary. (The story doesn't dwell on Amy's father. We learn that he and Amy's mother divorced when Amy was very young and that Amy never sees him.) Yet another adult male in her life has departed and Amy feels that she will never love anyone again. Her mother's explanations and reassurances don't seem to help but the presence of her extended family (grandparents, aunts, and uncles) reminds Amy that she does have people who love her and will be there for her. A useful story for the situation in which a child must come to terms with the end of a parent's romantic relationship. (Ages 4-8)

A Month of Sundays
by Rose Blue.
Illustrated by Ted Lewin.
Franklin Watts, 1972. 59 pages.

Simple black-and-white illustrations.
Read-aloud or advanced readers.

Ten-year-old Jeffrey's parents get divorced. That means a move and a new school for him. Jeffrey's feelings and adjustment problems are sensitively treated and his relationship with both of his parents is realistically depicted. Despite the age of this book, the story is realistic. A good choice for any child, particularly one whose adjustment includes a move. (Ages 9-12)

My Mother's House, My Father's House
by C. B. Christiansen.
Illustrated by Irene Trivas.
Atheneum, 1989. 32 pages.
Lovely, detailed watercolors.
Read-aloud or intermediate readers.
Out of print but available in libraries and used bookstores.

In this divorce story the focus is on houses and the moving back and forth between a young girl's mother's house and her father's house. She ends her story by emphasizing that when she is grown up she will live in only one house every day of the week and there will not be any suitcases. Her dream, true of many children of divorced parents, is that in her own house both her mother and her father will come to stay. A good vehicle for exploring the loss of home that occurs in many divorces. (Ages 6-9)

Priscilla Twice
by Judith Caseley.
Greenwillow Books, 1995. 32 pages.
Watercolors and colored pencils.
Read-aloud or intermediate readers.

At Priscilla's house, her parents talk to her but not to each other. They tell her that they are getting a divorce.

Priscilla tries hard to be well-behaved and do her chores without being asked. Her parents reassure her that her behavior has nothing to do with their divorce. Priscilla's father moves out but lives down the street. Everything is the different, yet the same. When Priscilla draws a picture of herself at home she draws herself twice, once at her mother's house and once at her father's. A realistic and touching book that will open discussion.(Ages 6-9)

Rope Burn
by Jan Siebold.
Albert Whitman & Company, 2000. 80 pages.
No illustrations.
Read-aloud or advanced readers.
Multicultural.

Narrated by a teenage boy, this is a realistic and humorous story of Richard who moves as the result of his parents' divorce. Richard tells his story through chapters named for proverbs and each chapter relates an experience that corresponds to the proverb. It's a witty, sympathetic, and poignant look at the problems kids face when their parents divorce. An excellent choice for an older child. (Ages 9-12)

Two Homes
by Claire Masurel.
Illustrated by Kady MacDonald Denton.
Candlewick Press, 2001. 32 pages.
Ink, watercolor, and gouache illustrations.
Read-aloud or intermediate readers.

Alex's parents are divorced so he spends time with each of them separately. There is no suggestion that Alex misses the parent with whom he isn't staying or of any negative feelings about the divorce. Best for younger children, to reassure them of their parents' love despite the change in living arrangements. (Ages 9-12)

Where Has Daddy Gone?
by Trudy Osman.
Illustrated by Joanna Carey.
Egmont Children's Books, 1994. 32 pages, with an
introduction by a psychiatrist.
Vivid watercolors.
Read-aloud or intermediate readers.
Out of print but available in libraries and used
bookstores.

A young boy describes his life when he was little
and his parents were happy. He describes his parents'
arguments and their eventual separation. He talks about
his feelings of sadness at not seeing his father often. As the
story ends, the boy has asked whether he could live with
his dad but he accepts his mother's statement that his parents decided together that he should live with his mom.
This simple story is best for young children who are bewildered both by their parents' decision to divorce and their
own strong emotions. (Ages 4-8)

REMARRIAGE

After a child has experienced divorce, a time may
come when his divorced parents become romantically
involved with other people. It can feel awkward or even
like a betrayal. Although it may result in a loving remarriage, it confirms the end of every child's hope that his
parents will reconcile. This is part of the painful acceptance of a different family life for children of divorce.

My Mother's Getting Married
by Joan Drescher.
Dial Books for Young Readers, 1986. 32 pages.
Ink and watercolors.
Read-aloud or intermediate readers.

Katy's mother is getting married and Katy thinks "it

stinks." She's happy with the way things are, just the two of them. Katy feels that things are different when Ben is around and she feels competitive with him. Nothing that anyone says or does changes the way she feels and she has no intention of welcoming Ben into the family. But she decides to behave at the wedding because her mother looks so happy. As the story ends, Katy finally shares her feelings with her mother and receives reassurance in return. A good choice for a child facing a parent's imminent remarriage. (Ages 5-9)

Totally Uncool
by Janice Levy.
Illustrated by Chris Monroe.
Carolrhoda Books, 1999. 32 pages.
Quirky illustrations.
Read-aloud or intermediate readers.

As the story begins, a young girl lists all the uncool things about her dad's latest girl friend. "She doesn't bake cookies. Her floor is too shiny. Mostly everything she eats is green." On the other hand, there are some cool things about this new woman in her dad's life. "She listens to me without the TV on. Keeps my secrets secret. Never interrupts me when I stutter." The story allows readers to acknowledge their parents' companions as whole people, with both attractive and unattractive traits. (Ages 7-10)

STEP-FAMILIES

With remarriage, a child may gain not only an additional parent but also new siblings. If a child is going to live with his new siblings he may feel both anticipation and anxiety. If his non-custodial parent will live with those new siblings he may feel anxious and jealous. This is a time when reading about the feelings and experiences of other children in the same situation can be immensely comforting.

Amelia's Family Ties
by Marissa Moss.
Pleasant Company Publications, 2000. 40 pages.
Detailed drawings.
Read-aloud or advanced readers.

Amelia, a young teenager, receives a letter from her father, the first she's ever received. He tells her that he is remarried and has a baby and wants to reconnect with her. Amelia has ambivalent feelings but she accepts his invitation to travel to Chicago to visit him and her stepbrother. She describes the visit in her teenage voice with accompanying drawings. Amelia loves her new baby brother but not her stepmother. There is an inevitable confrontation with her stepmother, and there is the beginning of a relationship with her father. This book will hit home with any older child or teenager coping with divorce and stepsiblings. (Ages 9-12)

Daddy's New Baby
by Judith Vigna.
Albert Whitman & Company, 1982. 32 pages.
Watercolors alternate with black-and-white drawings.
Read-aloud or intermediate readers.

In this narrative by a little girl, her parents are divorced and "Daddy has a new baby. She lives in Daddy's house with him and his new wife. Mommy and I live by ourselves." The young narrator's anger toward the new baby is demonstrated by an "accident" that almost ends in disaster. But by the end, she has more positive feelings toward her new sister. What distinguishes this story is its believable voice, filled with a child's insights as well as her confusion. (Ages 4-8)

I Want Answers and a Parachute
by P.J. Petersen.
Illustrated by Anna DiVito.
Simon and Schuster, 1993. 101 pages.
Occasional black-and-white illustrations.
Read-aloud or advanced readers.

The narrator, Matt, is an adolescent boy who takes a trip with his younger brother Jason to see their father who has just remarried. Matt worries that his brother is a pest and that their father has already replaced them with his new stepchildren. Matt also worries that if he and Jason aren't perfect, his father might be sorry that he invited them for a visit. With a mischievous younger brother like Jason, things are bound to go wrong and this story mixes humor and emotion beautifully. A good story for an older child who doesn't live with his father. (Ages 9-12)

If Daddy Only Knew Me
by Lila McGinnis.
Illustrated by Diane Paterson.
Albert Whitman & Company, 1995. 32 pages.
Watercolors.
Read-aloud or for intermediate reader.

A kindergartener, Kate, realizes that all the other kids know their fathers and she begins to ask questions about her father. Her mother explains that he left the family because he didn't want a family anymore. When Kate learns that he lives in the same town she convinces her sister to go with her to his house. After a long walk, they actually see him and his new baby. Their father overhears the little girl say her older sister's name and he watches them as they walk away. It is implied, but not stated that the door may be open for a possible reunion. Meanwhile, the story emphasizes that the children are loved by all the other people in the family-- mother, grandparents, and siblings. (Ages 4-8)

Sam is My Half-Brother
by Lizi Boyd.
Viking, 1990. 32 pages.
Quirky, appealing watercolors.
Read-aloud or advanced readers.

Hessie has accepted her father's remarriage. But now he has a new baby boy and Hessie visits him. She soon begins to wish that Sam, the baby, had never arrived and that there's no room for her. Hessie shares her feelings with her father. He reassures her and tells her about her babyhood. As the story ends, Hessie creates a picture book for Sam so that he will know all about her. A useful choice for children with a new stepsibling. (Ages 4-8)

FEELING SAFE IN A SCARY WORLD

GETTING LOST

Nothing strikes terror in a parent's heart more than a child who is lost. Children also have fears about getting lost. What would they do? How would their parents find them? In these thoughtful and sometimes humorous stories, getting lost is a problem that both parents and children learn to handle. Your child can be reassured that you will find him.

Come Along, Daisy
by Jane Simmons.
Little, Brown and Company, 1997. 32 pages.
Lavish, impressionistic illustrations.
Read-aloud or intermediate readers.

Mama Duck counsels baby Daisy to stay close but the world is so fascinating that Daisy forgets to heed her mother's advice. Suddenly Daisy finds that she is all alone and the world isn't as fascinating as it is scary. Just when it seems that whatever is out there is about to get her, it turns out to be Mama who has come back for her. This time Daisy stays close by no matter how enticing she finds the sights. A gentle tale for younger children. (Ages 3-7)

Ernie Gets Lost
by Liza Alexander.
Illustrated by Tom Cooke.
Golden Books, 1985. 24 pages.
Familiar Sesame Street characters fill the pages.
Read-aloud or intermediate readers.

Ernie goes shopping with Maria. Maria gives him a card with her name, address and phone number on it. She tells Ernie that if they get separated Ernie must stay where he is, talk to a salesperson, and give her the card. Ernie becomes distracted in the store and is separated from Maria. He initially forgets Maria's advice and wanders around the store. Then Ernie remembers and finds a salesperson who pages Maria. Although the story is predictable, for young Sesame Street fans it offers an opportunity to talk about the feelings when one is lost. (Ages 3-7)

I'm Lost
by Elizabeth Crary.
Illustrated by Marina Megale.
Parenting Press, 1985. 32 pages.
Simple black-and-white illustrations accompany extensive text.
Read-aloud only due to advice for parents.

Amy is going to the zoo with her father who is confined to a wheelchair. Amy gets separated from her father and must figure out what to do. Amy considers her choices, which include finding a helpful grownup such as a police officer or a woman with children. The story offers the opportunity to consider the probable consequences of each choice. Crary's books offer an interactive story in which children can explore choices and the consequences of each choice. An excellent vehicle for discussion. (Ages 5-9)

Left Behind
by Carol Carrick.
Illustrated by Donald Carrick.
Clarion Books, 1988. 32 pages.
Dark and busy illustrations.
Read-aloud or intermediate readers.

Christopher, an older elementary-school boy, takes a school trip to the city to visit the aquarium. On the ride home on the subway, Christopher is separated from the other kids by the crush of the crowds and inadvertently left behind at the wrong station. Christopher panics and then realizes that he needs to find a policeman. The policeman helps him to reconnect with his class but Christopher worries that his teacher will be angry and the other kids will think he is dumb. But his worries are unfounded; his teacher is very relieved and together they head for the rest of the class. A good story for an older child, offering realistic approaches. (Ages 7-10)

Sheila Rae the Brave
by Kevin Henkes.
Greenwillow Books, 1987. 32 pages.
Charming, humorous illustrations.
Read-aloud or intermediate readers.

Sheila Rae, a young mouse, isn't afraid of anything, unlike her sister Louise. Sheila Rae isn't afraid of the dark, thunder and lightening, the neighborhood big dog, or even bullies at school. One day Sheila Rae decides to walk home a new way and teases Louise for being afraid to come. But when Sheila Rae realizes that nothing looks familiar, she becomes scared and gives way to tears. It's her sister Louise who finds her and shows her the way home. When they reach home Sheila Rae tells her sister how brave she is and Louise responds that they both are. A delightful reminder that everyone is scared by something. (Ages 4-8)

STRANGERS

Today's parents and children are more careful about strangers than in the past. Yet it's never easy to broach this topic with kids. A good balance between appropriate caution and scaring kids is difficult to reach. Here is a useful selection for opening up discussion.

The Berenstain Bears Learn About Strangers
by Stan and Jan Berenstain.
Random House, 1985. 32 pages.
Familiar illustrations and characters.
Read-aloud or intermediate readers.

Sister Bear, a friendly bear cub, greets every stranger until Papa Bear tells his children the rules for behavior around strangers. Then Sister Bear becomes concerned about every stranger. Using the "bad apple in the barrel" analogy, Mama Bear explains the need for caution but also the importance of being open to new friends. In the end, it's Brother Bear who almost gets into a car with a stranger when he's tempted by a toy. The Bear Family's rules are provided on the last page of the story. While the story is openly didactic, this series appeals to many kids. If your child is a fan, a Berenstain Bears book is a good way to open discussion. (Ages 4-8)

ALCOHOLISM

It is difficult for any family member to comprehend the disease of alcoholism or to know how to help. It is even more mysterious to a child. Most children wonder if it's their fault or if they can do something to make it go away. Good books can be a useful resource.

Bottles Break
by Nancy Maria Grande Tabor.
Charlesbridge Publishing, 1999. 32 pages.
Unusual construction paper illustrations.
Read-aloud.
Available in Spanish.

A child feels "like a speck. Like I do not count," because his mother is an alcoholic. The child writes questions about alcoholism in a school journal. His teacher reads them and responds with factual information. The teacher says that sometimes the only thing you can do is to take good care of yourself, such as by riding a bike, reading a book, playing with a friend, or writing. The book explores the confusing emotions of children with alcoholic parents and emphasizes that alcoholism is never the fault of a child. At the end of the book the author includes a list of resources to help children of alcoholic parents. A useful resource. (Ages 7-10)

I Know the World's Worst Secret
by Doris Sanford.
Illustrated by Graci Evans.
Multnomah Press, 1987. 32 pages.
Detailed drawings, especially of faces.
Read-aloud or intermediate readers.

A little girl shares a terrible secret—her mother is an alcoholic. She is embarrassed to bring friends home because her mother is usually drunk. Nobody in the family will talk about it. The little girl takes an adult role in the family, doing the shopping, the cooking, and the cleaning. The little girl has one confidant, a doll she calls Friend. She asks Friend, "Why does Daddy put up with this?" Her mother has a serious auto accident while driving drunk and is put in a special hospital for alcoholics. The ending is deliberately vague. When the child asks her father if her mom will get better in the hospital, her father says "No one knows for sure." No comforting answers, but a realistic look at how a child might feel. (Ages 5-9)

I Wish Daddy Didn't Drink So Much
by Judith Vigna.
Albert Whitman & Company, 1988. 32 pages.
Simple childlike illustrations.
Read-aloud or intermediate to advanced readers.

A young girl talks about the sled her father gave her for Christmas as well as less happy moments, such as his boozy impersonation of Santa and breaking his promise to take her sledding. She is angry but her mother defends his alcoholism as an illness and suggests alternative ways to enjoy Christmas dinner. The ending is unrealistically rosy. However, the story offers the opportunity to explore alcoholism as a disease. (Ages 4-8)

Sometimes My Mom Drinks Too Much
by Kevin Kenny and Helen Krull.
Illustrated by Helen Cogancherry.
Raintree Steck-Vaughn Publishers, 1995. 32 pages.
Realistic watercolors.
Read-aloud or intermediate to advanced readers.

A young girl expresses her feelings about her mother's drinking. Her mother doesn't seem like herself when she drinks. She's unpredictably and alternately angry and sorry. It humiliates the girl when her mother is drunk in public. Her father explains that her mother has a disease and cannot help the way she behaves. The father is portrayed sensitively, as is the decision for her mother to be temporarily institutionalized. The ending offers no promises. A skillful and realistic portrayal of alcoholism in a family. (Ages 4-8)

DRUG ADDICTION

Children learn about drugs in many different ways. They may learn about medicine and later come to understand that medicines can be abused. They may hear discussions by their peers or adults about drugs, offering differing viewpoints. A child who experiences drug addiction firsthand sees a very different picture.

My Big Sister Takes Drugs
by Judith Vigna.
Albert Whitman & Company, 1990. 32 pages.
Gentle watercolors.
Read-aloud or intermediate readers.

A young boy describes his sister and how she has changed recently. Her new friends are disturbing and she has begun to skip school. In spite of the pressure on his family from his sister's troubling behavior, his own life goes on and he has made a good new friend. But after the police bring his sister home one night when she is caught smoking crack in the park, the little boy fears that he won't make any new friends ever again. He feels angry at the effect on his life of his sister's destructive behavior. His sister enters a rehabilitation facility. When she returns home he begins to feel compassion for her and to realize that she is even lonelier than he is. Remarkably, there are few books that deal with drugs that are written for a young audience. This story fills a niche that needs to be addressed. (Ages 6-9)

HOMELESSNESS

A Chance to Grow
by Sandy Powell.
Illustrated by Zulma Davila.
Carolrhoda Books, 1992. 32 pages.
Black-and-white sketches.

Picture Book for advanced readers.

In the voice of a young boy we hear how his family became homeless, what it felt like, and how things finally began to improve. The story is sympathetically told and has many realistic elements including drugs and people behaving in frightening ways. A good book to help an older child understand some of the problems of the homeless. (Ages 7-10)

Fly Away Home
by Eve Bunting.
Illustrated by Ronald Himler.
Clarion Books, 1991. 32 pages.
Sober, realistic illustrations.
Read-aloud or intermediate readers.
1991 NAPPA Award winner; 1992 California Books
Award winner.

A young boy, Andrew, lives in an airport with his father because they have no home. It hasn't always been this way. Andrew's father is working at one job and searching for more work. Their need to hide and to remain unnoticed is made clear as is the father's frustration at not finding work. A sensitive, reasonably realistic introduction for children who are wondering about homelessness. (Ages 6-9)

The Lady in the Box
by Ann McGovern.
Illustrated by Marni Backer.
Turtle Books, 1997. 32 pages, including a note
from the author.
Exquisite oil illustrations.
Read-aloud or advanced readers.
Available in Spanish.

A young boy and his sister are determined to help a homeless woman who sleeps in a box on the street. We don't see the face of the homeless woman until well into the story when she becomes more real by telling the children and their mother how she has come to be living on the street. As the story ends we see her smile. She has become a full person not only in the eyes of the children but, perhaps because of their caring, in her own eyes as well. An excellent way to talk to children about this tragic situation. (Ages 6-9)

Seeing Eye Willie
by Dale Gottlieb.
Alfred A. Knopf, 1992. 24 pages.
Distinctive, quirky, and colorful illustrations.
Read-aloud or advanced readers.

A young girl is very curious about a homeless man named Willie. She has many questions about him, especially how he came to be homeless. Everyone in the neighborhood has his own theories about Willie's life. The girl adds her own story about Willie, a story that is imaginative and explains all of Willie's disabilities and behaviors. She understands that her story might not be true and she is eager to hear the real story. "If he ever wants to tell it, I hope I'm there to listen." A good way to engage your child's thoughts about homeless people and how they become homeless. (Ages 6-9)

Someplace to Go
by Maria Testa.
Illustrated by Karen Ritz.
Albert Whitman & Company, 1996. 32 pages.
Realistic illustrations.
Read-aloud or advanced readers.

Davey, a young boy who is homeless, spends his time after school quite differently from children with stable homes. Davey has to fend for himself until the evenings when he, his brother and his mother are able to enter the shelter. He spends time in the public library until he falls asleep and is evicted by a security guard. He has a scary brush with drug dealers and remembers the death of his other brother from drugs. When he finally he meets up with his mother and brother, he gets good news: his brother has gotten a job. Sometimes the best way to understand another person's experience is to live it along with them, moment by moment. Realistic and unsparing, this is a book to help children understand the life of the homeless. (Ages 9-12)

VIOLENCE

Nobody Wants a Nuclear War
by Judith Vigna.
Albert Whitman & Company, 1986. 35 pages.
Watercolors alternate with black-and-white illustrations.
Read-aloud or intermediate readers.
1987 Jane Addams Children's Book Award winner.

The narrator, a young girl, shares her fears about the possibility of a nuclear war that might prevent her from growing up. She and her brother build a shelter and when her mother finds out she reassures the children that she and their father will try always to be with them, no matter what. She also encourages them to take action and the children decide to make a big banner that their mother photographs and mails for them to the President. A reassuring way to talk about fears that children have about war. (Ages 6-9)

Smoky Night
by Eve Bunting.
Illustrated by David Diaz.
Harcourt, 1994. 32 pages.
Striking, atmospheric acrylic and collage illustrations.
Read-aloud or advanced readers.
Multicultural.

Available in Spanish.
1995 Caldecott Award winner; 1995 California Book Award winner; 1995 Children's Literature Council of Southern California Award winner.

A mother and son witness rioting on the street below their apartment window. They try to sleep but are awakened by smoke and must evacuate the building. The text and illustrations together vividly convey the terror and confusion that the young boy is feels and his fear that his cat is trapped inside. He and his mother go to a shelter and there is brief happiness when his cat is brought in by a firefighter. As the story ends we see that from this event new friendships between people of different backgrounds are being forged. Diaz's striking and bold illustrations combine with Bunting's skillful writing in a rare rendition of a frightening experience. This book provides an opportunity for talking with children honestly, while offering hope for a positive outcome. (Ages 7-10)

A Terrible Thing Happened
by Margaret M. Holmes.
Illustrated by Cary Pillo.
Magination Press, 2000. 32 pages, including author's note to parents and a list of helpful resources.
Simple watercolors.
Read-aloud.

A young raccoon named Sherman sees "the most terrible thing." While we never learn what the terrible thing was, we know that it scares Sherman and affects his appetite, his sleep, and his behavior in school. Sherman doesn't know what to do but he begins to meet with an adult, Ms. Maple, who helps him think about his feelings. With her encouragement Sherman draws pictures of how he feels and his bad dreams. She also gives him an opportunity to ask whether it was his fault and to be reassured.

Best for younger children to encourage them to express their feelings and use the technique of drawing. (Ages 4-8)

FAMILY HEALTH: ILLNESS AND DISABILITIES

Chronic illnesses and disabilities have a profound impact on family life. Whether your child has just been diagnosed with a chronic illness, is trying to cope with a sibling's disability, or needs help facing the illness of a parent, books can help. In this section, all kinds of books are recommended about all kinds of illnesses. One theme is common to all—learning to accept and live with the reality of the illness.

GENERAL

Jim's Lion
by Russell Hoban.
Illustrated by Ian Andrew.
Candlewick Press, 2001. 40 pages.
Dreamy and evocative illustrations.
Read-aloud or intermediate to advanced readers.
Multicultural.

Jim is a young boy who is ill with an unspecified illness. As he lies in his hospital bed, Jim and his nurse Bami talk about his fears about surgery and the possibility of his death. Bami tells him a story about an animal in his head that can bring him back from wherever the doctors send him. Bami also helps him to visualize a place where he feels good. Bami gives Jim a "don't run stone" to help him with his fears. With Bami's help, Jim finds the strength to face surgery. The illustrations and the text work perfectly together to create a powerful experience for readers. (Ages 7-10)

AIDS

Alex, the Kid with AIDS
by Linda Walvoord Girard.
Illustrated by Blanche Sims.
Concept Books, 1993. 32 pages.
Colorful illustrations.
Read-aloud or intermediate to advanced readers.
Out of print but available in libraries and used bookstores.

Alex is a fourth-grader with AIDS. He also is funny and mischievous and he's not above using his illness to gain an advantage. His story is told from the perspective of another boy, Michael, who is assigned to be Alex's partner. The strength of the story lies in its willingness to allow Alex to be a full person, not just a sick child. He isn't perfect in his behavior, just as Michael is a normal boy too. This book is one of very few available fiction books for younger readers that deals with AIDS. A good book for a child who shares a classroom with a child with AIDS. (Ages 7-10)

ALLERGIES

Aaron's Awful Allergies
by Troon Harrison.
Illustrated by Eugenie Fernandes.
Kids Can Press, 2002. 32 pages.
Appealing, colorful illustrations.
Read-aloud or intermediate readers.

Aaron loves animals more than anything in the world, especially his big dog Clancy. His animal menagerie expands when he adds a stray cat and her six kittens to the animals that sleep in his room. Then he volunteers to babysit the class guinea pigs and their babies over the summer. But Aaron begins to feel miserable with itchy eyes, coughing, and sneezing. The doctor gives him bad news. He is allergic to animals. Every one of his animals has to have a new home including Clancy. Aaron is devastated and his mother's attempt to cheer him with a goldfish seems to fail. But he begins to take his goldfish with him everywhere and to find other critters to love as well, like frogs and snakes that don't make him sneeze. A warm if optimistic story. (Ages 4-8)

I'll Never Love Anything Ever Again
by Judy Delton.
Illustrated by Rodney Pate.
Albert Whitman & Company. 1985. 32 pages.
Simple, tricolor illustrations.
Read-aloud or intermediate readers.

The narrator, a young boy, is grieving because he will have to give up his dog Tinsel due to his allergies. As he tells the story we hear his anguish over giving up the dog he has had since he was born. We learn about all of his dog's likes and dislikes and about the narrator's ambivalent feelings on the question of whether Tinsel will be able to love anyone else. As the young boy tells the story, he fully shares his anger with the readers. The ending doesn't offer any answers. A good story to help a child express his feelings. (Ages 4-8)

ALZHEIMER'S DISEASE

A Beautiful Pearl
by Nancy Whitelaw.
Illustrated by Judith Friedman.
Albert Whitman & Company, 1991. 32 pages.
Simple, sepia-colored drawings.
Read-aloud or advanced readers.
Available in Spanish.

Every year Lisa receives a beautiful pearl from Grandmother. But Lisa's grandmother suffers from Alzheimer's. She forgets important events and is confused about the identities of familiar people. When Lisa is ten, she worries that Grandmother will forget to give her the pearl this year. In a rather contrived ending, Grandmother remembers the pearl. However, it is clear from the story that that may not always be true. An opportunity to discuss the progress of the disease. (Ages 4-8)

Great-Uncle Alfred Forgets
by Ben Schecter.
HarperCollins, 1996. 32 pages.
Impressionistic, childlike illustrations.
Read-aloud or intermediate readers.

Emily's great-uncle doesn't always remember who she is or what season it is. But he has stories to share with her about his childhood and Emily enjoys those stories. Both of them are glad that there still is time to be with each other. For any child with a relative in the early stages of Alzheimer's, this is a story about making the most of the time that remains. (Ages 4-8)

Sachiko Means Happiness
by Kimiko Sakai.
Illustrated by Tomie Arai.
Children's Book Press, 1990. 28 pages.
Pastels with Japanese motifs.
Read-aloud or intermediate to advanced readers.
Multicultural.
Available in Spanish.

Sachiko and her grandmother have enjoyed a special relationship but now that her grandmother suffers from Alzheimer's disease, Sachiko doesn't enjoy being with her. Her grandmother's confusion and insistence that she is five years old again anger Sachiko. But eventually Sachiko realizes that her grandmother really isn't the same anymore and that in her grandmother's mind, she is a little girl. With this realization it becomes easier to be kind and to find a new way to relate to her grandmother. A believable story that shows the frustrations of Alzheimer's disease. (Ages 4-8)

Singing with Momma Lou
by Linda Jacobs Altman.
Illustrated by Larry Johnson.
Lee & Low Books, 2002. 32 pages.
Vivid acrylic illustrations. Read-aloud or intermediate to advanced readers.
Multicultural.

Every week Tamika's family visits her grandmother Momma Lou in the nursing home and reintroduces themselves to a beloved woman who no longer recognizes them. When Tamika is bored her father decides to share with her Momma Lou's scrapbook. Together they relive her memories, from participating in civil rights demonstrations to composing music. Tamiko is moved and decides that maybe she can give back some of the lost memories to Momma Lou. Tamiko brings a different memento each week to share, even as Momma Lou deteriorates. But there is one last time that Momma Lou is herself again and Tamiko tries to reassure her that she will keep the memories safe forever. Later, even after Momma Lou is gone, the memory of sharing consoles Tamiko. (Ages 4-8)

The Memory Box
by Mary Bahr.
Illustrated by David Cunningham.
Albert Whitman & Company, 1995. 32 pages.
Muted illustrations on every other page.
Read-aloud or advanced readers.

Zach's grandfather tells him about an idea he has

for a special box that they could fill with family stories and traditions. Then, no matter what happens, the memories are saved forever. Zach objects to the phrase "no matter what happens" but his grandfather doesn't really explain. The two of them fill their box and as the days pass Zach notices a change in his beloved grandfather. Finally his grandmother explains to him about Alzheimer's disease and Zach uses the Memory Box to help his grandfather remember. A sweet idea that can give a child an opportunity to help a beloved relative remember. (Ages 4-8)

A Window of Time
by Audrey O. Leighton.
Illustrated by Rhonda Kyrias.
Nadja Publishing, 1995. 32 pages.
Haunting, lovely illustrations.
Read-aloud or intermediate readers.

Shawn's grandfather confuses reality with memories of his past. Sometimes he believes that he is still a young boy, living on a farm and playing with his good friend Jack. Shawn accepts his grandfather's confusion and enters into a kind of game where he indulges his grandfather's alternate reality. This is a story about acceptance and, when possible, finding a way to enjoy and treasure whatever reality an older person inhabits. (Ages 4-8)

ASTHMA

The Lion Who Had Asthma
by Jonathan London.
Illustrated by Nadine Bernard Westcott.
Albert Whitman & Company, 1997. 32 pages, including a foreword for parents.
Watercolors and ink.
Read-aloud.

Sean is a young boy with asthma serious enough to

require use of a nebulizer. Most of the time Sean feels strong, like a lion roaring. But unlike the lion he imagines himself to be, sometimes it's hard to breathe and then it's time to have his treatment. His mother tells him to put on his mask and be a pilot and he imagines that he is a jet pilot flying high. He breathes deeply and then comes down for a landing to resume his play. Helpful analogies for a child to consider while he's taking his treatment. (Ages 3-7)

ATTENTION DEFICIT DISORDER

Eddie Enough
by Debbie Zimmett.
Illustrated by Charlotte Murray Fremaux.
Woodbine House, 2001. 40 pages, including "note" from the main character.
Black-and-white sketches.
Read-aloud or advanced readers.

Eddie, a third-grader, tells about himself beginning with the fact that he's always in a hurry. He tells about a day at school when everything went wrong. When he ended up in the office of the principal, Mr. Thomas, he learned, to his surprise, that Mr. Thomas was a lot like Eddie in third grade. Eddie goes to a doctor who prescribes a medication that helps him and also sees a counselor. The story ends on a positive note with Eddie feeling better about himself and his self-control. For children who are struggling with attention deficit issues, a positive story. However, be advised that medication is prescribed in the book. (Ages 7-10)

Pay Attention Slosh!
by Mark Smith.
Illustrated by Gail Piazza.
Albert Whitman & Company, 1997. 56 pages.
Limited black-and-white illustrations.

Read-aloud or intermediate to advanced readers.

Eight year-old Joshua just can't keep still and he can't control himself either. It's hard to concentrate and he gets in trouble with his teacher and other children. His parents take him to see Dr. Harnett who doesn't seem to mind that Josh can't sit still or stop touching everything in her office. With her help Josh and his parents gain understanding of what will help Josh control himself, such as a token system for good behavior and working closely with his teacher. Dr. Harnett eventually prescribes medication as well, which calms him. Good descriptions of how Josh feels inside and how difficult it is for him to refrain from behaviors that get him into trouble. However, be advised that medication is prescribed in the book. (Ages 7-10)

Waiting for Mr. Goose
by Laurie Lears.
Illustrated by Karen Ritz.
Albert Whitman & Company, 1999. 32 pages.
Realistic watercolors.
Read-aloud or intermediate to advanced readers.

Stephen is a child who finds it difficult to wait or sit still. He wishes that he could be wild and free like the geese at the pond near his house. When he sees that one of the geese is caught in a metal trap, Stephen wants to help. But it will require patience and the ability to be quiet in order to gain the bird's trust. When Stephen is able to remove the trap and set the bird free, we feel his joy at what he has accomplished. Other books on this topic focus on the problem, so it's refreshing to find a story that recognizes the strengths in a child as well. A nice way to talk about attention issues by focusing on what children can do. (Ages 4-8)

AUTISM

Ian's Walk: A Story about Autism
by Laurie Lears.
Illustrated by Karen Ritz.
Albert Whitman & Company, 1998. 31 pages.
Soft but realistic watercolors.
Read-aloud or intermediate readers.

Eager to go on a walk, Julie is pestered by her younger brother Ian to take him as well. With some embarrassment Julie recounts some of the odd things Ian does, like staring at the ceiling fan in the diner, smelling the brick walls, and listening to the stones. But when Ian disappears at the park, Julie is able to find him because she remembers how fascinated he is by the park bell. Her remorse makes her willing to try to see things through his eyes. On the way home she tells him that it was a good walk. When, for "just a flash," he smiles at her, we can feel the joy she feels at connecting with him. It's easy to forget that siblings of a child with a disability also have a need to express themselves and work through their feelings. In this sensitive story about a girl with a younger brother who is autistic, her ambivalent feelings are recognized and respected. (Ages 7-10)

BLINDNESS

A Cane in Her Hand
by Ada Bassett Litchfield.
Illustrated by Eleanor Mill.
Albert Whitman and Company, 1987. 32 pages.
Dated illustrations.
Read-aloud or advanced readers.

The narrator tells us about her vision problems in a straightforward, believable way. Valerie does learn to use her cane and other skills as well but she still endures the

ignorance and teasing of children around her. There are few books available for elementary-school-age children on the subject of disabilities. Many of the available books have a preachy tone or seem dated. Here, the text is realistic but the illustrations show kids from another era.
(Ages 7-10)

Brian's Bird
by Patricia Davis.
Illustrated by Layne Johnson.
Albert Whitman & Company, 2000. 32 pages.
Vivid colorful illustrations.
Read-aloud or intermediate to advanced readers.
Multicultural.

Eight year-old Brian, a blind African-American boy, receives a parakeet for his birthday. Brian patiently teaches his bird to say "Hi Brian" and to return to his cage. The bird becomes a happy focus every day for Brian. But Brian's older brother Kevin demeans his efforts and accidentally leaves the front door open one day, which results in the bird flying outside. With Kevin's help, Brian is able to retrieve his bird. Both boys recognize something about each other's skills and frustrations and feel better about each other. Notable for its portrayal of a blind child, this is a good choice for children who are living with a disability as well as trying to understand it. The multicultural characters are unusual in fiction about disabilities.
(Ages 7-10)

The Secret Code
by Dana Meachen Rau.
Illustrated by Bari Weissman.
Children's Press, 1998. 32 pages.
Simple, childlike illustrations.
Read-aloud or beginning readers.

Oscar is a young blind boy in a regular classroom.

He shares his way of reading with Lucy, another child. The very simple story offers a positive view of a blind child's reading skills—that he knows a secret code he can share with sighted children. Best suited for helping sighted children understand the way blind children read. (Ages 4-8)

Other titles of interest, listed elsewhere:
Sarah's Sleepover

CANCER

Kathy's Hats: A Story of Hope
by Trudy Krisher.
Illustrated by Nadine Bernard Westcott.
Albert Whitman & Company, 1992. 32 pages.
Cheerful watercolors.
Read-aloud or intermediate readers.

A little girl describes all of the hats she has owned, from her first baby ribbon to her beach bonnet to her baseball cap. Recently she was diagnosed with cancer. She talks about the feelings and experiences she has had as a result of the cancer and especially about the worst part–losing her hair. Even though she had hats to wear it wasn't fun anymore. Her mother explained that the most important hat of all is a thinking cap, the invisible hat you wear when you are faced with a challenge you need to think about. Her mother's idea inspires her to put a favorite pin on her baseball cap and to add others that have special meaning. A positive idea for approaching hair loss that acknowledges children's angry and sad feelings. (Ages 5-9)

Promises
by Elizabeth Winthrop.
Illustrated by Betsy Lewin.
Clarion Books, 2000. 32 pages.
Cheerful watercolors.

Read-aloud or intermediate to advanced readers.

Sarah's mother is sick and spends a lot of time in the hospital. When she is home she and Sarah take slow, careful walks. Sarah remembers when her mother had lots of energy and ran marathons and still had her hair. Sarah's feelings are difficult, confusing, and painful even though she has a sympathetic teacher as well as her father to talk to. Her father reassures her that her mother is getting better and eventually her mother's hair begins to grow back as well. Even though her mother can't promise that she'll never be sick again, Sarah is happy with what her mother can promise—things about today and tonight. A good story for a younger child, with a positive message about cancer. (Ages 7-10)

Sammy's Mommy Has Cancer
by Sherry Kohlenberg.
Illustrated by Lauri Crow.
Gareth Stevens Publishing, 1994. 32 pages,
including an introduction from the author
and a glossary.
Gentle watercolors.
Read-aloud.

A young boy, Sammy, learns that his mother has cancer. He is too young to comprehend much about it but his parents give him age-appropriate information and explain each thing that happens including his mother's hair loss. Because of their explanations and reassurance, we do not see Sammy worrying about his mother. A very calm story for a very young child just learning about a parent's illness. (Ages 4-8)

There's a Little Bit of Me in Jamey
by Diana Amadeo.
Illustrated by Judith Friedman.
Albert Whitman & Company, 1989. 32 pages,

including a note from the author about
childhood cancer.
Sepia pencil sketches.
Read-aloud.

Brian's younger brother has leukemia. Brian is filled
with emotions, from anxiety about his brother's pain to
anger that his mother isn't paying more attention to him.
Even after Jamey comes home from the hospital things
aren't normal. Everyone is protective of Jamey and Brian
feels as though no one cares about his feelings. Jamey's
condition worsens and he returns to the hospital. That
night, Brian's parents make a huge request of Brian--a bone
marrow transplant. Brian is afraid but he loves Jamey and
he agrees. As the story ends, even though the operation
leaves Brian feeling sore, he doesn't mind, "[b]ecause of
that little bit of me in Jamey, he may come home, to stay." A
sensitive story about the feelings siblings may have when
they live with a brother or sister with a serious illness.
(Ages 7-10)

When Eric's Mom Fought Cancer
by Judith Vigna.
Albert Whitman & Company, 1993. 32 pages.
Gentle drawings and watercolors.
Read-aloud or intermediate readers.

Eric's mother had breast cancer and she had an
operation. Afterward, she reassured Eric that she expected to live for a long time. Now, even though the operation
is over his mother spends a lot of time resting or at the
hospital for treatments. Eric is young enough to feel frustrated that he hasn't gotten to use his new skis this winter.
His mother understands and Eric and his father have a special day on the mountain, skiing. It's also a good time for
a little more conversation to reassure Eric that nothing he
did caused the cancer. A good story for a younger child.
(Ages 4-8)

CEREBRAL PALSY

A Contest
by Sherry Neuwirth Payne
Illustrated by Jeff Kyle.
Carolrhoda Books, 1982. 40 pages.
Sepia-colored drawings.
Read-aloud or advanced readers.

Ten-year-old Mike has cerebral palsy and uses a wheelchair. Mike has just been mainstreamed into a new school where he needs assistance with everything from reaching a carton of milk in the cafeteria to opening bathroom doors. He's afraid to ask for help, hates it when people stare at him, and has been teased by a boy named Randy. But Mike tells his dad that he'll stick with it, and he does well in school academically. His teacher notices his sadness and realizes that she needs to show the other kids the ways Mike is not different. Mike tells her that he loves to arm wrestle, and when he and Randy arm wrestle, Mike wins. As the kids see that he has his own skills, they begin to accept him. A realistic look at the feelings of a child and the ways in which adults can help. (Ages 9-12)

My Brother, Matthew
by Mary Thompson.
Woodbine House, 1992. 25 pages.
Soft watercolors.
Read-aloud or advanced readers.

David's younger brother Matthew speaks, moves, and behaves differently from other children. Sometimes the extra attention Matthew needs or the way he behaves are a source of frustration and embarrassment for David. But David also enjoys his brother and is proud of his special ability to understand Matthew's speech. An honest story about the feelings of a sibling of a child with disabilities. (Ages 8-11)

DEAFNESS, HEARING IMPAIRED

Going with the Flow
by Claire H. Blatchford.
Illustrated by Janice Lee Porter.
Carolrhoda Books, 1998. 40 pages.
Bold, bright illustrations.
Read-aloud or intermediate to advanced readers.
Multicultural.
Out of print but available in libraries and used bookstores.

Mark, a fifth-grader, is starting a new school where he is the only deaf child and only his interpreter knows sign language. He feels lonely, angry, and embarrassed. Some of the kids ignore him while others tease him. But a few boys include him in their basketball game and he begins to feel a sense of belonging. For him, the message is to go with the flow and take it as it comes. Not a bad message when you think about it for any kid, deaf or hearing. A sympathetic and realistic story about the feelings of a deaf child. (Ages 9-12)

I Have a Sister—My Sister Is Deaf
Jeanne W. Peterson.
Illustrated by Deborah Kogan Ray.
HarperTrophy, 1984. 32 pages.
Muted black-and-white illustrations.
Read-aloud or intermediate to advanced readers.

The narrator, the sister of a deaf child, begins by saying that her sister is special and there aren't many sisters like hers. She talks about what her sister can and cannot do, like feeling the deep rumbling chords of the piano but not being able to hear the tune. The narrator demonstrates a deep love and acceptance of her sister and while she never voices any resentment of the special needs her sister undoubtedly has within the family, her feelings are believable. A warm book for a protective sibling. (Ages 7-10)

I'm Deaf and It's Okay
by Lorraine Aseltine, Evelyn Mueller
and Nancy Tait.
Illustrated by Helen Cogancherry.
Albert Whitman & Company, Illinois. 1987. 40 pages.
Sepia pencil drawings.
Read-aloud or intermediate to advanced readers.

This is a very unfortunate title for a book that otherwise offers a useful story. The narrator, a young deaf boy, has experiences that are both frightening and empowering. He feels jealousy toward his sibling, which is unusual in stories about children with disabilities. He is also angry at people who talk to him in loud voices. He longs for a time when he no longer would need his hearing aids and he is angry when his parents tell him that he will always need to wear them. When a deaf high-schooler visits his classroom he finds someone who understands his feelings. The title of this story gives the impression of a story that is uniformly positive. But this helpful and empathetic book is much more balanced. (Ages 7-10)

DEPRESSION

Please Don't Cry, Mom
by Helen DenBoer.
Illustrated by Janice Galanter Goldstein.
Carolrhoda Books, 1994. 32 pages.
Black-and-white illustrations.
Read-aloud or intermediate to advanced readers.
Multicultural.
Out of print but available in libraries and used bookstores.

The narrator, a young boy, describes his mother's behavior: she cries a lot, doesn't get out of bed, and doesn't eat. When he talks to his father he learns that his mother has depression, which his father describes as an illness. The father feels helpless and tells the boy not to worry but of course he does. After a month passes, his grandmother comes to live with them but her presence seems to worsen things, as she tells his mother to "snap out of this." Although his mother is put on medication, things deteriorate and the boy and his father share their sadness and frustration. Together they look at photos of happier times. Eventually the mother shows signs of improvement but there are no guarantees given in this thoughtful story. A good book for understanding not only depression but also the feelings it engenders in loved ones, from anger to frustration. (Ages 6-9)

Sad Days, Glad Days
by DeWitt Hamilton.
Illustrated by Gail Owens.
Albert Whitman & Company, 1995. 30 pages,
including a short forward about depression.
Dark pastel illustrations.
Read-aloud.

A young girl named Amanda Martha describes life in her family. Her mother is depressed and has moments when she tells her daughter that it "feels like darkness comes over her." On those days, her mother is angry for no reason and cries a lot. But on other days her mother is loving and insightful, shares information about her condition, and reassures Amanda Martha that she is loved. Both of her parents accept Amanda Martha's angry feelings. Good information about depression and the feelings of those affected. (Ages 7-10)

DIABETES

Tough Beans
by Betty Bates.
Illustrated by Leslie Morrill.
Yearling Books, 1992. 89 pages.

Occasional black-and-white drawings.
Read-aloud or advanced readers.

Nat Berger's story, told in his own words, is of a fourth-grade boy who learns that he has juvenile diabetes after he winds up in the emergency room. In realistic language Nat expresses his disbelief and frustration, as well as his horror of giving himself shots. He talks about his fears and shares his setbacks when he eats forbidden foods. (Note: this aspect of the story is outdated because more recent diabetes treatment allows any food to be eaten as long as the food is adequately covered by insulin injections.) In addition to diabetes, Nat has a problem with a school bully. As Nat learns how to handle the bully, he also comes to accept the need for his medical care and to feel more in charge of his own body. A good story for a child recently diagnosed with juvenile diabetes. (Ages 9-12)

DOWN SYNDROME

Making Room for Uncle Joe
by Ada B. Litchfield.
Illustrated by Gail Owens.
Albert Whitman & Company, 1984. 32 pages.
Tricolor pencil sketches.
Read-aloud or advanced readers.

The narrator, a young boy named Dan, and his family face the prospect of Uncle Joe moving in with them due to the closure of the state hospital where he has been living. Uncle Joe has Down Syndrome. No one else in the extended family is able to take care of him so Dan's family has to help out until another place can be found for Joe. Although Dan tries not to react as negatively as his sister Beth, privately he has his own fears and concerns. When Uncle Joe arrives some of Dan's fears are realized but he also discovers good qualities in Uncle Joe: he pays attention to the kids, appreciates their humor, and tries hard to be helpful around the house. When Joe's social worker finally locates a permanent home for him, Dan's family decides to invite him to stay permanently. An introduction to the fact that an adult can have disabilities too. (Ages 6-9)

Thumbs Up, Rico!
by Maria Testa.
Illustrated by Diane Paterson.
Albert Whitman & Company, 1994. 40 pages.
Bright watercolors on every other page.
Read-aloud or advanced readers.
Multicultural.

Rico, a boy with Down Syndrome, tells about his experiences playing basketball with another boy, Caesar. He also talks about his sister and about improving his art, in this three-chapter book. In the first chapter, Caesar hurts Rico's feelings by calling him "dummy" and insulting his ball playing abilities. But Rico is determined to improve his playing and to become friends with Caesar. His supportive older sister helps him in his quest and the story realistically describes their loving relationship. In the second chapter, Rico has an opportunity to respond to his sister's needs and he grows in doing so. In the final chapter, Rico copes with the limits of his artistic abilities and, with the help of his family and friends, learns to accept himself. A sensitive and kind story that portrays a child with Down Syndrome as a full human being. (Ages 7-10)

Epilepsy

What If They Knew?
by Patricia Hermes.
Dell, 1983. 128 pages.
No illustrations.
Read-aloud or advanced readers.
Out of print but available in libraries and used bookstores.

Jeremy is a ten-year-old girl who starts a new school in Brooklyn where she lives temporarily with her grandparents. Jeremy finds some good friends and an enemy as well, but she keeps to herself the secret that she has epilepsy. Over the weeks that follow Jeremy's secret is revealed and she learns some valuable lessons about being a friend to others. A kind and thoughtful story that explores the feelings of shame that may accompany epilepsy. (Ages 9-12)

Learning Disabilities

Other titles of interest, described elsewhere:
It's George!

Mental Illness

The Face at the Window
by Regina Hanson.
Illustrated by Linda Saport.
Clarion Books, 1997. 32 pages.
Vivid pastels.
Read-aloud or advanced readers.
Multicultural.
1997 Americas Award.

Dora, a young girl, joins her friends in stealing mangos from the garden of Miss Nella, an old woman who lives nearby. The children are afraid of Miss Nella because of her strange behavior. When heavy rains follow her actions, Dora is convinced that the rain is her fault. She tells her parents what she did and they respond by encouraging her to think of Miss Nella as a good person whose mind plays tricks on her. They take her to visit Miss Nella, which gives Dora an opportunity not only to apologize but also to discover the old woman's loneliness. The story takes place in Jamaica and is written in dialect. It's an opportunity to talk about mental illness and how the behaviors of the mentally ill may seem scary. (Ages 7-10)

PHYSICALLY DISABLED

My Buddy
by Audrey Osofsky.
Illustrated by Ted Rand.
Henry Holt & Company, 1994. 32 pages.
Colorful watercolors.
Read-aloud or intermediate to advanced readers.

The young boy who narrates this story has muscular dystrophy that confines him to a wheelchair. But with the help of his best friend, a golden retriever Service Dog named Buddy, the boy is able to realize his dream of being more independent. At his command, Buddy learns how to turn on lights, open doors, push elevator buttons, and even pay for items at a store. Because of Buddy, the narrator can go to school with other kids and Buddy helps him to make friends. A good way to talk about a disabled child's service dog. (Ages 7-10)

Princess Pooh
by Kathleen M. Muldoon.
Illustrated by Linda Shute.
Albert Whitman & Company, 1989. 32 pages.
Simple, old-fashioned watercolors.
Read-aloud or advanced readers.
Out of print but available in libraries and used bookstores.

The narrator, Patty Jean, is the sister of a ten-year-old girl confined to a wheelchair. Patty Jean calls her sister "Princess Pooh" because, from her perspective, her sister sits on a throne with wheels and tells everyone else what to do. Patty Jean's envy and frustration are palpable. To her it seems as though everyone favors her sister and makes life easy for her. One day while her sister is sleeping in a hammock, Patty Jean borrows the "throne" and goes for a joyride. She discovers that it's not as easy or as pleasant as it looks. As she tries to navigate through traffic and hills she experiences what it feels like to be teased by kids she passes and to have other people look away from her. Finally, she gets stuck in the mud in the rain. A realistic and sympathetic portrayal of a child's frustrations with her sister's disability. (Ages 7-10)

SCHIZOPHRENIA

My Sister, Then and Now: A Book about Mental Illness
by Virginia L. Kroll.
Illustrated by Mary Worcester.
Carolrhoda Books, 1992. 40 pages.
Soft black-and-white illustrations.
Read-aloud or advanced readers.

The narrator, a young girl, describes her older sister Karen who is schizophrenic. Karen's behavior didn't always seem odd. She and the narrator used to go to the beach together and enjoy feeding the seagulls. But now that the narrator is ten, she understands that there is something different about Karen. Karen cries a lot; she has strange fears and inexplicable behavior. Although the narrator's parents explain schizophrenia, the narrator doesn't understand and resents the extra attention Karen receives. She is ashamed of Karen's behavior in front of her friends and her anger spills over toward her parents. Eventually, the narrator's parents give her the opportunity to talk to a counselor about her feelings and she is able to accept her sister's illness. A thoughtful and realistic book. (Ages 8-11)

TALKING ABOUT DEATH

Children experience the loss of a pet, a friend, and a family member very differently, depending on their age and maturity. For some children, a chance to say goodbye is very important; others find comfort in memories or tangible reminders of the person or animal who has died. This is a time when books may be especially comforting, as the skilled authors of the books listed here demonstrate.

DEATH OF A PET

CAT

Goodbye, Mitch
by Ruth Wallace-Brodeur.
Illustrated by Kathryn Mitter.
Albert Whitman & Company, 1995. 32 pages.
Clear, crisp watercolors and colored pencils.
Read-aloud or intermediate to advanced readers.

A young boy, Michael, begins his narrative with these simple words, "My cat Mitch stopped eating on a Sunday. I know because it was my turn to feed him." Michael describes a touching and believable relationship in which his cat has always been a part of his life. But Mitch won't eat anymore. Michael's mom tells him that Mitch may be getting ready to die. Michael won't accept this and when Mitch finally eats, Michael sees it as a sign that Mitch is getting well. But Mitch continues to lose weight. One day, Mitch goes outside and doesn't return for several days. As Michael tells the story we feel his sadness and his determination to hold onto Mitch. Mitch dies and Michael and his family have a burial. This is a lovely, sensitive story about the inevitability of loss and how it feels. There is no attempt to sugarcoat it, yet the story is reassuring and ends on a positive note. (Ages 4-10)

Mustard
by Charlotte Graeber.
Illustrated by Donna Diamond.
Atheneum, 1982. 42 pages.
Occasional black-and-white illustrations.
Read-aloud or advanced readers.
Out of print but available in libraries and used bookstores.
1982 Irma S. and James H. Black Award for Excellence in Children's Literature Award winner; 1986 West Virginia Children's Book Award winner.

Mustard the cat has been a part of eight-year-old Joey's life since he was born. Joey resists facing the fact that Mustard is old but his fears are realized when the vet tells him that Mustard's heart is not as strong as it used to be. Time passes and Mustard seems stronger, then an encounter with a neighbor's dog causes Mustard to have a heart attack. Joey must face a hard decision—deciding to put Mustard to sleep so that he can die peacefully. (Oddly, having set up the conflict, the author then has Mustard die before the vet can put him down.) Joey wisely resists the urge to get another cat right away, recognizing that he isn't ready. A good choice for facing the decision to put a pet to sleep. (Ages 7-10)

The Tenth Good Thing About Barney
by Judith Viorst.
Illustrated by Erik Blegvad.
Aladdin Library, 1987. 32 pages.
Simple, soft drawings.
Read-aloud or intermediate readers.

The narrator, a young boy, is grieving the death of his cat, Barney. While comforting him, his mother suggests that they hold a funeral for Barney and that he should think of ten good things about Barney to share at the funeral. The boy thinks of nine good things before he falls asleep. At the funeral the boy lists nine things. Later, while working in the garden with his father, the little boy discovers the tenth good thing, the way that Barney will become a part of the earth and nurture the growth of trees and flowers. A sensitive portrayal of the cycle of life and death. (Ages 5-9)

When Lucy Went Away
by George Maxim Ross.
Illustrated by Ingrid Fetz.
E.P. Dutton, 1976. 32 pages.
Simple black-and-white drawings.
Read-aloud or intermediate readers.

The narrator tells about the cabin his family rents every summer that has a cat door for their cat Lucy, who always goes with them. Lucy likes to go out at night and hunt, although some nights she stays in and cuddles with the children. When the day arrives for leaving the cabin, no one knows where Lucy is. The family searches but they cannot find her. Finally, the family leaves without her, wondering whether Lucy will make it without them. The narrator fantasizes that when they return the next summer Lucy will be waiting for them. For a child whose beloved pet is missing, this gentle story will encourage discussion of why animals roam and whether they can survive on their own. (Ages 7-10)

DOG

The Accident
by Carol Carrick
Illustrated by Donald Carrick.
Houghton Mifflin, 1981. 32 pages.
Muted watercolors.
Read-aloud or advanced readers.
Out of print but available in libraries and used bookstores.

Christopher, a young boy, is waiting with his dog Bodger for his parents to pick him up. Bodger wanders to the other side of the road and just as a truck drives up Bodger runs across to join Christopher. The driver swerves but it is too late. He hits and kills Bodger. Christopher is angry that his parents don't blame the truck driver and he rages at the man when he offers Christopher a puppy. His anger continues when he learns that his father has buried Bodger without waiting for him. His father accepts his feelings and suggests that they find a stone to mark the grave. Finding just the right stone becomes a way for Christopher to finally express his grief and guilt and to let go of his anger. A sensitive story. (Ages 8-11)

A Dog like Jack
by DyAnne DiSalvo-Ryan.
Holiday House, 1999. 32 pages.
Warm, appealing watercolors.
Read-aloud or intermediate readers.
Irma S. and James H. Black Award for Excellence in Children's Literature.

A family adopts Jack, an eight-year old dog, from the animal shelter. Jack becomes such a part of the family that he even wears a costume when he goes trick-or-treating with the little boy, Mike. Jack especially loves when the family goes to the park and the beach. But Jack is getting old and the day comes when Jack can't walk far enough to go trick-or-treating. Jack finally dies. The family buries his ashes under a special pine tree at their summer house. Mike says, "Whenever I see a dog now, I always think of Jack…there will never be another dog like Jack." A gentle but very real story about loss. (Ages 4-8)

Goodbye, Max
by Holly Keller.
William Morrow, 1987. 32 pages.
Simple, mixed media illustrations.
Read-aloud or intermediate readers.

Ben is grieving the loss of his old dog Max and angrily rejects the new puppy his father brings home. When Ben delivers newspapers with his friend Zach the two boys reminisce about how Max used to help. Ben begins to cry and they cry together. When they return to Ben's house, Ben feels comforted and invites Zach to help him name the new puppy. A warm portrayal of friendship and grief make the story a good one for sparking discussion. The replacement of Max with another dog also may encourage discussion. (Ages 6-9)

I'll Always Love You
by Hans Wilhelm.
Crown Publishing, 1989. 32 pages.
Soft watercolors.
Read-aloud or beginning to intermediate readers.
Available in Spanish.

A little boy narrates the story of his dog Elfie. Everyone in his family loves Elfie but she is his dog. Through all the seasons they have fun together but the reference to seasons gently reminds us that time is passing. One morning the boy awakens to find that Elfie has died during the night. It helps him to remember that every night he told Elfie that he would always love her. A warm and loving story of the relationship between a child and his dog. (Ages 4-8)

Jasper's Day
by Marjorie Blain Parker.
Illustrated by Janet Wilson.
Kids Can Press, 2002. 32 pages.

Warm, richly colored pastels.
Read-aloud or intermediate to advanced readers.
2002 ASPCA Henry Bergh Children's Book Award winner.

Riley's dog Jasper has advanced cancer. It's time to let him go but before Riley's family takes him to the vet to be put to sleep they celebrate Jasper's life in a day devoted to him. As the story ends there are no easy answers. Riley feels his sadness but he's happy that his family shared one last day with their beloved dog. A useful idea, when it's time to accept the death of a pet, spending one wonderful day together can create a memory that eases the pain. (Ages 6-9)

Jim's Dog Muffins
by Miriam Cohen.
Illustrated by Lillian Hoban.
Picture Yearling, 1996. 32 pages.
Cheerful, childlike watercolors.
Read-aloud or intermediate readers.
Out of print but available in libraries and used bookstores.

Jim's dog Muffins was run over by a car and everyone is talking about it at school. But Jim doesn't want to talk about it, even after the other kids send him a letter to cheer him up. Jim's anger explodes when a classmate tries to tell him to cheer up. After that, his teacher wisely counsels the other children to give him time alone. Eventually Jim and his friend Paul talk about his memories and Paul consoles him. A loving story about grief and the important role friends can play. (Ages 6-9)

The Sounds of Summer
by David Updike.
Illustrated by Robert Andrew Parker.
Pippin Press, 1993. 32 pages.

Impressionistic, evocative illustrations.
Read-aloud or advanced readers.

Homer, a young boy, must deal with the aging and death of his beloved dog Sophocles. As the story opens, it is summertime and Homer has begun to notice that Sophocles is slowing down. The sense of time passing is conveyed by the descriptions of the seasons and the natural world. Homer and his friends go sailing and when they return Sophocles is gone. Eventually they find Sophocles but he is ill. Homer blames himself but his mother and the vet remind him of his dog's advanced age. The next morning, Sophocles dies. Homer's grief and eventual acceptance are sensitively portrayed. An excellent book for older children who are dealing with loss of a beloved pet. (Ages 6-9)

Toby
by Margaret Wild
Illustrated by Noella Young.
Ticknor & Fields, 1994. 32 pages.
Full-page watercolors.
Read-aloud or intermediate readers.
1995 COOL Award winner.

As Toby the family dog gets older, Sara, who has grown up with Toby, finds it hard to accept. When Toby no longer wants to walk or fetch, Sara is angry. Sara's younger brothers don't understand her attitude. Their mother explains that everything is changing in Sara's life now that she's about to start junior high. When the vet tells the family that it's time to put Toby to sleep, Sara says "Good" and storms up to her room. But in the middle of the night the whole family finds Sara cradling Toby. As the story ends, Toby is buried in the back yard and the whole family remembers him fondly. This story reminds us that children react differently to the aging of a beloved pet. (Ages 7-10)

Other Animals

Badger's Parting Gifts
by Susan Varley.
Lothrop, Lee and Shepard, 1984. 32 pages.
Impressionistic, muted drawings.
Read-aloud or intermediate readers.
Available in Spanish.
1985 Mother Goose Award winner; 1986 Kentucky
Bluegrass Award winner.

Badger is well-loved and wise but so old that his time to die is coming soon. His death is told in a gentle way as a marvelous passage through a long tunnel. His grieving friends find comfort in talking about him and the things he taught each of them. A well-written story that is also useful for discussion about the death of a family member. (Ages 4-8)

Goodbye Mousie
by Robie H. Harris.
Illustrated by Jan Ormerod.
Margaret K. McElderry Books, 2001. 32 pages.
Sensitively drawn.
Read-aloud or intermediate readers.
Available in Spanish.

Young children frequently connect death with going to sleep. This book helps by making it very clear that "dead is very different from sleeping." Mousie's young owner at first is angry at Mousie for dying. Then, in a realistic progression, he is sad that Mousie is dead. As he joins in plans to bury Mousie he begins to come to terms with the loss and to understand what death means. An excellent book, especially for young children to talk about death. (Ages 4-8)

Helen the Fish
by Virginia L. Kroll.
Illustrated by Teri Weidner.
Albert Whitman & Company, 1992. 32 pages.
Soft watercolors.
Read-aloud or intermediate to advanced readers.

For her third birthday, Hannah receives a goldfish from her older brother Seth that she names Helen. Hannah enjoys watching Helen play. But when Hannah is six, Helen dies. Seth comforts Hannah. He talks with her about life and death. As time goes by Hannah finds that the sadness does go away just as Seth told her it would. The story ends with Hannah buying a goldfish for her younger brother Noah. Most books about pet death feature dogs or cats. This one about a fish is unusual but for the many children for whom a fish is their only pet it's a good one. (Ages 6-9)

Other titles of interest, described elsewhere:
Good-bye, Vivi!

DEATH OF A FRIEND

If Nathan Were Here
by Mary Bahr.
Illustrated by Karen A. Jerome.
Eerdman's Publishing Company, 2000. 32 pages.
Richly-colored, impressionistic watercolors.
Read-aloud or intermediate readers.

A young boy is grieving the death of his best friend Nathan. We don't hear how he died but it seems recent and the sadness of the narrator is profound. At school, the class creates a Memory Box with things they recall about Nathan and questions they might want to ask him. But the narrator doesn't participate and his teacher compassionately understands. "She knows I'll talk to Nathan in my own time. In our tree fort." Inside the tree fort the sad boy asks, "What am I supposed to do without my best friend?" The author wisely doesn't answer. We see the narrator walking Nathan's dog and, finally, allowing Nathan's younger sister to enter the tree fort for the first time. A loving and powerful portrayal of a child's grief. (Ages 6-9)

A Taste of Blackberries
by Doris Buchanan Smith.
Illustrated by Mike Wimmer.
HarperTrophy, 1992, 96 pages.
Soft illustrations.
Read-aloud or advanced readers.
Available in Spanish.
1973 Josette Frank Award winner; 1975 Georgia Children's Book Award winner.

The narrator, a young boy, tells about his best friend Jamie who is an exuberant and mischievous show-off. When a neighbor offers to pay them to scrape Japanese beetles off her grapevines, it seems like a great opportunity. Jamie is horsing around, this time by shoving a stick into a bee hole. When his antics bring on a storm of bees, the narrator is annoyed with Jamie and walks away from him as Jamie is on the ground, gasping. But the narrator discovers that his anger was misplaced this time. Jamie is allergic and the stings have killed him. With great realism the narrator describes his guilt, the funeral, and above all, missing Jamie. When he reaches out to Jamie's little sister and mother, he finally begins to forgive himself. A powerful story about grief and guilt. (Ages 8-11)

DEATH OF A SIBLING

Lost and Found: Remembering a Sister
by Ellen Yeomans.
Illustrated by Dee deRosa.

Centering Corporation, 2000. 32 pages.
Smudged, evocative illustrations.
Read-aloud or advanced readers.

A preschool girl talks about her feelings since the death of her sister from cancer. When she begins her story the illustrations are a dull grey that mirror her numbness. As time passes she finds positive ways to remember her sister, such as wrapping herself in her sister's blanket and drawing a picture of herself with her sister. These small acts comfort her and the illustrations reflect her happier feelings. Her voice is believable if somewhat mature for a preschooler. A good book for talking about loss of a sibling. (Ages 4-8)

Molly's Rosebush

by Janice Cohn
Illustrated by Gail Owens.
Albert Whitman & Company, 1994. 32 pages,
including introduction by author and
advice for handling subject matter.
Gentle watercolors.
Read-aloud only due to advice for parents.
Out of print but available in libraries and used
bookstores.

Molly, a young girl, thinks about the special significance of the rosebush at her house. Several months ago her parents told her about her mother's miscarriage and that the new baby would not be born. Molly had lots of questions that her parents answered honestly. Then Molly spent time with her grandmother who shares her sadness. Together they decided to buy a rosebush for her mother that they would plant in the spring. It is this rosebush that Molly now looks at, which reminds her both of the loss and the possibility of better times ahead. A gentle, problem-solving book that offers good explanations. (Ages 4-8)

Stacy Had a Little Sister
by Wendie C. Old.
Illustrated by Judith Friedman.
Albert Whitman & Company, 1995. 32 pages,
including advice for parents.
Simple watercolors.
Read-aloud only due to advice for parents.

Stacy's baby sister Ashley dies unexpectedly from
Sudden Infant Death syndrome (SIDS). Stacy is concerned
that her own angry feelings toward the new baby might
have been responsible. She also wonders whether she
could die from SIDS. This is a story explicitly designed to
help a child with the death of a sibling from SIDS. It performs that job well by portraying all of the fears and concerns that a young child might have after a death in the
family. A useful entry in an area where there are few books.
(Ages 4-8)

DEATH OF A PARENT

FATHER

Everett Anderson's Goodbye
by Lucille Clifton.
Illustrated by Ann Grifalconi.
Henry Holt & Company, 1988. 20 pages.
Soft charcoal sketches.
Read-aloud or intermediate readers.
Multicultural.
1984 Coretta Scott King Award winner;
Reading Rainbow Choice.

Everett Anderson is a young boy whose father has
died. In this short but moving book we feel his grief. He
struggles through the stages of grieving, which are
described at the beginning of the book (perhaps unnec-

essarily, especially for the child who is reading this book on his own). The feelings ring true as does the ending in which time has passed and Everett Anderson has accepted that life goes on. (Ages 5-8)

Flamingo Dream
by Donna Jo Napoli.
Illustrated by Cathie Felstead.
Greenwillow Books, 2002. 32 pages.
Bright, collage illustrations.
Read-aloud or advanced readers.

The narrator, a young girl, describes wonderful experiences with her father, including a memorable trip to Florida to see where he grew up. But amidst the happiness is the reality that her father has cancer and is not expected to live much longer. With simple but affecting honesty the narrator describes how "sometimes we cried together, all three of us." Her father dies. The narrator describes her grief as well as her memories and how she will put it all together because now she knows "the story I want to tell." A good choice for children grieving the loss of a parent. (Ages 5-8)

Geranium Morning
by Sandy Powell.
Illustrated by Renee Graef.
First Avenue Editions, 1991, 40 pages.
Smudged black-and-white illustrations.
Read-aloud or intermediate to advanced readers.

A young boy tells of the changes in his life since the sudden death of his father in an automobile accident. There aren't any more outings and he is taking care of himself more. The narrator also talks about how his father's death gave him something very powerful in common with a new friend who also is grieving. His new friend helps him to accept the idea of counseling and to talk about his feelings. Very good for a child who may need to consider counseling. (Ages 4-8)

Saying Goodbye to Daddy
by Judith Vigna.
Albert Whitman & Company, 1991, 32 pages.
Gentle watercolors.
Read-aloud or intermediate to advanced readers.

A young girl, Clare, grieves for her father who died in a car accident. She worries that somehow it was her fault because she yelled at him after she broke his coffee cup. The other grownups in her life understand her confused feelings. They answer her questions and reassure her that they expect to live a long time. The story covers the funeral and Clare's feelings afterwards. She and her grandfather talk about heaven but the emphasis is on the memories that one has after a loved one has died. Best for a younger child because there is some simplification of feelings and Clare is shown feeling better rather quickly. (Ages 4-8)

Some of the Pieces
by Melissa Madenski.
Illustrated by Deborah Kogan Ray.
Little, Brown and Company, 1991. 32 pages.
Soft, simple watercolors.
Read-aloud or intermediate readers.
Out of print but available in libraries and used bookstores.

The narrator, a young boy named Dylan, begins his story a full year after his father's sudden death from a heart attack. His family goes to put his father's ashes in the river and as they sit there they reminisce. It feels good to talk and laugh about the funny things he did. With gentle simplicity, Dylan thinks about how hard it has been to accept that his father won't be home for dinner as he always had been. But he also realizes with surprise that the pain is less now, that a part of his father will always be with him, and that comforts him. A sensitive and gentle musing on feelings during the first year of grieving. (Ages 7-10)

Upside-Down Cake
by Carol Carrick.
Illustrated by Paddy Bouma.
Houghton Mifflin, 1999. 64 pages.
Pencil sketches.
Read-aloud or advanced readers.

A nine-year-old boy and his father always celebrate their birthdays together. His mother serves pineapple upside-down cake with whipped cream and two forks. He and his father laugh and have a great time. But it is one of their last happy times together. His father is diagnosed with cancer, has unsuccessful surgery, and is very ill from then on. This short novel covers the many stages of illness and explores the strong emotions that families experience with a dying parent. It describes the father's death at home, including the experience of seeing his body and attending a funeral. The story ends as the boy's tenth birthday approaches. At first he doesn't want a party. Finally he decides on a special kind of cake with forks all around, signifying the inevitable acceptance of loss. A thoughtful account of death. (Ages 8-11)

Other titles of interest, described elsewhere:
Badger's Parting Gifts

MOTHER

After Charlotte's Mom Died
by Cornelia Spelman.
Illustrated by Judith Friedman.

Albert Whitman & Company, 1996. 24 pages, including introduction by author and advice for handling subject matter.
Gentle watercolors.
Read-aloud only due to advice for parents.

    A six-year old girl, Charlotte, lives alone with her father since her mother's death in a car accident six months ago. Charlotte is confused by her father's behavior. He seems very busy all the time and sometimes he cries. Although Charlotte keeps up a brave front, she is "sad and mad and scared." One day at school, a classmate's teasing causes her to erupt in anger. When her father comes to talk to her teacher he is kind and loving to Charlotte and apologizes for being so unavailable to her. He tells her that they are going to see someone to help them express their feelings -- a therapist. With the therapist's help, they both learn how to talk about their sadness. Especially good for helping a child to accept the role of a therapist. (Ages 5-9)

Mama
by Eleanor Schick.
Marshall Cavendish, 2000. 32 pages.
Soft watercolors.
Read-aloud or intermediate readers.

    A dying mother and her daughter take their last trip to the park together. A housekeeper, Louise, begins coming to help. The mother goes to the hospital, so sick "you couldn't even tell me goodbye." Louise reassures the girl that her mother loved her always and that her mother always will be in her heart. As time passes, the story shows the young girl returning to her regular activities, realizing that there will always be times when she misses her mother. The father seems distant and not involved in the daughter's grief. The housekeeper plays a central role. Powerful and well-written. (Ages 4-8)

A Pillow for My Mom
by Charissa Sgouros.
Illustrated by Christine Ross.
Houghton Mifflin, Boston. 1998. 32 pages.
Muted realistic illustrations.
Read-aloud or intermediate readers.

In limited text and drawings filled with trees that represent the passage of time, a little girl tells the story of her mother's illness. In the spring the girl remembers their happy times filled with stories and games. During the summer her mother is uncomfortable so the little girl makes her a pillow. After her mother's death in the autumn the little girl uses the pillow to console herself whenever she misses her mother. A simple story that finds the heart of loss and grief. (Ages 4-8)

Sky Memories
by Pat Brisson.
Illustrated by Wendell Minor.
Delacorte Press, 1999. 80 pages.
Lovely watercolors.
Read-aloud or advanced readers.
Out of print but available in libraries and used bookstores.
2002 Children's Crown Award winner.

When Emily is ten years old her mother is diagnosed with cancer. Emily and her mother had just begun to "collect" sky memories, mental images of how the sky looks at a particular moment. Emily's mother is her only parent and she has difficult treatments that make her ill. Emily's Aunt Vicki moves in and for awhile it seems as though her mother is improving. In May her mother tells Emily that she is dying and the story concludes with her death. This is a powerful and moving book. The characters talk honestly with each other about many feelings. (Ages 9-12)

Winter Holding Spring
by Crescent Dragonwagon.
Illustrated by Ronald Himler.
Atheneum, 1990. 32 pages.
Soft black-and-white drawings.
Read-aloud or advanced readers.

Sarah and her father mourn the death of her mother. They talk about their memories and the change in seasons. Sarah is a fully realized character with her own thoughts, emotions, and ideas that she discusses with her father or muses about. There are no major events in this story but rather a wonderful evocation of the grieving process. A sensitive story about loss and acceptance. (Ages 8-11)

Other titles of interest, described elsewhere:
Badger's Parting Gifts

DEATH OF A GRANDPARENT

GRANDFATHER

Blackberries in the Dark
by Mavis Jukes.
Illustrated by Thomas B. Allen.
Yearling Books, 1994. 64 pages.
Black-and-white illustrations on every page.
Read-aloud or advanced readers.

Every summer, Austin, a young boy, visits his grandparents on their farm. This year is different because his grandfather has passed away. Being at the farm but not doing the things he traditionally shared with his grandfather just reminds Austin how much he misses him. His grandfather had promised that this summer he would teach Austin how to fly-fish. When his grandmother senses his sadness she is inspired to learn to do some of the things that the grandfather traditionally did with Austin. Together Austin and his grandmother learn to fly-fish. Believable and warm relationship between a grandson and grandmother. (Ages 8-11)

Grandpa Loved
by Josephine Nobisso.
Illustrated by Maureen Hyde.
Gingerbread House, 2000. 32 pages.
Colorful watercolors.
Read-aloud or intermediate readers.

An older boy reminisces about his grandfather whose love of life impressed him. Together they explored and delighted in the seashore, the forest, and the big city. Each page of the story reflects their joy in each other and in the ordinary happenings in everyday life. The boy believes that his grandfather will be there in spirit with his family always. A touching story of the relationship between a grandfather and grandson. (Ages 9-12)

Poppy's Chair
by Karen Hesse.
Illustrated by Kay Life.
Simon and Schuster, 1993. 32 pages.
Warm and comforting if somewhat dated illustrations.
Read-aloud or intermediate readers.

This is the first summer that Leah has spent with her grandparents since her beloved grandfather Poppy passed away. Now she and her grandmother take the bus but Poppy used to drive them. Neither of them sits in Poppy's chair because it doesn't feel right and Leah does not even want to look at Poppy's picture. When she can't fall asleep, she finds her grandmother asleep in Poppy's chair and voices her fear that her grandmother might die soon too. Her grandmother admits to the sadness she too feels but reassures Leah that she plans to live a lot longer. Later, they both sleep together in her grandmother's bed and say goodnight to the picture of Poppy. A realistic portrait of a young child's loss of a beloved grandparent. (Ages 4-8)

Sophie
by Mem Fox.
Illustrated by Aminah Brenda Lynn Robinson.
Voyager Books, 1997. 32 pages.
Bold, bright acrylic dye and paint.
Read-aloud or beginning to intermediate readers.
Multicultural.

This richly-illustrated book tells in simple language of a time when there was no Sophie "...and then there was." As Sophie grows, so does the bond between her and her Grandpa. They share many experiences until she is big enough to work with him and "look him in the eye." Then Grandpa begins to grow older and slower and smaller. But their love continues undiminished until his death. "And then there was no Grandpa, just emptiness and sadness for a while." At the end, we see Sophie has had a baby, whose arrival "fills the world, once again." A gentle reminder of the passage of time, the cycle of life and the inevitability of death. (Ages 4-8)

Sweet Sweet Memory
by Jacqueline Woodson.
Illustrated by Floyd Cooper.
Jump at the Sun/Hyperion Books, 2000. 32 pages.
Soft, muted pastels.
Read-aloud or advanced readers.
Multicultural.

Sarah, a young girl, mourns the death of her grandfather. She remembers his words, "The earth changes, like us it lives, it grows, like us, a part of it never dies.

Everything and everyone goes on and on." She also remembers experiences with him. Together Sarah and her grandmother enjoy sharing their memories. Her sadness doesn't go away but the memories are sweet and comforting. A simple and honest depiction of a child's feeling of loss. (Ages 4-8)

A Time for Remembering
by Chuck Thurman.
Illustrated by Elizabeth Sayles.
Simon & Schuster, 1989. 25 pages.
Blurry, appealing illustrations.
Read-aloud or intermediate readers.
Out of print but available in libraries and used bookstores.

A boy is alone, grieving his grandfather's recent death. He follows a ritual that his grandfather asked him to do the very last time they were together. He takes a flower given to him by his grandfather, sits by the fire, and remembers things about his grandfather. When he is finished he throws the flower into the fire just as his grandfather had requested. The simple ritual seems to comfort him. A moving description of the love between a boy and his grandfather. (Ages 4-8)

Other titles of interest, described elsewhere:
Badger's Parting Gifts

GRANDMOTHER

A Gift for Abuelita
by Nancy Luenn
Illustrated by Robert Chapman.
Rising Moon, 1998. 32 pages, including a glossary of terms.
Richly-illustrated with cast paper, wood, twine,

fabric and beads.
Read-aloud or advanced readers.
Multicultural.
Bilingual.

Rosita and her Abuelita are inseparable. The extraordinary illustrations and accompanying bilingual text show them cooking, singing, gardening and sewing together. When Abuelita dies, Rosita misses her terribly. In the Mexican tradition, the Day of the Dead is an opportunity for Rosita to remember and honor her grandmother with a gift. Rosita wonders whether Abuelita will join them on that day and her mother suggests that in her memories Abuelita will be with her. As Rosita works on her gift, her memories reassure her that the bond she shared with her grandmother will never be broken. A lovely story to identify with and to understand other cultures.(Ages 5-8)

Fox Song
by Joseph Bruchac.
Illustrated by Paul Morin.
Philomel Books, 1993. 26 pages.
Unusual illustrations in a variety of materials.
Read-aloud or advanced readers.
Multicultural.

The narrator, Jamie, begins her story after the death of her beloved grandmother. Jamie remembers the stories her grandmother told her and the things they loved to do together. The narration is in the spirit and culture of the Native American tribe to which Jamie and her grandmother belong. Many of Jamie's memories are of her grandmother's explanations of wild and natural things. Above all, her grandmother emphasized the cycle of life and assured her that in the natural world Jamie would always be able to find her grandmother, even after death. A unique and absorbing story that offers an opportunity to talk to your child about death and loss in other cultures. (Ages 4-8)

Ghost Wings
by Barbara M. Joosse.
Illustrated by Giselle Potter.
Chronicle Books, San Francisco. 2001.
40 pages including notes and a guide to using the book.
Watercolors and colored pencil.
Read-aloud only due to advice for parents.
Multicultural.
Available in Spanish

A young girl has lost her beloved grandmother who taught her how to make tortillas, chased the monsters from under her bed, and introduced her to the Magic Circle where the butterflies live in the forest. The little girl misses her grandmother terribly but she finds solace with her family and neighbors as they remember Grandmother with her favorite songs and foods. An opportunity to discuss the acceptance of death from a different cultural perspective. (Ages 5-8)

Good-bye, Vivi!
by Antonie Schneider.
Illustrated by Maja Dusikova.
North South Books, 1998. 32 pages.
Beautiful full-page paintings.
Read-aloud or intermediate readers.

A grandmother comes to live with the family and brings her yellow canary, Vivi. The family grows to love the little bird that figures in many of the grandmother's family stories. When the children find Vivi sitting on the bottom of her cage with eyes closed, their grandmother tells them that Vivi is old for a bird. The children take care of Vivi, cradling her and dripping water into her beak. When the little bird dies, the grandmother reminds the children of their many happy memories of Vivi and assures them that they will always have her in their memories. The grandmother becomes frail and in the spring she dies. The children find a book full of pictures and stories that their grandmother left them. The grandmother's acceptance of Vivi's death and her wise words help her family deal with their grief when she dies. A wonderful story. (Ages 4-8)

Marianne's Grandmother
by Bettina Egger.
Illustrated by Sita Jucker.
E. P. Dutton, 1987. 25 pages.
Somber, muted watercolors.
Read-aloud or intermediate readers.
Out of print but available in libraries and used bookstores.

Marianne thinks about her grandmother and her recent funeral. After the funeral, Marianne plays with the doll for whom her grandmother had sewed matching dresses. As she remembers her grandmother's gift, Marianne also thinks of other good times with her grandmother. Marianne realizes that remembering her grandmother is one way of knowing that she can always love her, even if her grandmother isn't there anymore. A simple but honest story. (Ages 4-8)

Nana Upstairs & Nana Downstairs
by Tomie de Paola.
Puffin Books, 2000. 32 pages.
Gentle tricolor drawings.
Read-aloud or intermediate readers.
Available in Spanish.

Tommy's grandmother and great-grandmother live together so he keeps them straight in his mind by thinking of them as his Nana who sleeps upstairs and his Nana who sleeps downstairs. From his visits to them every Sunday, Tommy has developed a loving routine with his Nanas that includes candy, conversation, and naps. One morning, Tommy's mother tells him that Nana Upstairs has died. It isn't real to him until he sees her empty bed. His mother answers his questions honestly, telling him that though Nana Upstairs won't come back she will always be there in his memory. Later, when he sees a falling star, his mother suggests that it was a kiss sent to him from Nana Upstairs. When his other Nana dies he comes to think of both of them as Nanas Upstairs. A gentle, loving way to think about those who have left our lives but not our memories. (Ages 4-8)

One More Wednesday
by Malika Doray.
Greenwillow Books. 2001. 46 pages.
Spare black-and-white drawings with dashes of color.
Read-aloud or intermediate readers.
2001 Parenting Best Books of the Year Award winner.

A little animal spends every Wednesday with Grandmother doing fun things. But one Wednesday his grandmother goes into the hospital and dies. The little animal wonders if "my granny was gone forever." His mother, while telling him that nobody knows for sure, also shares with him some of the beliefs that people have. "Some people say the spirit goes up to heaven. Other people say that when you die, your spirit comes back as a new baby, or maybe as a bird or a bee, or even a tree." A simple, sweet story to open discussion of life and death. (Ages 4-8)

Other titles of interest, described elsewhere:
Badger's Parting Gifts

AUTHORS AND ILLUSTRATORS

INDEX OF TITLES

SUBJECTS

INDEX OF MULTICULTURAL BOOKS

INDEX OF BOOKS AVAILABLE IN SPANISH

REFERENCES

Ballou, Mary, Editor. Psychological Interventions: A Guide to Strategies. Praeger. 1995.

Campbell, Laura Ann. Storybooks for Tough Times. Fulcrum Publishers. 1999.

Cornett, C.E., & Cornett, C.F. Bibliotherapy: The right book at the right time. Phi Delta Kappa Educational Foundation. 1980.

Doll, Beth, and Carol Doll. Bibliotherapy with Young People: Librarians and Mental Health Professionals Working Together. Libraries Unlimited, Inc. 1997.

Dreyer, S.S. The Bookfinder. American Guidance Services. 1977.

Forgan, James. Using Bibliotherapy to Teach Problem Solving. Intervention in School & Clinic, 10534512, Vol. 38, Issue 2. November 2002.

Grindler, Martha C. et al. The Right Book, The Right Time: Helping Children Cope. Allyn & Bacon. 1996.

Halsted, Judith Wynn. Some of My Best Friends Are Books. Arizona. Great Potential Press. 2002.

McCarty-Hynes, Arleen, and Mary Hynes-Berry. Bibliotherapy: The Interactive Process: A Handbook. North Star Press of St. Cloud, Inc. 1994.

Myracle, Lauren. "Molding the Minds of the Young: The History of Bibliotherapy as Applied to Children and Adolescents." Alan Review, Volume 22, Number 2. Winter 1995.

Pardeck, John, and Jean A. Pardeck. Bibliotherapy: A Guide to Using Books in Clinical Practice. Edwin Mellen Press. 1992.

Pardeck, John, and Jean A. Pardeck. Young People with Problems: A Guide to Bibliotherapy. Greenwood Publishing Group. 1986.

Rasinski, Timothy V., and Cindy S Gillespie. Sensitive Issues: An Annotated Guide to Children's Literature K-6. Oryx Press. 1992.

Rizza, Mary. "A Parent's Guide to Helping Children: Using Bibliotherapy at Home." Newsletter of the National Research Center on the Gifted and "Bibliotherapy for all: Enhancing reading comprehension, self-concept, and behavior." Teaching Exceptional Children, 33 (2), 74-82. 2000.

Tu, Wei. "Using Literature to Help Children Cope with Problems." ERIC Digest D148, ED436008. 1999.

ADDITIONAL RESOURCES

BOOKS IN SPANISH: WHERE TO OBTAIN THEM

AIMS International Books, Inc.
7709 Hamilton Avenue
Cincinnati, OH 45231-3103
800-733-2067 or 513-521-5590
fax: 513-521-5592

Lectorum Publications, Inc.
111 Eighth Avenue, Suite 804
New York, NY 10011
800-345-5946 or 212-929-2833
fax: 212-727-3035

Los Andes Publishing, Inc.
P.O. Box 2344
La Puente, CA 91746
800-LECTURA

Mariuccia Iaconi Book Imports
970 Tennessee Street
San Francisco, CA 94107
800-955-9577 or 415-821-1216
fax: 415-821-1596

Visit our website at www.lutrapress.com for an updated list of helpful websites. You'll also find a monthly newsletter with new books and our "Idea of the month."

Book Order Form

If you would like to obtain additional copies of *Books to Grow With: A Guide to Using the Best Children's Fiction for Everyday Issues and Tough Challenges* (Lutra Press; ISBN: 0-9748025-7-3; $17.95), please contact us in one of the following ways:

Telephone Orders: Call us at 503-291-0265 or Toll-free at 866-311-0265

E-mail orders: orders@lutrapress.com

Web orders: www.lutrapress.com (secure order form)

Fax Orders: 503-292-5697. Please send this form.

Name:_____

Address:_____

City:_____State___Zip:_____

Telephone:_____

E-mail address:_____

Shipping: Add $4.00 for the first book and $2.00 for each additional book.

Payment: __Check
            __Credit Card __VISA __MasterCard

Card Number:_____

Your signature:_____

Exact name on card:_____

Expiration date_____

Authorized amount:_____